THE
EXTRAORDINARY LIFE
OF AN ORDINARY MAN

A MEMOIR BY
AL HIRSHEN
WITH
RENATE STENDHAL

The Extraordinary Life of An Ordinary Man: A Memoir
Al Hirshen with Renate Stendhal
Published by Al Hirshen

ISBN 978-0-578-58486-7

Excerpts from this book have been previously published on the adventure travel website **www.RichardBangs.com.**

For further info, please contact the author at: **ahirshen@gmail.com**

PRAISE FOR
"THE EXTRAORDINARY LIFE
OF AN ORDINARY MAN"

An action-packed memoir both affecting and fun: from a boyhood in the Bronx to giving presidential lectures at Oxford to running anti-poverty programs in the US to wheeling and dealing for development projects overseas. Al Hirshen writes a disarmingly honest, introspective, and sensitive but realistic portrait of working in foreign cultures, hobnobbing with wealthy investors, and taking on officialdom and corruption, all the while trying to improve the lives of poor families and minorities. Donor governments, corporations, and international organizations will benefit from this book.

Al Hirshen's magnetic rapport with people, talent for networking, perceptiveness and insight into foreign practices—plus plain grit—led to successful developments, although he candidly admits how dreams and aspirations can be hopelessly dashed. A worldwide traveler, Al Hirshen shares vivid descriptions of his camel treks, elephant rides, bird watching expeditions, and trips to awesome historic temples, culminating in building a dream house in Bali. Despite his attraction to where "the action" is, he brings to the reader the deep spiritual wonders of communing with nature around the world. An extraordinary life well worth reading about.

ROBERTA COHEN, SPECIALIST IN HUMANITARIAN AND REFUGEE ISSUES
(UNITED NATIONS, US STATE DEPARTMENT, NGOs, AND ACADEMIA)

A hilarious and, at the same time, excoriating account of what can happen when a novice producer attempts to conquer the Byzantine world of Hollywood filmmaking.

JOHN WALCUTT, PRODUCER AND ACTOR (*THE TITANIC* AND *SEABISCUIT*)

––––––––––

Al Hirshen is an astute observer of the human condition in its beauty and its maddening shortcomings. His narrative seamlessly—with wit and kindness—demonstrates what I, as an educator, want all youth to understand: that we are all ordinary people living extraordinary lives.

CHARLIE PLANT, AWARD-WINNING TEACHER AND PRINCIPAL

––––––––––

Al's story is a coming-of-age story told by a tap-dancing eighty-year-old. He spins tales and distills wisdom. It is an extraordinary story because of his rampant curiosity, love of adventure, and capacity for wonder.

TERRY MYERS, PROFESSOR OF NATIONAL SECURITY STUDIES (RET)
FORMER USAID MISSION DIRECTOR, INDONESIA

––––––––––

What is so astonishing about Al Hirshen is not just that he had the guts, tenacity, and intelligence to go beyond the apparent limits of upbringing in 1940's Bronx, but that he describes his journey forward with such deep affection and generosity for all he encountered. His is a story of triumph against all odds, but also a tender, moving tale.

GILLETTE EDMUNDS JD, LLM, AUTHOR OF *HOW TO RETIRE EARLY, RETIRE ON THE HOUSE,* AND THE FORTHCOMING *WE WERE: A CALIFORNIA STORY*

This book truly is an account of an extraordinary life, a life overflowing with purpose, passion, adventure, and wonder. A life well lived and well observed. Al Hirshen has packed so much into his years and his travels that it seems almost impossible to capture it all in words—but he's done it! For inspiration and sheer pleasure, pick up a copy of this book!

KARIN EVANS, AUTHOR OF *THE LOST DAUGHTERS OF CHINA*

———

Al Hirshen eloquently describes Bill Young, an American version of Lawrence of Arabia in Southeast Asia, as a missionary and a warrior, doing God's work with his left hand while working deep under cover for the CIA and DEA with his right. Al's artistic eye and writer's pen inevitably spotted, at the far end of a long tunnel, the key ingredients of an exciting action-adventure-thriller motion picture. It will become apparent to the reader that Al's battles in the glamorous and treacherous trenches of Hollywood matched the thrills of his real warrior missionary, Bill.

DOUG APATOW, EXECUTIVE PRODUCER OF *BARNEY THOMSON* (WINNER OF BAFTA BEST FILM), FORMER TALENT AGENT AND BUSINESS AFFAIRS ATTORNEY (20TH CENTURY FOX AND PARAMOUNT PICTURES)

———

One of the most remarkable qualities of this life story is the author's honesty about his alcoholism and the devastation it caused to his brilliant career and his personal life. After more than thirty years of sobriety, this extraordinary man serves up life's lesson with wit, wisdom, and a twinkle in his eye.

SUSAN PAGE TILLETT, AUTHOR AND EXECUTIVE DIRECTOR, MESA REFUGE FOR WRITERS

The rationale for writing my memoir is to have my
grandchildren better understand a part of their family history.

I dedicate this book to Cooper, Hadley, Georgia, Jack,
and any grandchildren still to be born.
Also to Julie, my wife of twenty-five years,
who makes all good things possible.

"Don't stop yourself from doing anything."

AL HIRSHEN

CONTENTS

FOREWORD

If there is a common thread to exploration and adventure, it is a voracious inquisitiveness for all the world can offer. A fellow adventurer is Al Hirshen, a man of rapacious and unsated curiosity. Al is on a lifelong quest for understanding through travel, social change, and self-exploration.

Abridged versions of the travel memoir sections of Al's book were published on my blog, "Richard Bangs' Quests," and the reaction was overwhelmingly positive.

Whether the journey takes him to Mississippi, Washington D.C., Ukraine, Jordan, or Indonesia, curiosity, passion, and deep respect are mile markers for Al. These same traits are present in the "Recovery" chapter of the book. He takes the reader into the metaphoric traveler-through-life's mind, where the possibility for transformation (both of the world and of oneself) resides.

Through his travels, Al examines the emotional structures that make true discussions about race, ethnicity, and poverty difficult and distant for many of us. With clarity and compassion, he allows us to understand prejudice as a practice that is everywhere in the world. It is simply part of being human, but not something we have to accept. Through challenging these notions in his early life, and then through his work and travels, Al makes the case for societal change and social justice through productive visits and intimate cross-cultural relationships.

Al's incisive writings stitch together the cloth that binds us as Americans and as world citizens. He explores different ideologies without judging. For him, ideology is a personal choice. With riveting tales of his various adventures and misadventures, he provides a road map to empathy, and the antidote to bigotry: traveling and living with an open mind.

This remarkable book encourages all of us to embrace a more deeply nuanced exploration of the world and its cultures, and to make it all part of the conversation. Al's peregrinations and interpretations encourage us to relinquish ingrained hyper-attachment to individualism, and to celebrate diversity and inclusion.

And yet, is the exploration and betterment of oneself not the greatest, most harrowing journey of all? In a raw account of his path to sobriety, Al gives his audience a look at what it means to reflect upon and confront our innermost demons and ultimately come out on the other side. Much like the stories of his travels, Al is able to recognize the parts of himself that need change, while also approaching that change with compassion, hope, and an open mind.

Most of what Al needed to know about life was learned growing up as a young Jewish boy on the streets of the Bronx and coming of age in the Catskills. One of his guiding philosophies about life is that life experiences unplug one's prejudices. Al told me a story from his time spent working in the Civil Rights Division of the United States Justice Department in Carroll County, Mississippi, in the 1960s, when racial tensions were at an all-time high. He remembers walking into a bar with a group of black voting rights leaders when they were stopped by the local sheriff, who was a brusque white man. Al describes looking at him and making a snap judgment that the sheriff was a racist. After some back and forth, Al learned that the sheriff was not a racist, but in fact was an outspoken advocate for black voting rights. In an unexpected turn of events, it was Al who was the prejudiced one in this circumstance. Al's memoir is filled with such stories, which forced him to reflect on his worldview, and he encourages us to do the same.

With an unwavering conviction that change is possible, Al's message is clear: the levers for a better world lie beyond our comfort zone, out the door, around the bend, and somewhere in the unacquainted worlds of wonder.

—RICHARD BANGS

Richard Bangs is cofounder of MTSobek, was part of the founding executive team of Expedia.com, and is the cofounder of the travel storytelling platform www.steller.co.

He is the author of nineteen books and executive producer of the PBS series **Adventures with Purpose.**

ACKNOWLEDGMENTS

First, thanks to my friend Susan Tillet, who told me one day, "You should write a book," and followed up by arranging a breakfast meeting with Kim Chernin. Kudos to Kim, my first editor, for never saying I had a long way to go to be a writer! Kim worked her magic to get over five hundred pages out of me. Then, when my ego took over and I wanted more than only a manuscript for my grandchildren, she introduced me to her spouse, Renate Stendhal, who became my book editor. It has been a fun, rewarding, and stimulating three years. Her name is on the cover because my memoir would not be the book it is without her input and guidance. Thanks, Renate, for helping me find my voice!

Thanks to Howard VanEs for steering me through the shoals of self-publication. We both survived being East Coast Jewish boys with strong opinions.

Thanks go to my former and present assistants, Daniella Granados and Caroline Seroussi, who have lightened the load.

Many thanks to Susanne for the good times and our great children, Annik and Noel.

Special gratitude to Julie Allen for a million things, but especially for her artist's eye and editing skills.

Finally, my appreciation to all those who gave me the life experiences that make up this memoir.

CHAPTER 1

GROWING UP IN THE BRONX

I was six years old, having my lunch when my dad came home from work at the Bronx candy store he co-owned with "Hoffy," his brother-in-law. Suddenly he and my mom entered the kitchen arguing. The argument escalated. My father, with his face flushed red, banged his fist into one of the glass panels of a cabinet right next to me. Pieces of glass crashed to the floor with a clatter. My father stormed out of the apartment and, as it turned out, never returned.

My mother forbade me to leave the apartment. I later learned she was afraid he would kidnap me. My older brother, Sandy, who was not home at the time of the fight, told me they had been arguing over my not being properly dressed for the cold when I went out to play with the guys on the block. After a few hours I left the apartment anyway as I was never afraid of Pop. I was not kidnapped. This is my first childhood memory.

My parents never divorced, remarried, or to my knowledge had another romantic relationship. I never learned or understood why.

For four years after the split, my father lived on Sherman Avenue around the corner from us, with Hoffy and his wife, Gussie, who was my father's eldest sister. Thereafter he lived in a two-bedroom apartment with his two spinster sisters, Mitzi and Dottie, in a new six-story elevator apartment house diagonally across from us on 163rd Street.

The construction of this apartment building destroyed the "softball field" the guys on the block had just created on the vacant lot. Our gang had laid out baselines and bases made from vegetable crates on the dirt field. It was basic, but proudly ours. When the earthmovers came to start construction, it was a very sad day for us.

My father's and spinster aunts' apartment was a plastic mausoleum. Plastic covered the couch, the upholstered chairs in the living room, and the dining room chairs. Everything was to be preserved as if it were still brand new. Back then this was not uncommon for lower-middle-class Jewish households in the Bronx.

My mother, brother, and I continued to live three blocks east of the Grand Concourse, at 237 E. 163rd Street, a five-story walk-up, in apartment 4C. There were five apartments per landing. Our apartment had two bedrooms at opposite ends, a cramped kitchen, and a living room. You entered via a long, narrow entranceway with a transom above an open door to the living room. Brother Sandy or friends and I would play basketball with our pink Spaulding, using the open transom as a basket.

He and I shared one of the bedrooms for twenty-two years until he married. We never felt deprived that we didn't have our own rooms. To the contrary, it was fun to close the door, "mess around" together, and tell stories before bedtime. In my early youth I was comforted by Sandy's presence. Two incidents of our messing around in the apartment outside our room are still vivid in my memory. The first took place in my mother's bedroom while she was at work. We were wrestling and we crashed down on her bed and broke one of the legs. We put the leg back with wire without telling Mom about it. In the middle of the night there was a loud crash as the bed fell to the floor. Mom was not hurt, but we were in trouble. The second incident happened in the living room. Mom had a prized glass-top coffee table that broke into pieces when Sandy fell on it during another wrestling match. This time she made Sandy contribute part of his after-school working money to getting it fixed. I escaped scot-free as I was only ten and I had not yet started my delivery jobs.

In those days coal was delivered by truck down a shoot into the basement, and blocks of ice were delivered to our apartment for the icebox. We sent our garbage to the basement for collection by the superintendent via a dumbwaiter that was operated by heavy, coarse ropes. For me, an equally important function of the dumbwaiter was to exchange comic books with friends in apartments above and below ours.

It was always ironic to me that the neighborhood gang would go down past the coal bin and the garbage cans to the poorest family among us, the "Super's" dark basement apartment, to watch wrestling and the *Milton Berle Show*. He was the first on the block to own a TV. We were a tight-knit group of friends, and it was natural that we would be invited.

Across the street from our apartment building, between Grant and Sherman Avenues, was a series of mom-and-pop stores: shoe repair, groceries, vegetables, tailor, and Hirschman's (not a relative) candy store. Starting at eleven, I delivered orders for Ike, the vegetable man. Delivery jobs were my first lesson in business and learning how to maximize my tips. Having a smile on my face, being gracious and thankful would work wonders.

During the period of the '40s to early '60s, the Bronx was made of different economic neighborhoods in close proximity. The upper-middle-class Grand Concourse was only two blocks west of us, and the much poorer neighborhoods were twelve blocks south. The only time I entered the fancy apartment buildings was through the delivery side entrance, and then only at the direction of the doorman. Not until my junior year of high school did I walk through the main entrance into a lobby past the doorman, saying with a smile, "Visiting Bobbi Cohen's apartment." The scene reminded me of cockney boys in the British movies with their coal-dust-covered faces, tipping their caps to the guardians of the families in the grand manor.

During my college years I remember dating a young lady who lived in an apartment on Central Park West. I announced her name to the doorman and was escorted to the elevator where he, not I, pushed the floor button. I was in a state of mild shock when the door opened, not onto a hallway, but directly into an apartment. "Wow! Not bad," I thought. It was a step up the financial ladder from the Grand Concourse. As I grew into manhood, I learned that there is always another step up. The financial and educational class distinctions that were part of my youth acted as a motivator (consciously and unconsciously) to climb the ladder.

FIRST-GENERATION AMERICAN

My parents were immigrants. My father was fourteen and my mother eight when they arrived in America. Luckily World War I ended just months before my father was scheduled to ship out to fight in Europe. He came from a village outside Kiev,

Ukraine and she from the city of Brest-Litovsk, Poland (now part of Belarus.) Neither went beyond the fifth grade as they had to work to supplement their families' incomes. My mother worked in a hat factory in Holyoke, Massachusetts, and my father helped my grandfather in his candy store on the Lower East Side of New York City. Thereafter he joined the clothing business where he rose to chief quality tester. He had the bad luck of quitting his well-paying job just when the Depression hit. Then he and his brother-in-law, Hoffy, followed in my grandfather's footsteps and opened the candy store on 161st, eight blocks from our apartment, west of the Grand Concourse, between the Bronx County Courthouse and Yankee Stadium.

My mother was the eldest girl and third-born in a family of two girls and four boys. My father was the second child in a family of two boys and three girls.

Their marriage was never one of true love but rather of duty and expectation. Jews in their social station who emigrated from Europe married "because it was time." In effect, it was an arranged marriage. At the time my dad earned a good living. And my grandmother Eva thought, "Harry will do." My mother was five feet and five inches and always battled her weight. She was a direct, "get on with it" person. As was true of her mother, she did not spend any time bemoaning her life and had little tolerance for anyone who did. I inherited her "deal with it" mentality. At the same time she was a kind and helpful person to her friends and others. Although I knew she loved me, she was not a nurturing person. Maybe this was because from the time I was eight she worked full time at two different women's clothing stores. Maybe it was, as she told me much later, because she was advised by friends and family to be strict and tough with me because of my independent and rebellious nature. When I was ten she took me to the Woolworth Five and Dime on Morris Avenue and, after finding the manager, ordered me to tell him that I was returning several boxes of small toys I had stolen. I had to apologize and say, "It won't happen again." And it did not!

My Bubbe (grandmother) Eva shared my mother's bed for a number of years. Eva was a tough woman (my grandfather had died years earlier) who had moved her six children from Brest-Litovsk to Holyoke, Massachusetts by herself. Her cousin had made the guarantees to the American authorities. Clearly, my mother took after her mother.

Bubbe Eva and my mother mainly spoke to each other in Yiddish. Today I regret not learning Yiddish, but I was an American who wanted no part of the Old

World. I have three distinct memories involving my bubbe. The first was when I returned from school and witnessed her crying out loud. Worried, I called my mother at work; she said, "She was just praying." The second was when I returned home from school to find out she had given away my three-week-old puppy dog, King. (He was named after the Royal Canadian Mounties' Sergeant Preston's faithful Yukon dog of a very popular radio show.) I took the news as a matter of fact, without any resentment toward my grandmother. As I got older I understood she had been right. King lived in our bathtub where he did his "business," causing much disruption. I was too young to take good care of him without assistance. He was better off in his new home. Years later, however, I requested that our family dog (a standard poodle) be named King.

The last memory was at her funeral where my Aunt Esther was screaming and trying to jump into the grave. I always thought it made sense, given her nasty disposition. In my brother's memory, however, it was our mother and not Aunt Esther who was the "jumper." Years later we asked our Uncle Hymie to resolve the disagreement. He said, "Neither did." Both Sandy and I held to our memories of our graveside experience. It was just too strong for us to have made it up.

My father was five feet, eight inches, thin with a small potbelly. His parents had died before I was born. Unlike my mother, he was always nervous, insecure, liked to tell jokes and have fun. He passed these traits on to me. Whereas I looked like my father, my brother looked like my mother, but in our seventies we began to look more alike. People always remarked, "Al was more like Harry, and Sandy more like Mildred." Although we shared traits from both of our parents, they were right. I am a storyteller and like to do one-liner wisecracks to get people to laugh, and am at the same time a "get on with it" guy. My looks and my inherited personality may explain why I was Pop's favorite and why he liked to make fun of Sandy. But I never felt that Sandy was Mom's favorite. Sandy and I weren't rivals for the affections of our parents or in any other way. As he said to me once before he died: "It has always been us against the world." I agreed that our bond was strong and unbreakable.

Years later, after my brother had a heart attack, which he blamed on the stress of dealing with my mom's physical problems (I was living in Indonesia) he stopped visiting Mom in her nursing home. After my return to the Bay Area from Indonesia, I stepped in and took over. One day she said to me, "Who would have ever thought it would be Alvin who would take care of me." This was a quintessential Millie remark.

Although growing up I never heard Mom badmouth Pop, I learned years later, when she refused to shake my father's hand at my nephew's bar mitzvah, that she continued to harbor deep resentments against him. Dad never made fun of her or in any way badmouthed her.

After my parents split I saw my father on a regular basis. As a preteen I joined my brother on the first Sunday of each month to collect a $50 bill as a family-support payment. As a teenager I worked at the candy store; we had meals together at neighborhood cafeterias and went to the Yonkers track on Saturdays to bet on the horseracing trotters. We never had father-son conversations about how to be in the world. We spent our time with him telling jokes and laughing. He had very little knowledge about my life and never asked me about it. He had no idea of my feelings or struggles. I had no role model of a father. I had an Old-World relationship with my mother. She was Mom, an authority figure and protector, but not someone you talked with about feelings or life. My brother and the Bronx streets provided my education.

THE CANDY STORE

The Bronx had many neighborhood candy stores where locals would meet and exchange pleasantries. Given the location of my father's store between the courthouse and the stadium, it not only provided this service for the locals but also served a larger clientele. The store was never more crowded than during the summers when the Jehovah Witnesses held their convention at Yankee Stadium.

The store was part of a block with many small stores, ranging from a Jewish deli to a photo/portrait/driver's license shop. It had a large sign over the front that advertised "Law Blanks" for the lawyers at the courthouse. To the right of the entrance door, a sliding window opened to an outside wooden stand where newspapers and magazines were displayed. In the winter you were met with a cold rush of air when you opened the window to accept payment from customers. My brother and I spent many late Saturday nights putting together the sections of the Sunday *New York Times* (Arts and Culture, Finance, Magazine, etc.) with the early edition of the Sunday news that was delivered to the store at 10:00 p.m.

A few steps farther in, you came upon the classic soda fountain with five stools, and you would usually bump into a lawyer from the courthouse, a neighboring stor-eowner, a kid with her mom, and transients on the way to the subway nearby. To the left of the fountain sat the ice cream containers. A wall ledge behind the counter held three malted-milk machines. I made many malted milk shakes and egg cream sodas at that soda fountain. An egg cream soda is a famous New York City institution, best savored with a long stick pretzel and a chocolate halva. Of course there is no egg in an egg cream, only milk, chocolate syrup, and seltzer. The origin of the name is lost to history. Many say it comes from the Yiddish *echt keem,* meaning pure sweetness. The secret of a good egg cream soda was the order in which you put the ingredients into the glass. I will continue to keep that secret.

The narrow pathway to the back of the store took you to the racks of comic books. They were an endless, free supply for my friends and me. This was another example of generosity mixed with my desire to be liked. Our favorites were *Superman, Batman,* and the *Green Lantern.* With my father's approval, I used to hide several comic books inside a single one and shout out to my Uncle Hoffy, "Only one, and only one!" Hoffy was a short, wiry, sour man. In all the years I knew him, I never saw him smile. He was renowned in the family as being extremely parsimonious. It was said of him that you could steal the store blind when the stock markets closed and he was reading the financial news section for the daily results. Needless to say, Hoffy did not want his profits to go down the nephew drain. This experience taught me that all lies are not equal and some are benign.

For a short period of time my father allowed "numbers" to be run out of the store. I was very impressed by the fact that the numbers runner could keep all the bets in his head. As the enterprise was illegal, no records were kept. It was an exciting glimpse into the underworld. I later learned that my mother's best friend's husband was a numbers runner. This nice man who lived next door was a cog in the world of the mob. Just as all lies are not equal, all illegal acts are not equal either. You can be a nice man and still break the law. Don't be too fast to judge. I also learned that many times hope overcomes rationality. Given the betters' limited amount of disposable income and the incredible odds against winning, it was not a logical act. I was never tempted to partake.

On one occasion I was asked by a regular customer how my sister was doing.

Since I didn't have a sister, I was taken aback momentarily until I realized this had to be my father spinning his tales. I responded, "She is just fine!" Watching my father spin tales, tell jokes, and otherwise engage with the customers taught me that the personal touch was essential in business. Pop's behavior was in stark contrast with Hoffy's cold, downer demeanor and tight-fisted personality.

The times when Sandy and I worked at the store together, one of us was stationed outside at the news table while the other served behind the soda counter. Dad could sit down on one of the stools and rest his feet from the weariness of standing for many hours. But most of the time only one of us worked at the store so the other could enjoy Saturday night with friends or play ball with friends on Sunday when the Yankees had a weekend home game.

Over the years, I got to know some of the Saturday night *NY Times* purchasers. They were lawyers, accountants, doctors, stockbrokers, and professors. We would talk about a trial, the market, or the latest news. Without being aware of it, I was interacting with possible role models.

CHAPTER 2

COMING OF AGE
IN THE CATSKILLS

From the age of fifteen to twenty-four (1953–1962), on my way to becoming a lawyer and international development consultant, I worked as a busboy and waiter in resort-hotels in the Catskill Mountains. The Catskills were also known as the Borscht Belt, or the Jewish Alps. In the fifties, over a million Jews took a yearly summer break from noise, heat, smells, and disease. After driving ninety miles and about two hours on the old New York State Route 17, northwest of NYC, one reached the towns of Monticello, South Fallsburg, Liberty, and Swan Lake. There were hundreds of hotels, cottages, bungalow colonies, and kokh-aleyns (Yiddish for self-catered boarding houses) in Sullivan and Ulster County, New York. Although these counties have beautiful lakes, walking trails, and densely wooded rolling mountains, the guests at the hotels came mainly for the food, rest, entertainment, and the swimming pools.

The Catskill had accommodations that matched people's incomes. The more expensive hotels had nightclubs (one was named after Jerry Lewis), where top comedians Buddy Hackett, Mel Brooks, Jerry Lewis, Sid Caesar, Jackie Mason, Danny Kaye, and Rodney Dangerfield learned their craft. Famous singers like Eddie Fisher,

Eddie Cantor, and Sammy Davis Jr. all played the Catskills. At the less expensive hotels, nighttime entertainment was "Simon Says" or Bingo in the "game room."

BORN SERVING FROM A TRAY

I could make around $2000 for the summer, mostly from tips—usually $20 to $30 per person, per week. My earnings covered all my needs for a year, including my college fees at City College of New York (CCNY), and helping my mother with household expenses. From the age of eleven until I started working in the Catskills, I covered most of my expenses as a delivery boy for a grocer and a meat shop. I never thought this was all that unusual. Sandy had done it, and a few of my friends also had jobs. Only when I reached high school did I realize I was in a minority. My new friends did not have part-time jobs. They lived in the elevator apartments with uniformed doormen, where I delivered orders.

Sandy had spent two summers as a waiter in the Adirondacks at the Scaroon Manor Hotel. When I told him I wanted to be a busboy, he taught me how to hold two cups of coffee in one hand and stack three main dishes up my forearm while carrying a fourth in the other hand. He also told me the rules of service. Serve and remove plates from the left. Serve and remove beverages from the right. Never reach across a guest to do either. Then, armed with his draft card (you were supposed to be eighteen years of age) I visited the main NYC employment agency for jobs in the Catskills. I never thought about the skills needed to be a busboy beyond what my brother taught me. How hard could it be? It turned out I was right in not worrying about it. Later in life, at the Civil Rights Division of the Justice Department, in the Carter administration, and as a development consultant in numerous countries, I mainly followed the same modus operandi: Be prepared and thoughtful, but do not overly worry about the direction you are taking. These lessons came easily to me because they fit my personality. Even at fifteen I was up for any new challenge. When asked at the employment agency where I had worked before, I spouted out the name Scaroon Manor and the name of the maître d' my brother had given me. I had no trouble lying since the agency would only hire people with prior experience—as if busboys and waiters were "born serving from a tray." I thought the rule was absurd, and I had full confidence I could do the job without doing harm to my employer or the guests. My first job was as a busboy at the Long Beach Country Club over the Passover holiday. Luckily, it turned out I was right: being a top-notch busboy was no big deal. The next time I returned to the employment agency to get a summer job, I was able to add a real job to my resume.

SWAN LAKE RESORT

Herbie Strauss, the maître d' of the Swan Lake Resort in Swan Lake, NY, happened to be at the employment agency that day. He was an easily excitable, stocky man with tight, wavy hair and a thick Viennese accent. He interviewed me and hired me on the spot. I worked for Herbie for nine years, one as a busboy, five as a waiter, and the final three as his headwaiter. Over time we became friends. A busboy's basic job is to clear the dishes and serve beverages. A great relationship between a busboy and waiter is essential for first-class service. A waiter needs to be able to rely on a busboy to get a dessert, more salad, or bread and butter. The busboy needs to fill in for the waiter when needed, expertly polish the silverware for him, and sometimes do the setup for the next meal. A waiter's task is to keep the guests happy. This can take many different forms. Attentive, speedy service is paramount of course, but so is creating a friendly atmosphere. Although being headwaiter paid me little more, it gave me status with the dining room staff and tightened my relationship with Herbie. He by then already steered the bigger tippers toward me. I always had the greatest number of guests, serving thirty-two to forty people at tables of eight, whereas other dining room staff would serve a maximum of thirty-two guests. In exchange for his largess, and armed with my title of Headwaiter, I acted as mediator for any problems with the dining room staff without bothering Herbie. If my mediation did not prevail, vigilante justice would. One professional waitress tried to cut corners and save money. Rather than paying her busboy to polish the silverware, she stole polished silverware late at night from the drawers of other waiters. I told her to stop, but she ignored me. When this was discovered, the waiters and busboys joined together, and in the middle of the night moved her tables and chairs to the lake. I gave my approval to their revenge. When the waitress arrived in the morning ready to serve breakfast, she faced an empty space where her station was supposed to be. The stealing stopped. My work as headwaiter lowered Hebie's stress quotient, kept him calmer, and allowed him to focus on the guests. I can still see the shaking in his hands and the flush redness of his face from heightened blood pressure disappear, as if by magic, when I said, 'I will take care of it."

We worked three meals a day, seven days a week, for fourteen weeks. The breaks during the day were short, from one to three hours. We were young and played just as hard at night as we worked during the day. Many nights I would go to sleep at one in the morning and awake at seven. After serving breakfast I sometimes took a one-hour nap before returning to the dining room. Many times I awoke to the sound of my alarm, not knowing where I was. My sleep was very deep. My body was giving me a message: slow down. Some nights I would listen, but most nights I would not. On one occasion I nearly paid a high price for not listening.

My father, who could barely afford it, managed only one stay as a guest at the Swan Lake Resort. My mother never visited as she worked Saturdays, and in any event did not have the means for such a weekend. Of course, I served my father's table. It was great fun to see him taking pride in "his son the waiter." He took many pictures of me in my uniform—black bow tie, black pants, white shirt, and black cummerbund. At the end of his weekend stay I drove him back to the city to avoid his having to take a bus again. I did not take my morning nap that Monday but instead spent time with him before serving lunch. Half way home, I dozed-off for a moment and found myself hitting the brakes on the grassy highway divider. The incident could have been much worse; I could have easily veered into another car. It showed how draining the Catskills lifestyle was. On my first two nights home after the season, I usually slept fourteen to fifteen hours.

Different groups of the staff went out together, dancing and partying at different hotels. The fact that I loved to dance and was good at it was a definite plus. The evening usually ended with a late-night lox and bagel or pastrami or corned beef sandwich at the always-crowded delis in Monticello or South Fallsburg. We told jokes about our guests and the kitchen staff and laughed a lot. One of the bad jokes of the time was: Question: Why do seagulls fly over the sea? Answer: If they flew over the bay they'd be bagels. There was a great sense of camaraderie among most of the Swan Lake Resort staff that did not exist at the larger hotels. In Jackie Mason's one-man show on Broadway, he joked that the Christians in the audience were whispering about where they would go for a drink after the show, while the Jews were trying to decide where to go for a meal. However, I was one Jew who kept considering both. Years later, my idea of a great night used to start with two martinis and dinner at Windows of the World, at the top of the World Trade Center, followed by dancing at Club Le Jardin, at the Diplomat Hotel. I wished I could afford a black tie and tails on these nights; nonetheless my fantasy of being Fred Astaire was fulfilled. It could not get more sophisticated.

Grossinger's and its rivals, the Concord, Brown's, The Pines, the Waldmere, Kutcher's, and the Commodore were among the bigger and better-known hotels. Although I worked some of them during Passover and other Jewish holidays, I returned to the Swan Lake Resort and Herbie Strauss each summer. The money I could make would be less, but the stress would also be substantially less, given my relationship with Herbie and the dining room and kitchen staff. When I worked at the bigger hotels, I was usually low man on the totem pole, with a station farthest from the kitchen and an inexperienced busboy. This made it very difficult to give good service and avoid guest complaints. In addition, I sometimes had to put up with a crazy owner. One of them, an older woman, would station herself by the juice dispensers, dressed in her best evening wear, and yell at any of us who made the mistake of filling the glasses too generously. Talk about the absurd. She was not saving any overhead that would matter to the bottom line. This same owner prevented the dining room staff from eating the same meals as the guests. We were served less appetizing, cheaper meals. She carried her policy to the extreme of positioning herself in the kitchen on steak night and counting the steaks ordered by the guests to ensure we didn't whisk one away for ourselves. Her attitude inspired us to figure out ways to beat her system. One method was enlisting a trusted guest to order a second steak that was really for us. We called this "scoffing." We would sneak the steak back to our sleeping quarters, a converted kitchen space. The owner, in her evening attire, accompanied by the maître d', would then "sweep" our sleeping quarters to check for scoffed food. The waiters retaliated by setting off the smoke alarm, suppressing their laughter when she came rushing into the kitchen. The lesson I learned from this was to always treat my own staff with generosity and respect. This was not only the appropriate moral attitude but also made the most business sense—a happy confluence of the practical and the ideal.

Aside from Passover and other Jewish weekend holidays, the guests came for a week or two, a month or the entire summer. Couples, families, or singles made up the mix. Different hotels marketed to different groups. Usually when families spent the summer at a smaller, less expensive hotel, the men commuted to New York City for work and returned for the weekend. It reminds me of a joke told by Catskill comics: "What are the three words a woman never wants to hear when she is making love? Honey, I'm home." It was not uncommon for the staff to "look after" the left-behind moms during the week. Singles came for a weekend or a week to a hotel that catered to them, such as the Waldmere. The single women were looking for a husband, the men for sex. Both used to be successful. Husband-hunting single women were given the nickname "barracudas." It was a time when attitudes toward women were not exactly enlightened, to say the least.

Many hotels wanted the staff to mix with the guests at night to create a fun atmosphere. The Waldmere even had the requirement that the dining room staff draw straws to see who had to dance with the "ugliest" woman. The waiters usually provided her with a good time no matter what! On the several weekends I worked there, the maître d' learned that I was a good dancer, and pressured me to go dancing each night at the hotel's nightclub. Luckily we had the option to bail out of the drawing if we were not going to the Waldmere's nightclub. I could keep my relationship on an even keel with him by going to the hotel's nightclub on one night, on a second night joining other dining room staff at another hotel nightclub, or on a third simply going to sleep early. I have always thought it wise not to bite the hand that feeds you. As I only worked brief shifts at the Waldmere, the maître d' accepted my "nightclub solution."

EAT THE MENU

The main reason people went to the Catskills for their vacation was the food. Except for self-catering hotels, guests did not pay per dish for what they ate; all three meals where included in the daily price. You could not opt out of a meal and pay less. Of course, this meant everyone overate. Each meal consisted of hot and cold main dishes, salads, appetizers, melons, juices, and desserts. We labeled certain guests, "Eat the Menu" folks. This was not a figurative term. These guests literally ate every item listed on the menu. All the juices, melons, appetizers, salads, hot and cold main dishes, and desserts were consumed. This was an almost unbelievable feat to observe. Astonishingly, the "Eat the Menu" men and woman were not always fat.

People were often extremely picky around food, and very demanding. I remember vividly the first time I returned a hand-carved piece of roast beef because it was "not rare enough" for the guest. The chef dipped a brush in a cup of blood, painted the meat, and gave me back the plate to serve. At other times a guest requested his roast beef "well-done," and he then complained: "I ordered well-done!" In this case the chef took a bowl of "au jus" and rubbed it into the meat. I repeatedly heard a guest exclaim that for the first time in many years the roast beef was just as he wanted! This revelation then resulted in a bigger tip. I would chuckle to myself because people's fussiness was a function of their personality rather than their sophisticated taste. They simply were complainers!

Similarly, some of the older guests, especially women, were never satisfied that their tea was hot enough, even when you had washed out the cup in scalding water. In an extreme case, after discussion with the chef, the cup and water were put in the oven and served on a cool saucer. Needless to say, the unreasonable demands stopped without a word being spoken. To paraphrase a Catskills joke: "Question: What did a waiter say to a group of [older Jewish women]? Answer: Is anything okay?"

We never wrote down the orders but simply memorized them. Many times I earned extra money by betting a guest who sat at a table of eight that I would remember not only the entire order, but also each individual's choice. I found it all easy to recall by starting from the person I bet and going to his left, not taking anyone's order out of turn.

The better tippers were usually, but not always, the nicer guests. One guest stayed a month and tipped me $200 per week for him and his wife. He owned a bakery in NYC, and when his employees joined him for different parts of the month, he checked to see whether they had sufficiently tipped me. Even though I always responded in the affirmative, he would give me an additional tip for them. Of course I loved him, not only for the money, but because he genuinely cared about me. He wanted to know all about me: Where was I from, did I have a girlfriend, what did I want from life, how did I pick philosophy to study and teach? He also liked to laugh, something we had in common.

The Swan Lake Resort could accommodate four hundred guests. You entered the hotel via a long driveway that ran from the public highway wrapped around Swan Lake. The dining room was in the main building, as were the reception, a recreation hall for entertainment, and rooms for two hundred guests. The other guests were housed in a series of bungalows at a short distance from the main building and the swimming pool area.

The hotel's guests were 99 percent Jewish; the other 1 percent were Christians who found themselves lost in the Catskills and needed food and shelter. Saturday night was lobster night. Yes, you read that correctly. The resort did not keep a kosher kitchen (lobster is a shellfish and not kosher), and the guests knew this beforehand. They looked forward to lobster night. "It tastes good, it's probably not kosher," is an old joke. The Catskills mirrored Judaism itself, running from Chasidic to Orthodox, and from Conservative to Reform, with the many different gradations in each branch of the faith. But there were many "cultural" Jews who did not observe the rules of any of these divisions. I called these folks, of which I am one, the "sour kosher pickle, corned beef sandwich, and Nazi movie" Jews. There were also the Zionist Jews whose only tenet was belief in and support of the State of Israel. All these Jews were held together by two important facts: 1) in the best Talmudic tradition, they were all part of a "religion of lawyers" who loved to argue; 2) they were all subject to anti-Semitism, all "children of David" and survivors of the Holocaust. The Catskills had a resort for each and every type of Jew. Although the kitchen staff did not mirror the guests' ethnicity, the dining room staff did.

Getting back to the popular lobster night, it was very tricky to properly build up the bulky, very heavy plates stacked on your serving tray and carry them without incident to your station to serve to the guests. A way to prevent a lobster from falling off the tray was to limit the number of plates on it. Because of my relationship with the chef and Herbie, the maître d', I was allowed to exceed the limit that was in place for other waiters. I had the skill to properly stack the awkward plates, and the strength and dexterity to maneuver the tray through the narrow pathways of the dining room to my station dresser. This allowed me to give faster service to the guests. I remember the disapproving look from the chef the one and only time a plate dropped off my serving tray. He ordered his staff to clean up the peas and liquid butter that had splattered all over the kitchen floor. He never said a word about it, and I continued to carry the maximum amount of lobster plates I could handle.

Accidents did regularly happen over a season. A waiter or busboy would slip on a wet spot in the dining room, and all heads would turn to the sound of the crash and the breaking plates. One time a busboy carrying a pot of hot coffee slipped and splashed a small amount of coffee down the front of a woman's dress. I heard her shriek, and I was just in time to see a quick-witted guest at the next table jump up and pour the contents of a cream pitcher over her dress, successfully cooling off the coffee. "Wow," I thought, "bravo, and I hope I could think and act that fast."

The man who prepared the Maine lobsters for the chef to cook was the first person I met with a number tattooed on his forearm. Yes, a survivor of the concentration camps. He was a short, wiry man with a heavy Slavic accent and an ever-present stubble beard. He did not talk much, but as he hacked each lobster into the proper size, he shouted, "Himmler, Eichmann, Bormann, Hess, Göring, Goebbels!" He repeated these names in the same order until his lobsters were done. Strangely, he never mentioned Hitler! We never had a conversation, and I never asked him for the name of his concentration camp. In retrospect, I chalk this up to the self-centeredness of youth. To paraphrase an old TV program intro: "There are a million stories in the Catskills," but this was one story I did not get to know.

Paul, the sous chef, was a very large, well-educated man. He had been an engineer in Hungary and too vocal in his negative comments about the Communist government and Russia. Fearing for his life, he fled to Argentina, leaving his wife and child behind. Since he could not find work as an engineer, he became a chef. He was unable to get his wife and child out of Hungary. When things changed there it was too late—life had taken his profession and family away. He continued on in the States as best he could, with an underlying sadness that was visible and ever-present. My eyes began to open as to how many people had much more difficult lives than mine.

I also learned to be careful about assumptions. My long-term busboy of six years was an eighteen-year-old who had escaped with his family from Hungary, after the Russians forcibly ended the revolution. To my surprise, he deeply resented that he'd had to leave. He had been a top-rated wrestler, and had a life of privileges and a bright future. He lost it all when his family forced him to leave with them. He continued his resentment throughout the time I knew him. In direct contrast to my assumptions, he thought privilege was more important than freedom. Later in law school I was taught that assumptions were the enemy of a good lawyer.

One summer, a blond young man from a rural area in Kansas became the lifeguard at the pool. He told me he sought out the job so he could see for himself if Jews really had horns and tails. His story just made me laugh. He found out that he liked Jews.

ICE CREAM AND MURDER

Friday night dinner service was always a challenge. The kitchen was slow because each piece of roast beef was hand cut. Unlike other days when the guests came in at the same time, on Friday nights they would drive up from NYC and enter the dining room two, four, or eight at a time, usually over a period of thirty to forty-five minutes. This meant I sometimes had to be at the roast beef cutting station, the salad counter, and the dessert station at the same time. Coordination with my busboy was essential. If I got stuck on the main dish line, he had to pick up salads or desserts for the guests who had already finished their roast beef. Because of the Friday tension the kitchen usually decided to serve only one flavor of ice cream. One week it was butter pecan and of course a number of guests requested chocolate. I had just explained to these guests that we were serving only butter pecan ice cream when the kitchen ran out of butter pecan and started to serve up chocolate. Come on, why not vanilla, which at least looks like butter pecan? My eagle-eyed guests who had requested chocolate ice cream spotted the "brown gold" being served at nearby tables and demanded to know why I had said there was no chocolate ice cream. There was no way to quickly or satisfactorily explain the "why," and I had to expect a reduced tip because of kitchen stupidity.

While waiting for my next orders of ice cream at the counter, I started to curse the absurd system that gave me problems with my guests. Suddenly, out of the corner of my eye, I saw the dessert assistant, a French Canadian, come at me from the back of the serving station and swing his fist at my head. He thought I had cursed him. I jumped back, and he missed. My Hungarian busboy gripped him as he tried to jump over the counter to get at me. He shouted he was going to get his gun as soon as he could and shoot me. We all knew he had a gun. Most of the assistants on the kitchen staff, as well as the pot and plate washers, were guys down on their luck for different reasons. The majority of these men were alcoholics, aggressive, arrogant, and deeply insecure, often quick to take insult where none was intended.

Of course the chef and the owner came rushing over to see what was happening. I told them my busboy would continue the service while I would take a brief walk to the lake to cool off. I needed time to recapture my equilibrium. I imagined a headline in the next day's *Herald Tribune*: "Catskill Waiter Shot Dead over a Butter Pecan Ice Cream." By the time I returned to the dining room a few minutes later, the local police had already put the guy on a bus back to Quebec. During my absence my busboy had expertly handled the dessert requests. Yes, this included chocolate ice cream. "Thanks a lot, folks," was all I could mutter to myself. Everything had happened in the kitchen out of sight of my guests, so they had no idea about my pending demise.

A word about the chef, whose name was Frank. We worked together for seven summers. He was a very talented, handsome, diminutive man who ran his kitchen with a strong hand but without the temperamental outbursts of many other chefs I worked with. He and Herbie taught me about food and wine. One of Frank's specialties that he would make as a treat for the three of us was carved melon balls soaked overnight in brandy. I learned about kirschwasser, Riesling, German Pinot Noir, and life. They also taught me about formal silverware setups and which knife and fork to use first. They regaled me with stories of their life, of growing up in Austria and Germany. I learned about wives they hardly saw, and their divorces. Like the professional waitresses I worked with, they led nomad lives. In the winter they worked in Miami Beach, and in the Catskills in the summer. Separation apparently did not make the heart grow fonder. I remembered this lesson years later when I too led a nomad life, working as an international consultant in numerous countries such as Russia, Albania, Moldova, India, Indonesia, and Cambodia. I tried very hard to keep my absences from home down to three weeks at a time.

Breakfast chefs were essential to the hotel kitchen. They were often of Asian background. One or two breakfast chefs would handle the orders of 200 to 600 guests. They prided themselves on remembering each order and to which waiter it belonged. They remembered whether it was fried, poached, or shirred eggs, omelets, pancakes, or waffles. They would bellow a string of expletives, sometimes in Chinese, at anyone who tried to pick up another waiter's order. It was great fun to yell in an order of "huffin' on the makin'" and watch them pick up an omelet pan, put in some butter and then strain to remember what the order was. When they got that I was joshing them, they would threaten to throw a hatchet at me, but with a smile on their face.

BOILED EGGS AND CAMUS

In the big hotels, we did not have any protection against someone stealing our boiled eggs. Waiters made their own boiled eggs. We placed up to two eggs in a metal container of a machine that automatically lowered them along a metal spine into boiling water. Each machine had individual timers from two to four minutes. It was impossible to tell whose egg was whose. So taking whatever eggs were ready was the order of the day. Sometimes this resulted in a shouting match between waiters. It was as if a Rube Goldberg cartoon had come to life.

My summers at the Swan Lake Resort were enhanced by my relationship with the owner who, Herbie informed me, wanted me to marry his daughter. Although she and I went out dancing a few times, there was no click. Dancing told me if there was a sensual spark that would act as a touchstone for a deeper, meaningful connection. Her father was a decent man with an intellectual bent. His desire for me as a son-in-law was probably influenced by who he thought I was: assistant professor of philosophy at the University of Chicago. As I had lied about my age when I started working in the Catskills, over the years I developed a story to match my "adopted" age. I was still in high school when my brother helped me purchase a Columbia University sports jacket. It made sense to say I was attending Columbia University. Didn't the jacket prove it? My reality was Taft High School in the Bronx, and then CCNY. After starting law school at the University of Chicago, I changed my school and title because it's easier to remember details of a lie that are based on facts. Another reason to perpetuate the myth of being an assistant professor was my giving poolside lectures to the guests on Existentialism, especially Camus. I remember the guests in bathing suits, some in their minks in spite of the summer heat, gathered next to the pool. They usually numbered between thirty and fifty. They were mainly women. To my surprise they often asked pertinent and insightful questions. Juxtaposed to the lectures were martial art lessons conducted once a week by my Hungarian busboy, George. My soon-to-become wife, Linda (1963–1966), who was a waitress at the resort, and I alternated as "attackers" with fake knives to allow George to demonstrate how to disarm us.

The lectures were a success, and the *Herald Tribune* wrote a flattering article about them. The incongruity of this once-a-week scene at the pool was not lost on me. What was also not lost was the fact that this article gave me too high a profile.

Afraid of more press coverage and being found out, I abandoned my "professorial" lectures at the poolside.

My time in the Catskills ended more with a whimper than a bang. Increased income, especially among the guests of the middle and smaller sized hotels, the development of the airline industry, and the availability of resorts elsewhere that were open to Jews helped begin the slide that resulted in the demise of the Catskills. By 1961, my guest load was down by one quarter. And in the summer of 1962, Linda and I took a two-week break from the hotel due to lack of guests. My nine-year run in the Catskills was over. One of my favorite jokes from the Catskills is this: "Let me give you a short summary of every Jewish holiday: They tried to kill us. We won. Let's eat."

CHAPTER 3

MUCH OF WHAT I NEEDED TO KNOW IN LIFE I LEARNED IN THE BRONX

During my school years, blacks and Puerto Ricans would arrive and turn their enclaves into their own neighborhoods, while the long-term ethnic residents fled for the all-white areas in the Bronx and Queens. While many neighborhoods changed their racial and ethnic mix in the '60s and '70s, my college and law school friend Paul Marino's neighborhood in the northeast Bronx stayed Italian. Some (including Marino) say this was due to the efforts of the Mafia members who lived there.

My friends—Conway, O'Neil, Duggan, and Nash, to name a few—never hurled any anti-Semitic slur words in my direction, whereas they had no restraint when it came to blacks or Puerto Ricans, especially when members of those groups moved closer to our block. My brother was not so lucky, and a kid named Skates harassed him for being Jewish. Sandy's close friends, all Jews, lived a block or two away in a fancier neighborhood. Thus he had no one on the block to protect him from Skates. It probably did not help with the tougher kids on the block that he would wear his Club Scout and Boy Scout uniforms when he went to meetings. No one else on the block, his generation or mine, were members. I refused to join either organization, loudly expressing to my mother my opinion that they were "like the World War II Fascist organizations with their uniforms and mind-manipulation patriotism."

MOVIE ADVENTURES

Growing up, every other Saturday was movie theater time with Sandy or a few friends. We had many choices of theaters. The Earl on 161st Street and the Fleetwood on Morris Avenue were the closest. You could see a double feature plus the cartoons for thirty-four to fifty-two cents. Roy Rogers and his sidekick Gabby Hayes, Gene Autry, Randolph Scott and Hopalong Cassidy were the top cowboy movie stars. Roy Rogers and Gabby Hayes were my favorites. John Wayne, William Holden, Humphrey "Bogey" Bogart, James Cagney, Edward G. Robinson, Peter Lorre, and Sydney Greenstreet were the war and gangster movie stars. My favorites were Bogey, Peter Lorre, and Sidney Greenstreet.

The Lowe's Paradise Theatre, although more expensive, was a special treat. My second major childhood memory took place at this theater, when I was seven and my brother was eleven. We went to see *The Spanish Main* with Paul Henreid, watching the movie from the balcony. We loved sitting in the balcony, especially during a pirate movie, because at the end we could "sword"-stick duel down the spiral staircase to the ground floor. But on that day, there was no dueling. Toward the end of the movie, my leg joints suddenly froze, and I was unable to move or walk. There was no panic on Sandy's or my part. He simply carried me downstairs and called my mother. Our family doctor, Dr. Holtzman, met us at the hospital. It turned out I had rheumatic fever. I was in the hospital for six days. Penicillin, which had just begun to be widely produced, saved me and prevented severe damage to my heart, but I still could not walk when I was discharged from the hospital. An appointment had been scheduled at Dr. Holtzman's office the next day, and I decided that I would not be carried into his office. It would be too embarrassing. I was old enough to walk!

The morning of the appointment I was seated at the kitchen table. I pushed my chair away from the table and decided to walk the few steps to the cabinet of "shattered glass" fame. On my first try I fell back into the chair. On the second, I found myself standing but unable to walk. I closed my eyes and said to myself: "Do it!" It worked and I walked the four steps to the cabinet. I repeated this three times and later that day proudly walked into Dr. Holtzman's office unaided. Tenacity became a part of my personality. A funny thing about this momentous moment in my life was that my mother had no recollection of it. Later, when I became a parent myself, I realized that momentous events for a child might not be the same for the parent. We all go through life in our own world.

As I said, my mother was not the nurturing type, but I always knew she loved me and was concerned about my physical health. After my bout with rheumatic fever she set me up with a charge account at Hirschman's candy store across the street from our apartment so I could "put meat on my bones" with milkshakes. I would add egg creams and candy for the guys on the block. This was a combination of my natural generosity and a wish to be popular. My mother stored a rasher of bacon outside on the fire-escape for me, even though she kept a kosher home. She knew I loved it, and I still do. Sandy had no burning desire to share the bacon.

Years later my brother told me he thought these were examples of how my mother spoiled me. But did she? In putting aside her religious beliefs, was she spoiling me or, as with the Hirschman's charge account, simply acting as my protector? BLT sandwiches and milkshakes did put weight on me.

YANKEE STADIUM, AUTOGRAPHS, AND LEARNING STREET SMARTS

Between the age of eight and fifteen, I went to a lot of games at Yankee Stadium, but I rarely paid to get in. Many times my friends and I would hang around the entrances before the game started, asking for "extra tickets." Almost without fail, a man and his friends would invite us to join them for the game. They often had the best box seats on the Yankee side. A Coke and hotdog were normally part of the bargain. I gave their generosity no thought at the time, but now I surmise these season ticket holders, rather than have a ticket go to waste, would "take pity" on the poor kids from the neighborhood. Other times, our group of friends bunched up at an entrance to the outfield at the beginning of the seventh inning, and at the count of three ran inside. Of course the four or five of us were too many and the guards were too slow to catch us. We then walked around looking for empty seats. Sometimes we also watched World Series games from the roof of an apartment house across from the Stadium. The view was partially obstructed and far away from home plate, but still it was a thrill to watch a World Series game live.

Most of us collected autographs of the players—my collection included all the greats (Joe DiMaggio, Ted Williams, Jackie Robinson) and the not-so-famous (including Yankee relief pitcher Randy Gumpert and Giants pitcher Sal Maglie). I got to know and understand the power of being a groupie. I gave my autograph book to one of the "Yankee ladies" (they were young, beautiful, and always very kind to me) who returned it the next day with some of the harder-to-get Yankee players such as Allie Reynolds. I often took the subway (D train) to downtown Manhattan and went to the hotels (the New Yorker for the American League, and the Commodore for the National League) where the visiting players stayed, and snatched autographs as they entered or emerged. These were the first-class hotels of the day with large, fancy lobbies and chandeliers. It was important to make friends with the doormen so they would allow you to stand around the entrance. Other National League players' autographs I obtained by waiting outside the players' entrance of the Polo Grounds, the home field of the Giants before they moved to San Francisco. I was particularly lucky to get Johnny Mize's autograph at the World Series party celebration at the Plaza Hotel on 161st Street and the Grand Concourse, three blocks from home. Mize was drunk at the time, slurring his words and unsteady, which turned out to be to my advantage as he was known to be a belligerent man who rarely gave autographs when sober.

One time the great Ted Williams was walking into the hotel where I stood guard. He said, "Kid, I will get you on my way out." Later I spotted him at a window of the team bus as it was starting to drive away. I yelled out, "You promised, you promised!" The bus stopped, he opened the window, and signed my book.

I had two "album books," one for each league. There was room for four or five autographs per page. I didn't add pictures. Unlike some of my buddies, I was not into picture baseball cards that were sold with chewing gum. They did not seem genuine to me, but simply a merchandising device. We competed to see who could get the most difficult to obtain and the most famous players to sign. My collection was one of the very best. Getting Williams to sign my book was an early example of my tenacity and successful negotiation.

Years later, my son Noel was heartbroken (as was I) to learn that my mother had given my autograph collection and PM2 mitt to my cousin Stephen. I guess she thought I had outgrown both and did not think about a grandchild. At that late date I didn't want to ask to get them back. I never found out if he passed them on to his son or just disposed of them.

STREET GAMES

Jackie Nash was our neighborhood gang leader because he was a few years older and the best athlete on the block. He was fast, tall, muscular, and good-looking. He threw a football and hit a baseball farther than anyone else. Nash did well enough at school, and at eighteen went on to college to become a civil engineer. But smarts did not count for much on the streets, which was demonstrated by our next leader, "Winkie." He was a sixteen-year-old pockmarked, skinny kid who was a terrible student and always in trouble at school for truancy and stealing. Nonetheless his strong personality and athletic ability made him the head of our group for a year or so. His first big-time criminal job after high school was to rob a federal armory for guns. He was caught and sentenced to a number of years in a federal penitentiary.

The streets were our sports field. We played stickball, curb ball, and pitching in. All three of these games involved a pink rubber Spaulding ball. For stickball we used a broomstick. The brush part of the broom was sawed off, and the front fenders of parked cars served as first and third base. The round sewer holes in the middle of the street were second base and home plate. A "two-sewer man" meant you hit the ball on the fly for three- to four-hundred feet and thus were a power hitter.

Curb ball was played at a street intersection. The home and second base corners had a rain sewer with an open part on the curb of the sidewalk and a closed grated part in the street. You had to throw the ball at the top edge of the home base curb to get a hit. When the ball went down into the sewer we would remove the grated metal part and lower a boy down to retrieve the ball. He would use the end of a metal hanger twisted into a cup-like shape at its end to spoon up our Spaulding. The retrieval required a steady hand. When he had completed the task, his clothes would be dirty from lying on his stomach in the street. This guy was on the lower rung of the athletic gang pecking order and didn't have the personality to say, "Not me."

On my first trip to Venice seven years later, I wrote a postcard to the guys from the block who I remained in touch with, saying that here a "two-sewer man" would lose the ball in the canals.

"Pitching in" was a simple game. We would chalk a rectangle box on a wall that approximated the batter's strike zone, and pitch in from across the street. Hellerstein and I endlessly played this game. The batter would use the same broomstick we used in stickball. The streets also served as our football field for two-hands-below-the-waist touch football. Quarterback instructions were, "Alvin, go to red Ford and break left, and Jerry, go to white Chrysler and break right." We played "ice hockey" and roller derby in the streets with clamp-on metal roller skates. By using vegetable wood crates for the body and wooden planks from the crates for handles, and attaching our metal skates to two-by-fours that were in turn nailed to the body, we built "skate scooters" for racing.

The streets were my playground, and I loved them. I would spend two to three hours on a weekday and five hours on the weekend with the gang. Although I was not a natural athlete and not the first guy chosen when we were dividing up sides from the group, I discovered that by showing heart, grit, and a desire to win, I would be chosen in the second group. My determination allowed me to play above my physical abilities. These same qualities often served me well as an adult, although I could go overboard. For example, during a friendly tennis doubles match with my then-wife Susanne, she often threatened to stop playing with me because of my aggressive competitiveness.

My speed allowed me to make catches in the outfield or in touch football. Being part of the key play to win a game was exhilarating. I would fantasize doing it in a professional or college game even though given my skill level, there was no way for me to participate in either.

Although my modest athletic talents prevented me from being the leader on the block, I was always part of the top group of guys. The streets taught me that being on the winning side was often a matter of being chosen by or choosing the best athletes. This was a lesson I applied years later in choosing staff in the Carter administration and as the director of an anti-poverty law center (the National Housing Law Project). It also served me well in choosing business partners in Indonesia. I always liked motivating and leading a team effort. I recognized I could achieve more by hiring strong, outstanding folks. I was not afraid to hire people smarter than myself who were not afraid to argue with me as we developed strategies and programs Starting in college, I recognized I could inspire people and have them follow my lead. My debating skills and lack of fear making decisions overcame my limitations from my mild dyslexia. The embarrassment of not being able to spell (pre-spellcheck) or accurately proofread a page faded.

In sports, my performance exceeded my brother's. I could always beat him at one-on-one basketball. This added to my enjoyment. Matching his academic excellence was another matter. My dyslexia (only recognized after my daughter was diagnosed with this problem) also created difficulties with standardized tests that made this competition impossible.

Street play with the gang was the catalyst for one of my first successful negotiations. Going to Hebrew School after my public-school classes interfered with my play time with the boys. When my bar mitzvah approached at age thirteen, everyone was concerned that I was not properly preparing for my reading (havtorah) of the Torah. I kept skipping Hebrew School, and it was clear that my heart was not in it. To his credit, the Rabbi recognized the problem and we made a deal. He gave me a recording of my reading; I could study and memorize it at home and did not have to come to Hebrew School. I remained free to play with the boys. To the surprise of the Rabbi, my mother, my father, and members of the congregation, I "nailed" it.

Another example of the pull of the streets was how playing ball with the gang and their expectations superseded another passion of mine—tap dancing. My tap-dancing career was short-lived and ended somewhere between twelve and fifteen. My mother had spent money from her tight budget on tap shoes and lessons. My tap-dance teachers had told me that I was a natural, and they wanted to arrange an audition for a TV program called *The Children's Hour*. But I declined. Tap dancing simply was not what the boys on the block did. As an adult I have often wondered what path my life might have taken if I had accepted the audition. Would I have had a career as a dancer in the mode of Fred Astaire? Then my next thought would be, "But I cannot sing on tune. No way." My Aunt Esther who lived with us for a year carried on about how irresponsible I was for making my mother spend the money on the tap shoes when I didn't use them. Needless to say, I never liked my Aunt Esther. She was an unhappy, judgmental, and negative person. My mother once told me a failed love affair was the cause. I never found out what occurred to make her move in with us and share my mother's bed.

DETERMINATION IS NOT ALWAYS ENOUGH

Years later, when I was forty, I decided to take ballet lessons. This was a hilarious mistake. It was an example of my Don Quixote "What was I thinking?" personality. I cramped when I tried to curl my toes for the *retiré devant* position. The list of things I could not do went on until I gave it up. Why I didn't choose tap lessons, given my earlier promise and my love of Fred Astaire, is a mystery. Similarly, I chose to learn classical guitar over basic folk music, again demonstrating the unreal fantasy part of myself. Full steam ahead. With determination, I thought I could do anything, as I had conquered rheumatic fever or prevailed in the street games. Sometimes yes, but sometimes no, and again no! I continued to love watching ballet and to dance to all kinds of music from Zydeco to Latin and ballroom.

A joyful event that fulfilled a boy's sports fantasy was the intramural Jordan L. Mott Junior High School Basketball Tournament. I sunk two free throws at the buzzer to win the game for my team. "Al, the hero." This was an example of my street resolve making up for natural talent.

Another youthful sports "claim to fame" was running in the 500-meter race at the High School Indoor Nationals in Madison Square Garden. Only the "best" participated. My mom and Sandy attended. The track at the Garden was very steeply banked. As it turned out, there were too many runners bunched together in my qualifying heat. The gun went off, there was a lot of shoving, and about three meters after we came off the first high-banked turn, I tripped over the heel of the runner in front of me and stumbled. Although I recovered before actually falling to the ground, the other runners were by then too far ahead. I came in dead last. Given the talent gathered in my heat, I would have come in last anyway. But now I had my excuse. Sad—yes, but not entirely. I learned that sometimes what appears to be a disaster is a lucky break and that determination doesn't always win the day.

In the streets, our favorite evening game was ring-a-levio. Depending on the season, we played it before or after supper. The fading daylight was not good enough for ball sports. We divided ourselves into teams of between four and five per side.

One of us was the jailer-protector of a rectangle box drawn with chalk on the sidewalk. The aim of the game was to capture all your opponents and put them in jail in the rectangle box. You could free your teammates by putting one foot into the jail and yelling three times, "Ring-a-levio, one, two, and three." All manner of mayhem was allowed. My competitive resolve made it hard to stop me. I had to free my team members from jail at any cost.

On one occasion two boys grabbed me, lifted me high off the ground, and dropped me. I put my arm out to break the fall. The pain in my arm stopped me from playing on. After dinner that night I complained, and my mother instructed me to go to the emergency room of the neighborhood hospital in the morning and have it checked out. Morrisania was a public hospital with very long waiting times. I told my mother I would go, but I had no intention of waiting forever (several hours) to be seen. I simply set foot in the emergency room, turned around, and left. When my mom asked if I had gone to the hospital I said yes. For me it was a fib rather than a lie. Even at an early age the streets taught me to be in charge of myself. Luckily, my arm was not broken; it healed.

MOVING ON FROM THE BLOCK

After high school ended, a number of us moved away to attend college or a seminary. Several of the guys, including myself, attended "subway colleges" (we lived at home and commuted to school every day) such as CCNY or Brooklyn College. Over the next four years the "street" was less the center of our social life. Although gathering on the block never fully stopped, college friends and activities now became our focus.

My friend and neighbor Hellerstein started Harvard Law School during my last year of college. Since my mother worked a few nights a week and I hated eating alone, I offered to make dinner for his father (his mother had died several years earlier) on Thursday nights. He was a short, stocky man with a twinkle in his eyes. I loved his stories about Russia before and after the revolution, and how he had avoided the army by absenting himself from his village when he learned soldiers were going around to villages to enlist young men. He repeated his being absent on several soldier visits until his family left for America. On other occasions I enjoyed the arguments Mr. Hellerstein had with a lifelong friend from the old country about the glory of socialism versus communism. Before Thanksgiving, he stopped me on the street to tell me his son was coming home for the holiday and it was his turn to cook dinner. That night was filled with laughter and a father's pride for his son, the "law student." We were eating dessert and laughing when "Mr. H" (this is how I addressed him) collapsed from what turned out be a heart attack, hitting his head on the table on his way to the floor. I looked at his vacant eyes and purple face and ran to the phone to dial 911. His son held him in his arms. It was clear to me that he was dead. After the paramedics arrived and pronounced him dead, I called my mother who had just arrived home. She came over to Mr. H's apartment, comforted his son, and invited him to stay with us. The next day Hellerstein and I made funeral arrangements. I helped him pick a wooden casket from the depths of the funeral home. "From dust to dust." Life was making me an adult.

I stopped living full time at 237 East 163rd street in 1961, when I went to the University of Chicago Law School and subsequently married my first wife, Linda, in 1963.

The last time I stayed at my mom's apartment was the summer of 1964. Mom had gone to live with a friend around the corner so that my law school friend Dave Madway and I could study for the NY State bar exam. Linda and Dave's wife, Nancy, also stayed with us.

After two weeks of cramming Dave and I decided we needed a break, and a movie was in order. All four of us went down the street to my car, which was parked in front of St. Angela, on Grant. I had lent the car to another friend, and I saw that my Ford was banged up and the rear trunk was tied shut with strong rope. It was quite a sight. Once a good-looking car, it was now in need of substantial repair. My car had its own wild street life!

We got in and I turned the ignition key, but nothing happened. Madway joked, "What have you done to the battery, Hirshen?" I got out of the car and opened the hood. There was no battery. It had been stolen. We took a bus to get to the movie just in time. The next morning when I went down to take care of the car, I saw a Puerto Rican family (husband, wife, and three kids) removing the four tires along with other parts from the engine. I said to them, "Good pickings?" They did not respond but simply walked away. The following day, the four doors had been removed. The neighborhood had become even rougher than I remembered. Given the pressure of studying for the bar, and the fact that not a lot of money was lost, I took no action. It pleased me that Madway had had a firsthand view of what I had been telling him about the streets of the Bronx. After the exam we would find our own apartments and start our jobs.

I landed a job as a law clerk for a federal court judge for the Southern District of New York. I was helped by a maxim learned in the Bronx: "Don't stop yourself from doing anything. Let the other guy say no." Although I was only in the top 25 percent of my class at the University of Chicago Law School (not Harvard or Yale), I pursued the clerkship. It turned out that the judge wanted to break the mold. He related to my modest upbringing and hired me.

My mother did not move from the block to an apartment in the northwest section of the Bronx until 1965, when I moved to DC with Linda to join the Civil Rights Division of the Justice Department. Mom had told me that no matter how much she cleaned, cockroaches kept appearing. She blamed this on the inadequate cleaning performance of her new Puerto Rican neighbors. I flew up from DC after she moved, and at her request went to the apartment for a last checkout. I was met with a sea of wall-to-wall cockroaches everywhere. They did not flee into the crevices even when I put on the lights. It was clearly time for my mother to move on. Neighborhoods in cities run in cycles from great to terrible. Ours was going down as crime skyrocketed and the buildings deteriorated from age and lack of landlord care. All my friends and their families had moved on. The Bronx chapter of my life was over.

CHAPTER 4

STUDENT YEARS AT CCNY

I started at the College of the City of New York (CCNY) in the fall of 1956 as a mechanical engineering student. Since I could not draw, I thought it was the closest field to my brother studying architecture. As an aptitude test later demonstrated, it was a terrible choice for me. I was at the bottom of the scale for spatial relations, an essential skill for a mechanical engineer. After two years of getting mediocre grades and not enjoying school, I transferred to being a philosophy/political science major. Except for French, I excelled. I felt at home in these subjects. My intellect was ignited. I learned that sometimes you grow only by going down a wrong path, and experience teaches you that a course correction works wonders.

CCNY was the older version of the present City University of New York. It is a subway school. There are no dormitories. It was the first public college in the US. Its graduates have received more advanced degrees than students from any other college and count nine Nobel Laureates among them. From the 1930s through 1950s, it was a tuition-free school for the working class of New York City. It attracted many of the best students from NYC high schools for whom the top-flight private colleges were unavailable due to race and religious restrictions. This was not my situation. Although I was a member of the National Honor Society (Arista), I was not accepted at the University of Michigan or Bucknell University. I never did well (just average) at standardized tests such as the SAT or later the LSAT; maybe it was my dyslexia problem? At that time anyone with above a B average in the NYC schools had to be accepted at CCNY. So CCNY it would be. It turned out to be the right place for me.

In addition to finding my intellectual home, I soon had the fun of being in the fray as captain of the Debate Society and as president of the Young Democrats chapter. I could use my ever-expanding speaking skills that were first used on the streets of the Bronx.

As president of the CCNY Young Democrats, I attended the Democratic Student mock convention held at Harvard University in 1960. Part of my delegation was my friend Al Linden, president of the CCNY student body. We went as supporters of Adlai Stevenson for president. At that convention I met many young leaders within the Democratic Party, among them Chuck Manatt. Chuck would go on to be chairman of the Democratic National Committee and co-chair of the Clinton-Gore campaign. At that time he was national chairman of the Young Democrats and chairman of Students for Kennedy. When it was clear that Stevenson could not win, and after many hours of conversations with Manatt and members of the NYC delegation, I made an impassioned speech to move the Stevenson votes to Kennedy. It worked, and Kennedy won by a landslide. It was an exhilarating experience and let me know I had the speaking skills to lead.

After our return to NYC, Al Linden and I met with the president of the college, Buell Gallagher, and asked him to send a letter on behalf of CCNY, the Young Democrats chapter, and the students inviting President Harry Truman to speak in support of Senator Kennedy. I enlisted the assistance of Chuck Manatt in this endeavor. He told us where to send the letter and whose support within the New York Democratic Party we needed. To our delight, President Truman accepted. He was so popular that the largest auditorium at the college could not accommodate all the students who wished to hear him speak. We arranged to pipe his speech into an overflow room. Before we entered the auditorium, I had the honor of a private time with him. What I remember most about our conversation was how at ease he made me feel. He was just a normal, nice person. He said his wife did not join him because she did not like to fly. Funny how this detail of our small talk is the only part I remember clearly. I have met a number of famous or powerful people, and what struck me about many of them is how simply kind they were. No need for their ego to be on display. This was a continuing lesson for me about the importance of humility. Of course anyone who becomes president or gains political office or business power has a healthy ego. Over time, I have learned from my own experience not to feel superior to others and to understand how much my success depended on good luck. I also understood that a sense of humor about achievements and failures was a useful tool in staying rightsized. Someone gave me the advice to remember that neither the good nor the bad lasts forever. Both are part of life. Learning these lessons is easier said than done.

Another unforgettable moment of that day was President Truman laughing at an Eisenhower joke I told and clapping for me after the punch line. Pictures on my office wall of us being together on the stage keep the remembrance alive.

This was the joke: One day Dwight D. Eisenhower comes up to heaven and says to St Peter, "My name is Dwight D. Eisenhower, and I would like to get into heaven." St Peter says, "How do I know you are General Eisenhower?" He muses out loud that Pablo Casals knocked on the gates the other day saying he was Pablo Casals and to prove it he played the cello. A few days later a man claiming to be Pablo Picasso wanted to get into heaven, and to prove who he was he sketched a beautiful woman. "What can you do to prove you are General Eisenhower?" At this point Eisenhower asks, "Who is Casals? Who is Picasso?" And St. Peter says: "Come right in, Dwight D. Eisenhower!"

I graduated in January of 1961. I had to repeat a semester of French I had flunked. I told my mother that I was not going to graduation because it made no sense. There would be a cast of thousands, and I had not won any award that would make it special to me. Two days after this conversation my friend Bob Glassman entered our apartment and, holding a copy of the *New York Times*, excitedly exclaimed, "You won, you won a prize!" As it turned out I had won the John Kelly Esq. Prize for Debate. (My debate faculty coach had not mentioned it to me.) I have never regretted my decision not to attend. The size of the graduation remained too mammoth to have any meaning for me. I showed my mother the beautiful prize medal and watched her grin with pride. Luckily, I had already been accepted to the University of Chicago Law School, and I said that she should rather come to that graduation, given that it would be a small graduating class and would be special. She did attend, and it was special, even though I won no award.

CHAPTER 5

BIGOTRY, AMERICA'S ACHILLES HEEL: THREE FRIENDS ON A ROAD TRIP

In September of 1961, two college friends and I picked up a yellow-and-green Ford taxicab in New York City, to be delivered to its new owner in Kennewick, Washington. Anyone who wanted to purchase a new or secondhand car in NYC, without having to pick it up in person, used a driveaway agency. It was a cheap way to travel to other parts of the US. We only had to pay for gas and tolls.

All of us were recent graduates of CCNY and, as was typical of the time, we were the first or second in our families to go to college. You could call us a diverse group of Americans: I was a Bronx son of Ukrainian-Polish Jewish immigrant parents; Oliver, a Queens black man and son of a Seventh Day Adventist mother; and Walter, a Polish Catholic from the Lower East Side of Manhattan. Oliver was a dark-skinned, muscular man with a kind, mustached face. People felt his warmth and immediately liked him. Walter was the fairest and tallest and the most reserved of us. I was the skinny guy who loved to laugh and argue. Hadn't I been the Captain of the CCNY debate team?

We had five days to drive across the country and deliver the car. Afterward we planned to go south to Orange County, California, lie back with our CCNY friend Joe, and enjoy his apartment's swimming pool.

We left NYC in ninety-degree heat, headed toward Chicago, and because we were going to Southern California, we were dressed in short-sleeve shirts and summer pants.

It was lightly snowing in the late afternoon when we arrived in Sundance, Wyoming. The scene reminded me of James Joyce's "The Dead": "The snow was falling, faintly falling over the crosses where Michael Furey lay buried." We were totally unprepared for this drastic change of weather. Perhaps as New Yorkers we had in mind the maps of our country where New York and California make up 99 percent of America. It was the kind of mistake the young are prone to make.

A loud, grinding sound suddenly came from the car. The first garage mechanic in Sundance abruptly told us he could not be of any assistance. Was the car going to die on us two thirds of the way to our destination? The second mechanic said the rear differential was a goner. He could fix it, but would have to have the necessary parts delivered the next day. If the parts arrived on time, the car would be ready late that day. We called the owner and received the go ahead.

We carried our luggage from the mechanic's to a hotel we had noticed on the main road in town. Without sweaters or coats, it was a chilling walk.

When we entered, a six-foot, six-inch, 280-pound man towering behind a desk told us he had no rooms available. We found shelter from the snow at a bar near the hotel. Without the burden of luggage, I went to check out a motel we had spotted on our way into town. I was the guy who had set up the driveaway, and as I had the most forceful personality of us three, it seemed natural that I would be the one to venture forth. But first, I gave the hotel another try. I told the owner we would happily pay to use the lobby overnight. The lobby had a few stuffed chairs and a sofa. He curtly said, "My wife wouldn't like that." I sensed this refusal was a cover for something else.

I trudged on to the motel, shivering from the cold. The owner, an older man, at first stated he had rooms, but then hesitated and asked, "Are you with the colored boy?" When I said yes, he exclaimed, "I will not rent to coloreds." Shocked, I asked him to repeat what he had said. He repeated it word for word. How did he know I was with a "colored boy"? Was it so strange to see a person of color in Sundance that the news of Oliver's presence was spreading like wild fire? Had the hotel owner quickly called him with the news? Back at the bar, rubbing my hands together for warmth, I told my friends they would not rent to college boys. I was not going to tell Oliver that the color of his skin would prevent us from getting a room. It just was too hurtful. Water said, "You got to be kidding!" Oliver said nothing. I then offered to walk around and see what else I could discover.

On the main street I spotted an official-looking man who turned out to be the night marshal. He could have been any average man going about his business except for the badge pinned to his heavy brown jacket. After explaining our predicament, I asked if we could sleep the night in the town jail. At first he indicated that we could, but then he asked if I was with the "colored boy." Again I said yes, but quickly added that we did not intend to freeze to death. Either he let us sleep there the one night voluntarily, or we would find reasons for him to lock us up. After what seemed an eternity, he said okay. I asked if the jail had heat. There was a potbellied stove, he told me. He would supply some wood and coal. I was elated and thanked him profusely, and told Oliver and Walter the good news that we were going to spend the night in jail.

As we were walking toward the jail, a car with men we recognized from the bar swerved toward us, causing us to throw our luggage and jump to the side of the road. They continued on their way. Walter and I gave each other a glance that said, "We need to get out of Sundance as soon as possible."

When the night marshal opened the door to the jail, there were only two simple cells, each with a single-person bed, and a large table. We lit up the stove and stood around it to get warm, then tossed a coin to decide who would sleep on the beds in the cells, and who had the bad luck of the small "table bed." Walter, who was without any "butt padding," accepted his fate with good cheer. We had been given thin blankets by the night marshal. Luckily, we awoke in the night in time to discover that the fire had gone out; we were able to relight it and avoid hypothermia. We awoke with a start as the front door was thrown open with a jolt by the day marshal. Although we had not discussed our recognition that we were the subject of bigotry and potential violence, each of us had a two-by-four firmly in our grasp. Boys from the streets of NYC have the same instincts of self-protection.

Of course we knew that racial discrimination existed in New York City and elsewhere in America, but we did not comprehend the depth of bigotry we would encounter. In Mississippi, yes, but in Wyoming—no way.

We were in luck. The parts had been delivered, and the car was fixed late in the day. Unwilling to spend another night in jail, we left shouting, "Fuck you, Sundance." As the light was fading, we found a motel and decided to enter together so we would know immediately where we stood. To our relief, there was no hesitation and the clerk rented us three rooms. It felt as if we were back to NYC normal. With a good night's sleep behind us, we headed off toward our destination: Kennewick.

Somewhere in the mountains between Yellowstone and Rexburg, Idaho, we heard a thumping under the car. It turned out we had lost one of the brackets on the gas tank. We found some wire in the trunk, rigged the gas tank, and nervously headed for Rexburg. The mechanic at the Ford dealership flat-out told us he would not fix our car because of Oliver. We could hardly believe our ears. We hastily accepted his offer of strong wire to patch up the tank. We managed to make it to Kennewick without further incident and handed the car over to its new owner. As we drove away in a taxi to get a bus to San Francisco, we broke into a spontaneous cheer.

Our friend Joe was a good-looking, energetic, always curious Italian-Catholic from the tough Bedford-Stuyvesant section of Brooklyn. He lived in a typical Southern California apartment, a stucco-style horseshoe building around a swimming pool. After spending a few relaxed days together, there was a knock at the door. The landlord announced that "the Negro" could not stay. We were dumbstruck. Joe had the presence of mind to negotiate and asked, "If all the tenants said it's okay for Oliver to stay, would that be okay?" He then went to each of his neighbors, who all responded in the affirmative. However, some of them said, "But only if he doesn't use the swimming pool." Fear that Oliver's color might wash off, or ...? Oliver agreed to do without swimming for the time of our visit. Walter stayed on with Joe, while Oliver and I left for Chicago to begin graduate and law school. Not a word was said among us about this shameful incident. What was the point? Oliver knew we were horrified and shared his pain. Leaving a day earlier was no big deal. We had to start our classes.

A short time later, as I approached the Law School building, I saw Oliver sitting on the steps to the entrance. His five-foot, ten-inch body was hunched over. The usual sparkle in his eyes was missing. I was surprised to see him there, as his classes were several blocks away. "What's up?" I asked him. He said, "I will never again enter into a new friendship—black, white, or whatever." I was taken aback. He told me two Jamaican blacks had made friends with him over the last few weeks and had repeatedly talked about race relations in America. Early that morning they had declared, "A black can't save money in a white man's bank." He told them they were nuts. He himself had money in such a bank. They didn't believe him. They said, "Prove it." He went home, retrieved his passbook, and showed it to them. At that point they pulled a gun and ordered him to take them to his bank and withdraw all his funds. With one of them directly behind him and a gun in his back, Oliver withdrew his funds. They drove him around for twenty or so minutes, and then to his surprise, stopped the car and let him go. "I thought I was going to die," Oliver told me.

The Chicago Police later affirmed Oliver's story. The people involved had targeted black university students in both Indiana and Illinois. His experience showed the impact of our road trip on Oliver. Because he had been deeply hurt by the bigotry he encountered, he was overeager to make new black friends and let his New York City street smarts desert him.

The following fall, Oliver and I planned to share an apartment together with another CCNY friend who was starting at the law school. A number of apartments in the paper appeared promising, but when we visited them they suddenly turned out to be unavailable. Racism was alive and well in Chicago. We were dejected but decided to try one more address. I knocked on the door, and a black man answered. We grabbed Oliver, who was behind us, and moved him to the front. Luckily the owner was not prejudiced against whites! We had our new apartment for the year. We never discussed the discrimination Oliver faced. We just dealt with it and moved on in a matter-of-fact way.

The impact of our trip and the continuing reality of racial discrimination were major reasons for my joining the Civil Rights Division of the Justice Department in 1965. Over the last fifty-six years, whenever we get together, we joke about the jail, the swimming pool, and our Chicago apartment. Recently, we have been worrying that too large a segment of the American public is again accepting bigotry. Whether we are laughing about our experience or stating our present concern, I always see a flicker of pain in Oliver's eyes.

CHAPTER 6

CIVIL RIGHTS

After my graduation from the University of Chicago Law School in 1964 and my one-year clerkship (for Judge Irving Ben Cooper) at the Federal District Court for the Southern District of New York, I was lucky enough to be presented with two job choices: one in the office of the US Attorney for the Southern District of New York, and the other in the Civil Rights Division of the Justice Department. It was a no-brainer for me. The effect of discrimination I had witnessed and the pain racism was causing my friends and the whole society led me to choose the Civil Rights Division and move to Washington, DC. Moreover, as a Jew, I was painfully aware how the horrors of bigotry had led to the Holocaust. I could not idly stand by.

MY FRIEND CECIL

I encountered bigotry early on in my neighborhood and in high school. I ran the mile on the track team at Taft High School, in the Bronx. The team consisted of a majority of blacks, and they were my friends. I did not appreciate the racist comments of some of my Irish neighborhood buddies. From time to time I mentioned that I ran track with "them" and they were good guys. I never really understood why the Irish and

Italians I grew up with were so virulently anti-black and anti-Puerto Rican. Their prejudice made me uncomfortable and angry. The boys knew I disapproved and toned it down around me.

My closest friend on the team was Cecil Harris, who happened to be black. He specialized in running the 440 and 880 and could run the mile faster than I. He was handsome and had a magnetic personality. Everyone liked him, especially the girls. We were the second-best track team in the country, after Boys High School in Brooklyn. Cecil was the only black man on the team to go to college.

Cecil and I spent hours together at each other's homes, went to black college fraternity parties, and took the D subway train to visit his aunt who was a dancer at a night bar in Greenwich Village. Both our mothers worked, so it was a golden opportunity to bring girls to our apartments to dance and party. Whenever I went over to Cecil's place he locked his ferocious dog (called "Killer" by me) in the kitchen. At that time many blacks used "biting" dogs for protection. Until years later when I had my own dog, I was afraid of dogs. My brother was supportive of my hanging with Cecil, and my mom never said anything negative about it. For me, if I liked someone I liked them, no matter their race, religion, sexual preference, financial status, or their dog. This has been a lifelong trait.

In my senior year of high school, black college fraternity parties became the focus of my social life. After attending several of these weekend parties, I was accepted by Cecil's friends. Usually six of us, some wearing bucket hats with the logo of a fraternity, would set out together in one of their cars (this was the era of the front bench seat). In the '50s it was commonplace for blacks to use the N-word, either as a salutation or in a put-down. We all loved to play "The Dozens" (a fast, verbal put-down interaction). At some point we were such good buddies that they would even use the N-word in addressing me. However, many times when we were around whites they used "Reggin," the N-word spelled backward. I think the use of this substitute word was a tacit recognition of the negative impact the N-word had on all of us.

The Fraternity House parties offered wonderful music, and there were hot young women looking to have fun. The dance floor was filled with hip-gyrating bodies dancing to slow blues music, or cool style (faster hip motion but not too energetic) to jazz tunes. At either speed it was great foreplay.

Cecil and a white cheerleader at Taft fell in love and wanted to marry, but her parents were violently opposed. They enlisted officials at the school to break up the relationship. They threatened Cecil with blocking his application to Dartmouth College unless he relented—and they acted on their threat. The pressure on the cheerleader turned out to be too much for her, and she broke off the relationship.

After years of trying, with the help of Google (my kids' suggestion), I finally located Cecil. Along with his grandson, he joined me at our fiftieth high school reunion. I watched as the women still flocked to talk with him. He had not lost his natural charm. We reminisced about "the incident," and he was gratified that I remembered the injustice done. I saw the fleeting pain in his eyes as we talked about how he lost his first love and his life changed forever. He said, "I never trusted whites in the same way thereafter." We talked about kids and grandkids and traced our lives since high school. He had attended Morgan State (on a track scholarship), got a PhD in psychology from the University of Texas, and rose to the rank of deputy commander of administration (the top-ranked "shrink") at Fort Ord in California. "As a noncombat officer, I would never make general," he told me. "I had gone as high as I could, so I retired." He mentioned what a good man General Powell was when he served under him at the Pentagon. I said, "Glad to hear that about a CCNY man." We laughed about our time together at Taft and the vagaries of life. It was as if fifty years had not passed.

LIMITED AMBITIONS

As captain of the debate team at CCNY, I had another experience that demonstrated the corrosive effect of prejudice on all parties involved. Our team attended the Middle Atlantic Debate Tournament at Hampton Institute in Hampton, Virginia. It turned out that among the seven schools participating, we were the only white team. At the dinner before the tournament, conversation turned to what we were going to do with our lives after graduation. The difference in our stated ambitions was startling. The whites wanted to be lawyers, doctors, congressmen. The blacks wanted to be school principals. Discrimination in our society had limited the expectations of my fellow debaters. What a loss to our society, not to speak of the pain inflicted on each one of them by the cap placed on their dreams.

When we returned to CCNY, having won the tournament, a number of my friends and acquaintances joked, "Of course you won. All the other teams were black." They were sadly unaware of both the stupidity and hurtfulness of their "joke." I told them that not only was their comment a put-down to all involved, but also particularly to me as the person named "Best Debater." In the fifties and early sixties, the acceptance in some academic circles of the "scientific proof" of the "inferiority of the Negro" was outrageous. This was some fifteen to twenty years after the adoption of the Nazi Nuremberg race laws. I thought, "Shame on them all!"

Coupled with my trip across America with my black friend Oliver (described in Chapter 4), these incidents informed my view of bigotry and discrimination.

DANGEROUS LESSONS: CIVIL RIGHTS DIVISION, MISSISSIPPI

During my time in the Civil Rights Division (1965–1968), I made several trips to Carroll County, Mississippi in connection with the 1966 election for US Senator. Mississippi was over one-third black, and a number of counties had a black majority. Their vote could make a difference to the outcome. The *Delta-Times* of Greenville reported ten killings and uncounted beatings, bombings, and shootings over a six-month period. The Voting Rights Act had become law on August 6, 1965, but officials in Mississippi continued to place stumbling blocks that were unlawful under the act. (In time the act would alter the elections of local officials, from local school boards and sheriffs to US Senators.) James Eastland, who had opposed the Voting Rights Act, won the 1966 election by playing to the racist element in Mississippi. He resigned in 1987 rather than lose re-election. Change and compliance with federal law would not come easily. I learned that to achieve changes to deep, long-standing, and ingrained racial discrimination, people would have to take many risks, including death. Carroll County had two county seats, Vaiden and Carrollton. Most of my time was spent in and around Vaiden, a town that was typical of most small towns in the South. A courthouse dominated a treelined square with a statue of General Lee or another prominent Confederate soldier. The department protocol was to first meet with the county judge (who was the person in charge of implementing the Voting Rights Act of 1965) and then the county registrar of voters. The judge was supposed to advise the registrar and lay out his obligation to cooperate in order to show full compliance with the law.

The judge in Vaiden was pleasant and business-like. He said he would talk to the registrar and alert him to my visit the next day. Back at my rental car that was parked in front of the courthouse, I discovered I had left the keys in the ignition and locked all the doors. I returned to the judge's office to ask his secretary for a metal hanger. Her Southern politeness prevented her from asking why I needed one. Armed with the hanger and in broad daylight, I used the Bronx technique of straightening the hanger, maneuvering it between the door and window, and pulling up the lock button. I chuckled over how the tricks of my youth could come in handy later in life. But if I had been black, breaking into my car in the Town Square, how would the townsfolk have reacted? Would they have been so nonchalant? I doubt it.

The next day, I visited the registrar, showed him my badge, and introduced myself. In a rage, he threw the papers in his hands in my direction and called me a "Lyndon Baines Johnson bastard." He was a very large man, at least six feet, four inches tall and 275 lbs. The force of his anger and the flying papers led to my quick retreat toward his office door. Without a word I returned to my car. I saw several men getting into a pickup truck behind me. The truck had the rifle rack filled with rifles across the back window that was standard in the rural South. I started driving toward Greenwood, where I planned to call folks in the Division to get instructions for my next step, when I noticed in my rearview mirror that the truck was still behind me. As I increased my speed the truck appeared to do the same. I was on the Civil Rights Division team that had written the appeals brief in the Viola Liuzzo case. The Klan had murdered her on an Alabama highway between Montgomery and Selma. It was not a difficult mental jump to think I might meet the same fate. I made a Sterling Moss left turn onto a dirt road leading into a black community that I had already visited. Given their experience with Klan violence, I thought they would be able to help me. Just how, I had not figured out. When I checked my rearview mirror again, the truck was no longer behind me. Rifles in gun racks are usually meant for hunting. For me, they symbolized racial violence.

When I got back to my hotel, I spoke directly with John Doar, the head of the division. He started the conversation by joking that he'd heard I was causing trouble in Vaiden. He instructed me to revisit the county judge and registrar the next day. In the interim, the department would have a serious conversation with them both. I later learned that the registrar had been enraged by a dust-up he had with the Civil

Rights Division and John Doar personally. Southern officials in general were upset with "outsider" federal officials telling them what to do. He was in fact a good and fair registrar who was respected by the blacks in the county. He was professional and helpful when I visited him the next day. This was a lesson in assumptions based on negative experiences.

On another trip to Carroll County, I had just left a county road and was driving uphill on a long dirt road toward the house of a black voting rights leader, when from nowhere dogs started racing toward my car, barking loudly. My heart started beating hard. I was not fond of large barking dogs. By the time I reached the house, the sound of the dogs was deafening. The black leader came out to meet me. He shouted at the dogs, and their barking and growling stopped. He told me they were his alarm system.

The two of us drove back to town where he wanted me to meet other black voting rights leaders. We were about to enter a bar to meet them but were stopped by the sheriff. With his beer belly, patchy white skin, and brusque demeanor, I assumed he was a racist. He was joined by several of his deputies, whose look and manner were similar, reinforcing my assumption. The sheriff asked me, "What finance company are you from?" Showing him my Justice Department badge, I responded in my best "smartass Bronx kid on the block" manner: "I am from the largest finance company in America." Looking at my badge, he could not know I was referring to the US Government. I should have parked my attitude, prejudice, and assumptions at the door. I learned that he was not a racist; he had been very supportive of blacks in their effort to vote. He was simply trying to prevent me from attempting to collect money owed on bills from people in the bar who might be drunk. "Do not judge a book by its cover." For the second time in two days I learned that lesson.

The day before and the day of the election I was under instructions to call the FBI every hour. The department was afraid of potential violence. This was a way for the bureau to keep a check on my whereabouts and to receive intelligence on exactly what was going on in the county. The day before the election I stopped in a general store frequented by Klan members. In my best NYC accent, I feigned a call to the department. I said, "This is Al making my hourly FBI call-in per instructions. All is well." I just thought it wise to let folks know the feds were on the scene.

Late that night I received a call from a black leader who was equally concerned about violence and turnout. I told him I would be at the polling place in the morning before it opened. When I arrived, the leader was there along with a few other blacks and the people running the polling station. I got out of my car, shook hands with him and the others, and left. I do not know whether my actions were noticed and helped the high turnout, but nonetheless it was gratifying.

SCHOOL VS. SEGREGATION: SHELBY COUNTY, TENNESSEE

On another occasion I traveled to Shelby County, Tennessee, on a school desegregation case. Shelby County is south of Memphis and borders Mississippi. At the time it was the most violent county in the South. I interviewed an eleven-year-old girl who was walking by herself to her new "white school." She was a small, very dark-skinned, pigtailed girl who wore a homemade dress. Each day she was met with a torrent of nasty catcalls, including "N-Witch" and "Go home, you're not wanted here." I asked her if she had been contacted by CORFU, CORE, SNCC, NAACP, or any other black organization. She said no. I then asked her why she went against the wishes of her grandmother with whom she lived, and suffered the epithets hurled at her at the "white school". With quiet dignity she said, "I want a better education." I was deeply moved by her response. The power of the human spirit is found everywhere, in all ages, colors, and genders. The black leaders in Mississippi and a twelve-year-old girl in Tennessee gave me faith that I would see a lessening of discrimination.

Thirty-one years later, in November 1998, I was standing with Indonesian staff members on the roof of my apartment house, watching Jakarta's Chinatown burn for the second time in a year. The first time had been in May, during the overthrow of the dictator Suharto. Prejudice against the Chinese had been long-standing and nasty. To my knowledge, it was the only Chinatown in the world where signs in the Chinese alphabet were forbidden. Celebration of the Chinese New Year was also forbidden until a few years after I arrived in Indonesia. Many Chinese Indonesian colleagues told me how during the May and November riots they would huddle in their apartments in other sections of Jakarta in fear of being killed. When I asked different Indonesians why they hated the Chinese, they said, "The Dutch treated the Chinese-Indonesians better than us." I said, "But the businesses you burned were not

51

created by the Dutch, nor do you hate the Dutch." Prejudice has its own logic.

This bizarre exchange reminded me of the time I was in Mississippi on a school desegregation case and had to get permission from a landowner to interview share-croppers who lived on his land. The owner was an elegantly dressed, quintessential patrician with perfect manners who lived in a stately Palladio portico mansion with manicured green lawns. He said, "Go back there and see how those animals live." The landowner neither saw his role in their misery nor how the corrosive nature of bigotry created the very thing he was condemning.

CALIFORNIA AND THE TEAMSTERS UNION

Although I was still based in DC, working on appellate briefs, over my last nine months in the division (until October 1968) I regularly traveled on assignment to the San Francisco Bay Area to develop discrimination cases. The division recognized that bigotry and discrimination are not limited geographically. I headed investigations into the Sailors' Union of the Pacific, and the long-haul Teamsters Union.

The Vietnam War was creating many well-paying jobs on ocean-going ships, but blacks were being shut out. The ruse the union used was to require a union card before you could get a job on a ship. At the same time, in order to get a union card you had to have at least one job offer on a ship. This policy was enforced selectively. Favoritism was also in place. Friends or important people with access to the head of the union could use their influence to obtain a union card.

I paid a visit to Morris Weisberger, the president of the union, and explained that the department suspected discrimination against blacks in the admission policies and sought his permission to examine his records. I told him agents of the Federal Bureau of Investigation would photograph the records for further analysis. The department would appreciate his cooperation and permission to photograph, but if he did not give his permission voluntarily, we would get a federal court order. I emphatically stated that there was enough preliminary evidence showing the practices of the union were discriminatory. Obtaining the court order would be a simple task. He gave his consent.

Under my overall direction, a team of bureau (FBI) agents proceeded to photograph the records. I gained a great deal of respect for the agents during this time.

They were very professional and efficient, even though civil rights cases, unlike bank robberies, usually took a long time to close. As I understood it, promotion within their ranks was, at least in part, based on the speed of closing cases.

While the bureau was doing its work I had many conversations with Mr. Weisberger. A number of these took place at Original Joe's restaurant in San Francisco. He mused that a system of "first come, first serve" would relieve him of the pressure he felt from people of influence who wanted jobs for the men they sponsored. I listened without comment at the time. When we completed our analysis of the records, it was absolutely clear that union policy had discriminated against blacks. I presented these findings to him and added that if he would agree to a consent order he would be free of the pressure of influential people and friends because it gave him the ready excuse that his hands were tied. I also pointed out that he could not be blamed for signing such an order, given the overwhelming evidence of discrimination. Consenting would be best for the union and for him. He agreed and signed the Consent Order sometime after I left the department.

The Teamsters' short-haul drivers' hiring hall was located near the Oakland Airport. We had received complaints that blacks were not given the better-paying, long-haul driving jobs. To remain as inconspicuous as possible, I did not wear a suit but dressed in my brother's old University of California sweatshirt and his paint-stained khaki pants (he and his family lived in Berkeley). It was important not to place these black men in a difficult position with the union. Over a period of days, seated in my rental car in the Teamster Hall parking lot, I interviewed six black short-haul drivers per day, one at a time. I had a go-between who knew when I would be in the parking lot. He would tell me the names of the day's interviewees. My brother and some friends joked about my ending up at the bottom of San Francisco Bay. I did not think that was a realistic possibility.

My interviews demonstrated a likely discrimination case warranting further investigation by the department, and I conveyed my conclusion to my superiors. I never found out if any follow-up action was taken. It would not surprise me if none were taken. To my knowledge, no one from the division took up my role after I left. The division became actively involved in police brutality cases brought on by demonstrations at the University of California, Berkeley. Also, once I had resigned I had no ability to effect division policy. Therefore I just let go of the situation.

I moved to California in October; my resignation from the Civil Rights Division became official in December of 1968, and in January of 1969 I started my new life as director of the National Housing Law Project (Law Project).

Before I officially resigned from the Justice Department, I returned to Washington, DC, to close out my apartment and get sworn in to the Bar of the United States Supreme Court. I thought it would be cool to take advantage of the perk (as a Justice Department lawyer) of having the solicitor general "move my admission" (by filing a motion to formally support my becoming a member of the Supreme Court Bar). The majesty of the courtroom impressed me. After returning to California I was informed by the clerk's office that my check for admission to the court had bounced. In moving banks from DC to Berkeley I had not allowed sufficient time for my transfer of funds to take place. This was an auspicious and humorous beginning to my career before the Supreme Court.

CHAPTER 7

ANTI-POVERTY PROGRAM

It was a natural progression for me to join President Johnson's newly formed Anti-Poverty Legal Services Program. The program was designed to assist the poor in everyday legal matters and to take on the forces of the status quo that were aligned against them. It fit my personality to become part of the law reform part of the movement. I liked the intellectual and practical challengers this opportunity provided. I wanted to have a real impact on addressing the conditions the poor were in. It was essential to level the playing field if the poor were going to have a chance to alter their situation. I was part of what Attorney General Nicholas deBelleville Katzenbach called, "[A] new breed of lawyers … dedicated to using the law as an instrument of orderly and constructive change."

NATIONAL HOUSING LAW PROJECT

In January of 1968, I entered President Lyndon Johnson's "War on Poverty" through the National Housing Law Project (known as the Law Project or NHLP). It specialized in housing and community development law and provided in-depth, specialized legal assistance to the overworked legal services lawyers in local neighborhoods nationwide.

I was well aware that the lawyers in the Legal Services Program worked for a third of what they could command at the large private law firms for corporate/real estate development. The neighborhood offices would have low rents and be easily accessible to clients. No offices with great views of San Francisco, New York, or Chicago skylines! No large conference rooms with redwood tables and wonderful paintings on the walls. The Law Project started with offices in the University of California Law School in Berkeley and, when the staff expanded a year later, moved to an unused sorority building.

When I started at the Law Project in January, 1969, 260 legal service grants had been made in every state except North Dakota (the Governor had opposed a grant by the Office of Economic Opportunity), and the NHLP was the second "backup" center (support center to provide expert backup to the neighborhood legal services lawyers). By 1980, there were 1,406 local field offices employing 6,559 attorneys and 2,901 paralegals, and there were sixteen "backup" centers.

During my nine years at the Law Project, I watched many of my clients struggle on a daily basis against all the odds to make a better life for their kids and themselves. I thought then, and I think now, how could I not try to change the legal imbalance that existed for the poor? America had provided me with a basically free and excellent public education (including college) that allowed me to improve my path in life. But the public education system that had helped me had fallen into disrepair and did not provide the same assistance to my clients. I was amazed and shocked to read that in 2015, the Southern Education Fund found a majority of public-school students living in poverty. I had not been locked into, or limited by, circumstances of my parents or my race. Many of my clients were not that lucky. When I saw how my assistance affected their lives for the better, it reaffirmed my desire to offer a helping hand. I felt I was doing meaningful work pioneering law reform.

At my time at the Law Project, I was able to explore many skills, first as the lawyer in charge of our public housing efforts and then as director: I expanded my leadership, negotiation, article-writing, teaching, motion/appellate argument, and statutory writing skills. In giving hands-on advice to local legal service lawyers, setting up training programs, and speaking at legal services and state bar conferences, I worked in many of America's ghettos, barrios, depressed rural areas, and reservations.

One particular experience opened my eyes even wider to the extent of segregation in our country. A National Tenant Organization (NTO) conference took me to the black city within the city of Las Vegas—a copy of the hotels and gambling casinos of the "white" Las Vegas, albeit less extravagant. The 15,000 blacks of the city (10 percent of the population) were forced to live in this segregated section called Westside. Resort casinos barred African Americans from gambling, attending shows, and staying in their establishments. Blacks were not allowed to own or sell businesses or houses beyond the Westside district. This had only slowly changed with the Moulin Rouge Agreement that abolished these restrictions in 1960. Wow, I never had a clue that there were two Las Vegas cities, one for whites, the other for blacks. By the '70s we had done away with "separate but equal" in the schools, but not yet fully in the gambling casinos of Las Vegas. This was a striking example for me of the tie between economic and racial justice that Martin Luther King talked about.

"YOU'RE A COMMUNIST"

The first big task of the Law Project in 1969 was the development of the *Handbook on Housing Law*. This became a 1000-plus-page manual designed to be of assistance to poverty lawyers in the field. It covered public and FHA housing, the Model Cities program for community development, urban renewal, and landlord-tenant law. I wrote the Public Housing section. As an appendix, the section contained a model lease and a model "due process grievance procedure." It was a technical book, not designed for nighttime reading, unless you wanted a nonnarcotic "sleeping pill." I was totally surprised when a Georgia congressman attacked the *Handbook* on the floor of the House of Representatives as the work of Communists. Today I regret to say that a number of congressmen, not only from Georgia, continue to attack those who are simply trying to make our democracy work by protecting minorities and the poor and giving them a voice in our system. I have learned by experience that the forces of the status quo neither disappear nor change easily—continued pressure is ever necessary.

Together with the legislative assistant of Senator Edward Brooke (a black liberal Republican from Massachusetts), I wrote in 1969 what became known as the Brooke Amendment to the National Housing Act. It limited the rent tenants had to pay to 25 percent of their income. It established that people without income had the right to live in public housing. This part of the amendment was repealed within a year or so. It was an example of youthful overreach. It required too big a subsidy and had the moral hazard effect of encouraging people not to work. Although the 25 percent ratio has been increased over the years, the concept of rent being capped at a fixed percentage of income is still in effect all these years later.

The Brooke Amendment initiated me into the legislative process in Congress. Brooke's legislative assistant and I negotiated the provisions of the proposed statute with officials at the Department of Housing and Urban Development. As if we were in a Keystone Cop movie, we would run down the stairs from the office of the General Counsel (who opposed any limit on the percentage of income to be paid for rent) to the office of the assistant secretary (who supported it) to gain their approval of certain language in the amendment. Senator Brooke then used this approval to move forward with the legislation.

This experience taught me that a bureaucracy is not always monolithic and it is important to take advantage of any differences within. No mention was ever made to HUD's Office of the General Counsel of our back channel and the role we played in developing their position. During my time at the Civil Rights Division, I had met key attorneys from the office at friends' houses or at dinner parties at my house. Networking had been an essential tool for success throughout my career. In no small part, my connections helped us win the bureaucratic battle.

But the battle to get the amendment passed in Congress was quite a different matter. Here politics was the determinative factor. Being on the "side of right" was not enough. My connections at the St. Louis Neighborhood Legal Services helped me enlist the head of the Teamsters Union (Local 688 in St. Louis) to be our champion: Harold J Gibbons, who was also the vice president of the International Brotherhood of Teamsters and heir apparent to Jimmy Hoffa. As heir apparent, he had enormous political power. Congressmen listened carefully to what he said. He opened doors we could not. He had a long history of progressive positions for improving the lot of the poor. These views and his work to make them a reality landed him on the Nixon enemy list. He was a wonderful man to work with, down to earth and kind. As if by magic, he could arrange appointments with members of Congress that on our own we could not have obtained. We could at best get an appointment with a relevant senior staff member. Gibbons' active support was critical in getting the amendment passed.

My eyes were opened wide as to how our legislative process works. All constituents are not equal. Power begets power. To get legislation passed you need to get powerful interests on your side. These powerful constituencies can either be large-dollar political contributors, suppliers of large numbers of voters, suppliers of large numbers of election time volunteers, or all three.

LEASE AND GRIEVANCE REGULATIONS: "NO MORE LIVING UNDER PLANTATION RULES!"

In early 1970 I started a yearlong negotiation on behalf of the National Tenants Organization (NTO) against the long-standing abuse of tenants by managers of their units. The managers had absolute power. The leases were weighted heavily in favor of the Public Housing Authority. Tenants could be evicted for any reason—real or false. No due process hearing was required. It was common practice for managers to threaten female tenants with fines or eviction unless they consented to having sex with them. The tenants called their situation, "living under plantation rules."

The US Department of Housing and Urban Development (HUD) understood that it was in their interest to issue regulations on these matters as neighborhood legal services around the country were beginning to win lawsuits on illegal lease clauses and evictions. Instead of spending its resources on defending numerous lawsuits and having the embarrassment of losing them, HUD might get the stakeholders to agree on regulations that would redress the abuses in the management of public housing. The poor were slowly winning the battle against the federal and local governments that oversaw and ran federally funded public housing.

Two national organizations were representing the constituents of HUD that would be directly affected by the proposed model Lease and Grievance Procedure: NTO and National Association of Housing and Redevelopment Officials (NAHRO). It was vital for the successful implementation of the model to have both groups supportive of its issuance. NAHRO members had close connections with mayors and governors. They in turn had influence on members of Congress who funded the programs of HUD. HUD would not issue the regulations over the objection of NAHRO and risk a fight with Public Housing Authority supporters in Congress over their issuance. If it was not to their liking, NTO was free to reject HUD's proposed regulation and return to fighting the local housing authorities in the courts.

Jesse Gray was the chairman of NTO. He was a short, wiry, charismatic man whose energy poured out of him. Originally from Louisiana, after spending years in NYC he had led a famous tenant rent strike in Harlem in 1963–64. He was a savvy grassroots organizer who understood how to create a tenants organization. It is very difficult to organize a tenant rent strike in one apartment house let alone in many apartment houses. Tenants would be afraid that their nonpayment of rent would get them evicted. Eviction is a potentially devastating result for poor people with nowhere else to go. Landlords would try to peel off tenants from the strike by threatening eviction, sending eviction notices, and taking those who were most vulnerable (tenants with a large family) to court. Jesse had to keep the trust of the tenants in his strategy of withholding rents as leverage to force the landlords to make repairs and exterminate the rats in the apartments and buildings. For the rent strike to be successful it needed maximum tenant participation—as close as possible to 100 percent. The economic loss to the landlord had to bite. Forty or fifty-percent participation would not get the landlord to capitulate. But Jesse would not conduct the negotiations with HUD. Instead, Rose Wylie would undertake that task, while Jesse Gray would continue to organize tenants in private and public housing using the very effective tool of rent strikes.

Rose Wylie was a short grandmotherly type who was tough as nails but with a kind demeanor. She had cut her teeth organizing the Philadelphia public housing tenants. She led them in their fights for better housing over a number of years, including a successful negotiation of how HUD modernization money for the Public Housing Authority in Philadelphia would be spent. Not everyone who has the skills to move crowds of people to organize and force a response to their legitimate demands also has the skills to negotiate a positive result once inside the board room. Forceful rhetoric filled with buzzwords that appeals to deeply felt, already-formed opinions of the audience, is what moves people to action. Jesse Gray only had the first rhetoric skill; Rose Wylie had them both. Inside the board room, her personality was outwardly less aggressive. Although she had the same toughness as Gray, she also had the ability to make you trust her and think she was a person with whom you could do business. She did not rant, but quietly put forth her demands. She understood just how far her opponent would go in negotiations.

My confidence that HUD would issue these negotiated regulations was fifty-fifty. A number of Housing Authority members of NAHRO had expressed their strong opposition—publicly and privately—to HUD and Bob Maffin, the executive director of NAHRO. I was concerned that a potential schism within the organization would prevent NAHRO from approving, and HUD from issuing, the regulations. These local public housing authority officials did not want to give up their absolute power over the eviction of tenants. But Bob Maffin's negotiating skills, his understanding of the direction in which the courts were ruling, and his savvy political management of his members prevailed. Without him there would not have been any Public Housing Lease and Grievance Procedure regulations. Rose Wylie, Bob Maffin, and I kept moving the process forward together, while I kept worrying. In February 1971, after a year of negotiations, HUD finally issued the Public Housing Lease and Grievance Procedure. I was happy and somewhat surprised. I was also delighted to know, for example, that female tenants would no longer be evicted simply for refusing to have sex with a manager of public housing units.

My concerns about the retrograde Housing Authorities' ability to cause trouble were eventually borne out when the Public Housing Authority of Omaha, Nebraska, along with eight other Housing Authorities, filed an action to have the regulations ruled illegal by the Omaha US Federal District Court. I learned that the district court judge was a former Housing Authority lawyer—which was not a per se cause for having him removed. But I decided to intervene in the lawsuit on behalf of the NTO.

I flew into Omaha to meet and coordinate strategies with the local legal service lawyer representing the Omaha public housing tenants. He was not your pinstriped version of a lawyer. He was a long-haired guy who made his own wine, had no big ego, and believed in the tenants he represented. I should add that he was very good at his job.

Chairman Jesse Gray came to Omaha to organize demonstrations in support of the lawsuit. The newspapers were full of physical threats against Jesse. Fear of violence against him and the tenants was a realistic concern. Many in the community had strong feelings against blacks and public housing. I would not have been surprised to learn that members of the Omaha Housing Authority hierarchy were stoking these feelings. Nevertheless, Jesse went ahead organizing the tenants for a possible rent strike. After NTO agreed to my proposed legal strategy, I outlined the documents we would file and returned to Berkeley to write the necessary motion documents. We coordinated our strategy with Justice Department lawyers representing HUD.

A month later I returned to Omaha to argue the case. I had a 102-degree fever but was determined to move forward anyway. Plaintiffs had venue-shopped cleverly (found the right judge to preside over their lawsuit) and the district court ruled in their favor. HUD and I were in mild shock. NTO was in severe shock as they were afraid the gains made in local communities nationwide would be lost. I assured Jesse and the members of the NTO board that the ruling would not stand. We immediately appealed to the Eighth Circuit Court of Appeals.

When I arrived in St. Louis (where the Eighth Circuit is located) to argue the case, I was nervous but prepared. A brilliant UC Berkeley Law School professor had graciously volunteered to assist me on my brief. We held a number of moot court sessions to prepare me for the oral argument. I scoped out the judges who would hear my case with a friend who was one of their past law clerks.

The three judges that heard the case sat behind an elevated polished wood bench in a large room with wooden panels. We stood at a lectern in front of them. In their long black robes they were intimidating.

The department lawyer representing HUD and I split our allotted time, but I suspected he had a lack of in-depth knowledge as this was but one of many cases he handled. Although I thought we won the argument, I remained concerned, but six weeks later a broad smile broke on my face upon reading the letter from the appeals court. They had ruled 3 to 0 to reverse the district court. I was especially pleased that the decision was unanimous. Plaintiffs did not prevail in their court-shopping gambit. They did file a petition for the US Supreme Court to hear the case on appeal and hired a distinguished lawyer from a prominent Chicago law firm. He and I had a cordial relationship (no need for professionals to be otherwise). After their petition was denied he wrote me a tongue-in-cheek congratulations letter which stated I had ruined what was possibly his last chance to argue before the Justices of the Supreme Court. I wrote back, "It could not happen to a nicer guy."

In a letter to me dated January 3,1972 (and printed in the Congressional Record, Volume 119, Part 20 [July 20, 1973 to July 27, 1973], page 25649), the outgoing assistant secretary of HUD, Norm Watson, wrote "I wanted to personally thank you for the efforts in assisting the Department over the last four years. More particularly, the advice and counsel given HUD during the negotiations between HUD, NAHRO, and NTO on developing the Lease and Grievance Procedure that resulted in the Department issuing a policy agreeable to two very volatile national organizations. Our General Counsel's office informs me that your representation during subsequent litigation was outstanding and instrumental in getting a favorable ruling for the Department … [our] association has been rewarding and I wish you all the best for the future."

David Maxwell, the general counsel of HUD, also wrote to me and said, "This letter is to express the appreciation of [HUD] both to you personally and to the Project for your assistance in the case. … Your participation in this litigation, especially your involvement in the negotiations with the plaintiffs, as well as your excellent briefs and oral presentations materially contributed to the successful outcome before the Court of Appeals for the Eighth Circuit." Maxwell asked me to come to DC for a training session of HUD lawyers. I consented because I saw this as a way to achieve faster positive results for our clients through future negotiations. It was important for all to understand where we had a mutual interest in avoiding time-consuming litigation. I also thought we could widen the understanding of the HUD lawyers as to what was in our "mutual interest."

In a second letter Maxwell wrote, "We are deeply grateful for your taking the time … to make such a fine contribution to our meeting. … The panel made a tremendous impression on everyone, and I believe your candid and comprehensive approach was a particularly valuable experience for our lawyers in the field." Maxwell's letters are preserved on the same page in the Congressional Record as Watson's. I was proud of what had been accomplished.

Maxwell was key to the issuance of the Lease and Grievance Procedure regulations. The general counsel of any agency can kill changes in policy and regulation by manufactured interpretations of the law. He was a forward-thinking Republican with many important political connections in the White House and in the Congress. He understood from the beginning that legal "times were a changin'." He later became chairman of the all-important billion-dollar buyer of mortgages institution, Fannie Mae (Federal National Mortgage Association). Under his watch the mortgage market expanded exponentially. *Fortune* magazine named him one of ten of the greatest CEOs of all time. We developed a friendship but lost contact after I moved to Indonesia.

SAN FRANCISCO HOUSING AUTHORITY

After the Lease and Grievance Procedure regulations were issued and we won the court battle, the head of the Tenants Union in San Francisco Public Housing thought it was time for the Housing Authority to follow suit, and I agreed. Together with the San Francisco Legal Services, we began a long negotiation on behalf of the Tenants Union to gain their adoption. By this time I had a history of working with the Housing Authority as well as with the SF Public Housing Tenants Union. The woman who was the head of the union was a smart, tough welfare mother with an imposing presence, and she was a no-nonsense leader. In her day-to-day life she carried an ice pick for protection. She was the real thing, someone who used her power to help her fellow tenants instead of aggrandizing herself.

The Board of the Housing Authority had scheduled an evening meeting to vote on the Lease and Grievance Procedure. The vote was to be covered by the local TV news stations. During the debate, a black "preacher" from the neighborhood of the projects started to rail against the Lease and Grievance Procedure and the outsider white lawyer—Al Hirshen. He motioned to his two very large "bodyguards," and they started to move menacingly toward me. I stayed calm and wondered in which movie had I already seen this scene. At the same moment the head of the Tenants Union rushed across the room with her ice pick in hand. She shouted, "Al has been with us from the beginning! You are the outsider here." I was relieved and thankful for her intervention. It totally deflated the tension, and potential violence was avoided. The Housing Authority board voted to adopt the new Lease and Grievance Procedure.

I should mention I saw a rerun of the events later that night on the eleven o'clock news. We never found out if the "preacher" was in the employ of someone from the Housing Authority. It continues to be my bet this was the case.

For many years later I would hear from folks in San Francisco and nationwide about how the Lease and Grievance Procedure regulations saved tenants from un-lawful eviction and rent hikes.

CHAPTER 8

TRAVELING ABROAD: MOROCCO

Throughout my work life, I always made sure that I also had fun. Travel, and especially travel abroad, were a particular source of pleasure. I loved experiencing different cultures, art, architecture, landscapes, and food, and leaving the land of lawyer arguments behind. Travel just expands who I am. This feeling started with my first trip to Europe in 1963, but my time in Morocco ignited a passion that has led to a lifetime of travel and eventually to working and living abroad. Let us take a break from work and dip our toes into travel. I shall return to work thereafter.

In September 1969, my ex-wife Susanne and I took a TWA flight from New York City to Rabat, Morocco. We had just seen a movie filmed on a Moroccan beach. The cinematography captured the beauty, romance, and exotic nature of the scene: Berbers and Arabs dressed in their colorful clothes, fabulous large Berber tents with red, black, and yellow rugs and old leather saddlebags strewn about. White stallions dotted the beach. When we left the theater, I said, "Why don't we go there?" We were in our early thirties, without children, and my job gave me plenty of flexibility. We could follow a whim. TWA had a cheap ticket promotion at the time, and off we went to Morocco for a month.

An hour before we were scheduled to land in Rabat, the pilot announced that

King Hassan of Morocco had called an Emergency Arab Summit, and Moroccan authorities had closed the airport to commercial travel. We would be the last commercial flight to land. He said there would be no services at the airport, including rental cars. We wondered about the Avis car we had booked, and the representative who was supposed to meet our flight. The pilot said buses would take us from the airport into the city.

It turned out the Emergency Arab Summit had been called to discuss forming the Organization of Islamic Cooperation. Planes carrying leaders of fifty-seven Arab countries would be landing in Rabat to end the disunity of the Arab states that had been caused by the loss of the Arab-Israeli Six-Day War of 1967. A united policy toward Israel was the goal.

After our landing, I called our Avis representative. To my great relief, he answered his phone. He said he would meet our bus when it arrived in the city center. He warned us that in all probability we had lost our hotel reservation to the visiting dignitaries.

On the road into town, armed soldiers were stationed every seventy-five feet with their eyes glued on the highway. This was a Jewish boy's introduction to his first Arab country.

At the bus stop we overheard a conversation in French and broken English between a Moroccan official and three elderly passengers from Kansas. The official was telling them that without a doubt the Hilton hotel had given their rooms away to the visiting Arab leaders. He offered to assist them in finding new accommodations. They appeared stunned and unable to get the message. The man in the group said he did not believe the Hilton would give away their reserved rooms. He walked up the steep hill to the hotel to make inquiries and after a short period of time, he returned dejected. The Hilton had trampled his faith in this American institution.

The "Avis Man" made many phone calls, and then we drove in our rental car to a hotel he thought would have a room. While I parked the car, he and Susanne entered the hotel. There was a long hallway from the front door to the front desk. When I reached it, the receptionist said they had no vacancies. As we left the hotel Susanne was visibly upset. She thought he had said they had a room available and only changed his mind when he saw me enter the front door. My blonde wife of English-Irish extraction thought the man could tell the difference between an Arab

Semite and a Jewish Semite at over a hundred feet. But perhaps her French was simply rusty.

Our "Avis Man" made another suggestion. The hotel was "not the best," but would give us a place to stay overnight. Again, I let the two of them off in front of the hotel and parked the car. I saw the hotel needed a paint job badly, not to speak of the faded, torn furniture in the lobby. Susanne had her brave face on: "It will do." She had already paid for the night without first seeing the room. I asked the "Avis Man" to wait while we had a look. I should note that a joke between Susanne and me was how differently we had traveled to Europe before we met. Susanne had driven in limos, stayed at expensive hotels, and paid a visit in England to the Queen's doctor for her broken ankle. Her first husband's father was head of the American Nickel Corporation. I had traveled on less than five dollars a day.

We entered the room, and it was horrible. The toilet was backed up, and when I pulled back the bed covers every nationality's body hair greeted me. It turned out we were in a Moroccan whorehouse. Susanne was willing to rough it. I was not. After securing reimbursement of most of our money, we thanked "Avis Man" for his help, gave up on Rabat, and drove south several hours to Casablanca in search of a room for the night. Alas, due to the spillover from Rabat the situation was the same. We continued farther south to the exquisite Portuguese fortress town of El Jadida, where our luck changed. We found a room in a wonderful beachfront hotel with views of the Atlantic Ocean. After twenty-four hours of traveling, we fell into a deep sleep.

I awoke to a brilliant blue sky and a shimmering ocean. Susanne was gone. I showered and went to find her on the beach talking to a handsome young Moroccan man (nineteen years old) named Mohammad. I learned they had just met a few minutes ago and already were in deep conversation. Susanne's inquisitive nature was at work as she peppered Mohammad with questions about himself and Morocco. He turned out to be a young man with a curious mind who spoke English. "Why did you choose Morocco to visit?" "What cities are you going to visit?" "What other Arab countries have you visited?"

After an hour of conversation he invited us to visit his home (not an unusual occurrence in many Arab countries), where his mother served us many sweets and Nana (the traditional Moroccan sweet Maghrebi mint tea). As she showed us her house with pictures of the family, lace embroideries, and small multicolored rugs everywhere, we had to be careful not to overly admire the decorations. My friends had told us, and my reading confirmed, that Arabs have a deep-seated tradition of warm hospitality and might insist we take anything we admired with us as a gift.

After talking with Mohammad and obtaining his mother's permission, we invited him to accompany us to Marrakech. We would pay for his food and hotel there, and he would be our guide.

On the highway to Marrakech we passed a camel souk where several men were butchering a camel. They were dressed in their long, flowing, hooded djellabas (an outer garment) and soft yellow babouche slippers. We watched as one of the men, with great expertise, separated the skin from a muscle of the camel. The others were carving the meat into smaller pieces for sale. Rivers of blood with squadrons of flies were everywhere. The smell of decay was in the air. Meat in rural Morocco did not come in hygienic, plastic-covered, individualized packages.

Marrakech is Morocco's fourth largest city, founded around 1062 and built by the Berber empire. Red clay walls from the Sadyaan dynasty (1549-1669) surround the old city. As in other Moroccan cities, the French built their new quarters outside the walls, thus preserving the ancient city. No urban renewal here. As the French left after independence, the rich Arab population moved from the old city to the comforts of the new.

Marrakech is set in the foothills of the snow-covered Atlas Mountains. With the very tall Koutoubia Minaret in Djemma el-Fna Square, framed by a crimson sky at sunset and the Atlas as a backdrop, you felt you were on a Hollywood stage setting. The sounds and sights of Djemma el-Fna —the musicians, snake charmers, sword swallowers, storytellers, and food stalls—enhanced this feeling. We could check out the action from the balcony of our hotel room before deciding what food stall and entertainment to aim for and then immerse ourselves in the tempo and vibrations of the Square.

To "stay safe" and eat in the hotel would have meant missing out on the exotic nature of Morocco, the very attraction of the Morocco we had seen in the movie. We chose a stall consisting of a grill and two small tables because we spotted locals eating there. The smells of the spices (garlic, cumin, turmeric, coriander) of our traditional Moroccan grilled chicken dish, the sounds of the music by the numerous musicians mixed with the smell of the after-dinner hashish (offered by our stall owner) filled our senses and enhanced the glow we felt.

The Raba Kedinia (Spice Square) also assaulted our senses. There was a fusion of Africa and Arabia in this chaotic square with owners hawking their goods—cumin, saffron, anise, cinnamon, and more. Men ran the stalls, and the customers were overwhelmingly women.

The souks of Marrakech are the largest in Morocco. The winding labyrinth of stores would have been overwhelming without Mohammad. But because he could be our interpreter and advisor, we decided to act on our desire to buy two rugs. He chose the rug store based on the quality of the rugs he could see on display.

The travel guides told us not to pay more than half the asking price. After several minutes Mohammad indicated he wanted to talk with me outside the store. He said the owner had told him he would give Mohammad a fee if he helped him cheat us. Mohammad wanted us to leave, but I responded that, on the contrary, we now had an advantage. He could discretely tell me what the owner said to him in Arabic. Nana (Moroccan sweet tea) was served, and the bargaining began in earnest. The storeowner's opening price for the two rugs was $600. He spoke in French to Susanne, and she translated what he said. I thought he probably spoke English as well. Bargaining was not part of Susanne's DNA or background. "Only a schmuck pays retail prices" was not her motto. The process made her very anxious, whereas it took me right back to Orchard Street on the Lower East Side of NYC, watching my mother haggle over the price of a suit for me. Each bargaining interchange brought a smile of fond remembrance to my face. To follow the guidebook's advice and offer half still seemed too high a price for the two rugs. With the spirit of my mother and all the Jewish Bronx mothers I knew as guides, I jumped in with a $150 counteroffer. The game was on.

He shouted that I had just insulted his mother because she did not raise a stupid son. I said, "But we are just poor students." (Of course we were not.) After more Nana and more negotiations, we agreed on the price of $225 for both rugs. Afterward it was obvious that Mohammad was disappointed in me. He thought we paid $25 too much. I was happy with the transaction. I knew no tourist would ever get the same price as a local, and near the end of the trip this truism was brought home to me as I bought some grilled sardines on a beach. After bargaining, I purchased them at twenty-five cents each. My chest was out with pride as I thought I had mastered Moroccan bargaining. To my amusement, soon after my purchase, a local bought the same sardines for five cents apiece.

We went to celebrate our rug adventure and thank Mohammad for his assistance in beating the guidebook percentages. We entered the ornate lobby of the famous hotel La Marmouna with colorful, mainly blue and green ceramic tiles and large glass chandeliers. I sought advice as to where lunch was being served. I was told rather straightforwardly that while we were welcome, Mohammad was not. Was it his lack of status (too dark), not being dressed richly enough, not being from the right social class? All of these I think contributed to the rejection of him as a suitable customer for lunch. Of course to us he looked just fine, and not at all underdressed. Prejudice is everywhere in the world, in Russia or the Ukraine against blacks, in Indonesia against the Chinese, in India against darker Indians and the "Untouchables," and in Australia against the Aborigines. The list goes on. Pick any country (of course including America) and you will find prejudice in its many forms—class, ethnicity, race, religion. It just seems to be part of being human that we do not like the fellow who is different from us.

We did not accept the invitation for only the two of us to stay for lunch, and politely expressed our displeasure. We walked out together, just as we had walked in. Of course our action would not affect the policy, but at least it would send a message and not diminish Mohammad's humanity.

Our next stop was the Festival of the Fiancée (Imilchil Marriage Festival) that took place high in the middle Atlas Mountains. Traditionally, Berber women would choose a man who had found a way into their hearts and then marry in one grand collective ceremony. We knew our timing was off to see the actual ceremony on the last of the three-day festival, but decided anyway to go for one day because we knew from friends that we would see the young Berber teenage fiancées in their entire splendor and partake in a massive souk.

We started from Tinerhir, a town that gained notoriety when Winston Churchill painted landscapes there. I bought a round trip for the two of us in the cab of a truck. The back was filled with Berber and Arab men. The truck slowly climbed up a dry, black-and-brown rock riverbed through the Todgha Gorge high into the Atlas Mountains. The mountains were many shades of purple, and the ground around the riverbed was a shining dark green with date palms everywhere. The views took your breath away. Susanne, who had drunk the tap water at the Club Med in Quarzazate (she had not read the warning in the hotel) bravely fought off feelings of nausea and a blistering headache. When we arrived in the green valley with cypress-like trees, there were horses, camels, goats, and lambs everywhere on the purple hills. The numerous large black Berber tents we had seen in the movie were dotted across the valley. Each tent was similar to stores we had visited in the city souks with different things to sell, ranging from western kids clothes and cheap bed linens to kitchen utensils, from pots and pans to colorful plastic dishes and matching coffee cups. The blue, pink, and brown plastic sandals for kids and grownups were new to us. The valley was jammed with many thousands of Berbers, a small number of Arabs, and an even smaller number of Westerners. As we moved around the souk I would at times lose sight of Susanne, but suddenly I would spot her blue-and-white headscarf in the sea of turbans, wool ski caps, and wrapped headscarves.

The numerous teenage brides-to-be walking around the souk were a fantastic sight. They were decked out to impress, and impress they did. Their young cheeks were painted red with a blue stripe on their chin. Their mainly dark-indigo blue and black wrapped head scarves were held down by red rope ties and adorned with strands of silver coins. Many of them also wore very large silver necklaces. They were dressed in full-length gray, blue, or black wool blanket-type capes, with red, white, and green stripes. They walked with or among older women in similar outer garments, but without makeup or jewelry. The grooms and men did not wear any particular outfit.

Susanne looked in vain for traditional women's garments or other handcrafted textiles. None were to be found. As is often the case, the locals want Western style goods when they have the ability to afford them. They buy what we buy, which is a sign of their economic progress. But for us this is a loss because the crafts and way of life that attracted us in the first place are disappearing. The world spins forward without our permission.

Although we did not witness the marriage ceremony, the festival did not disappoint. The ride to the festival, the valley itself with the tents and animals, and most of all the people we saw left an indelible mark. You could not have this experience anywhere else.

In Tinehir, before we started our drive up the riverbed, we had an encounter that underlined the self-evident truth that international travel means you are in a foreign country. Foreign means a place with a different culture, law, and rules of behavior. What you might expect in America in terms of legal protections, cultural norms, and mores does not necessarily apply.

We had asked two local policemen about the road to the riverbed. We struck up a conversation and decided to have lunch together. One of the policemen had an aggressive personality. I was surprised to see him have a beer or two—something that just isn't done in public in a Muslim country, especially with foreigners. In French, he suggested to Susanne she should leave me and run away with him. Many times Moroccan men asked me how I got so lucky to find a French woman. I was often mistaken for an Arab because I liked to wear the country's traditional dress, a djellaba (a kaftan with a hood), and instead of shoes, balgha (yellowish soft leather slippers with flattened heel.) The policeman's behavior made me nervous and put me on guard. Soon thereafter he offered to buy hashish for me. I declined. It's not smart to buy drugs from someone you do not know in America, and even less in a foreign country. There are no entrapment laws or due process in Morocco. Of course I already knew this. What went through my mind was a possible setup by the policeman to get rid of me so he could pursue Susanne. I will never know if this was the case or not. When we left, the other policeman apologized for his colleague's behavior.

By contrast, accepting the offer of an after-dinner hashish pipe from the owner of a stall in Djemaa el-Fna (the main square in Marrakech) was not a problem. It was the equivalent of an after-dinner liquor. Clearly it was no setup, but just Moroccan tourist hospitality.

The most alluring scene in the movie that inspired our trip showed Arabian stallions on a beach. In my imagination I added a scene: at the end of the ride I would turn my stallion to face the sunset. I realized this dream in Agadir, in the southwest part of Morocco, the land of the "blue people" (who get their name from the dye on their djellabas that colors their skin blue). We found a place to rent two marvelous white Arabian stallions. I should note that Susanne was a horsewoman with great experience. By contrast, I only had a few rides under my belt from a stable in Yonkers. When the horses hit the beach, they took off at a gallop. I called out to Susanne, "Isn't this marvelous?" She nervously shouted back, "No, they are running away with us." Sometimes ignorance can be bliss. On the ride back to the stables we were able to walk the horses ankle-deep into the calm, blue-green ocean and watch the sunset form with deep pink clouds. Fantasies can sometimes come true.

Another day in Agadir we watched the ancient Guerda dance, a dance performed to rhythmic "trance music" provided by a single pot-shaped drum. No other instrument is played. There is ever-quickening chanting and hand clapping by several "blue men" as well as onlookers (in our case, a few tourists and numerous Moroccans). It starts with a woman on her knees covered by a black veil, looking like a shapeless black mass. Her hands and fingers emerge and move, flickering, tapping, and vibrating with slow purpose as the momentum builds. The rhythm quickens as she rotates, leans forward, undulates, and bends backward until her head touches the ground. As she accelerates to the music, the very macho-looking Moroccan men in the audience shout their incitement. Her hair, face, and silver jewelry headdress become visible as she gradually removes the veil and rises from her knees, but her hands continue to be the focus of the dance. Then she stops, and there is abrupt silence. The drum, chanting, and clapping begin anew, and another dancer takes over repeating the same dance. The Moroccan men, with smiles on their faces, twist dirham notes in the dancers' braided hair to show their admiration. *Wow*, I thought, although there was no cleavage or pelvic grinding, the dance was an indelible lesson of sensuality, radiating a magnetism that connected the viewer to physical pleasure and sexuality.

We left Agadir in a state of bliss and traveled to Fez, the cultural capital of Morocco. We saw the famous walled Medina, the red, pink, and blue dyeing pots of the tanner quarter, and the exquisite blue-green Fassi tiles of the Royal Palace. As I parked our car at different sites and restaurants, young men approached and asked, "Would you like me to wash your windows and keep your car safe?" I immediately said yes! To do otherwise was to guarantee a break-in.

The Medina (a UNESCO site) is one of the largest car-free zones in any city in the world. The high walls make it impossible for a tourist to identify a landmark by which you could get your bearing. I hired a young boy of fourteen to show us the way. When I told him I wanted to see the Jewish Quarter and Maimonides' home, he said, "They are dirty and you don't want to go there." He did not understand why I laughed in response.

We accepted an invitation for cocktails at the home of a young man who had been seated next to us on the plane. His manservant brought us our drinks in a beautiful inner court with several walls partially covered in Fassi tiles. The mosaic tile floor was covered with several small red rugs and red, pink, and yellow flowerpots everywhere. It was a delightful way to observe the cocktail hour, and we felt privileged to enjoy this aspect of Fez life.

Three days before we left Morocco, we decided to drive from Meknes to the Mediterranean Sea that abutted the famous "Hashish" Rif. (My friend Steve who had camped out there for two years had told me of his ample supplies from the nearby mountains). The Rif, originally a part of the Spanish Protectorate and only recently ceded to Morocco, was open to tourists. We left the main road and, armed with only a hand-drawn map, we made many turns in the unmarked desert until we finally arrived at the sea. The mountains we had just driven through framed the long, brown sand beach that ran down to the green-blue water of the Mediterranean. We took a swim and ate our packed lunch. It was getting late. On our return, we had been driving for fifteen minutes on the dirt road, and after a few wrong turns to nowhere, I noticed with mild anxiety that the "running out of gas" light was blinking more vigorously. Susanne started to panic as it became clear we were lost in a maze of dirt roads with no idea how to get back to the highway. The lights of small villages were coming on. A glorious sunset was beginning to form, taking me away from our potentially serious situation. I snapped back to attention and said, "Don't worry, if worse comes to worse, I'll will walk to a village and ask for help. Don't forget Arabs and Berbers are famous for their hospitality." Just as I was finishing my words of comfort to a disbelieving Susanne, a car appeared out of nowhere, and the driver told us how to get to the highway and buy gas. We were saved! Our month in Morocco had begun and was ending with a potentially problematic situation, but in both instances the kindness of the Moroccans saved the day.

We spent our last two days in the seventh largest city and capital, Rabat. Now that the Emergency Arab Summit leaders had left, we were able to get a decent hotel room. Rabat, with commanding views of the Atlantic, is a delightful mixture of an architecturally interesting modern city with a historically significant older one. Unlike other cities in Morocco it is not dependent on tourist income and is therefore more relaxed. The twelfth-century Kasbah is predominately residential, and its narrow streets are lined with whitewashed houses, mostly built by Muslim refugees from Spain. The most dramatic entry to the Kasbah is the enormous ceremonial Almohad gate of Bab Oudaia (1195), built by the Almohad Berber Dynasty that ruled Northern Africa and Iberia (Moorish Spain) from 1122 to1269. Within the

Kasbah rises the oldest mosque in Rabat, built in the twelfth century and restored in the eighteenth.

Rabat's most famous landmark is also a mosque, one that was never completed due to the death of Sultan al-Mansur (1184–1199). It would have been the second-largest mosque of its time after Samarra in Iraq. The part of the mosque that was built was later destroyed in an earthquake in 1755. The well-tendered gardens next to a forest of shattered pillars demonstrate the grandiosity of the Sultan's plans, and the views make it a must-see.

As we buckled our seatbelts on the airplane for the ride home to California, I marveled how a spontaneous fantasy about Morocco had turned into a wonderful reality. Whenever you can, follow your whimsy.

As was the case after each of my travels, I returned to the battle recharged and ready to enter the fray with all the necessary energy at my command.

CHAPTER 9

RURAL HOUSING

In 1971, the Office of Economic Opportunity (OLEO), the U.S. Government agency charged with implementing President Johnson's poverty program, asked me to join a task force that would create an entity to support the development of low-income rural housing. A product of this effort was the Housing Assistance Council (HAC) that is still in existence today. It provides technical assistance and training to local nonprofit, low-income developers. Through a subsidiary it also makes different types of loans to assist these developers.

I was elected president of the board of HAC and held this position until I had to resign when I joined the Carter administration in 1978. Both the black and Hispanic members of the board trusted me to make independent decisions that were not racially motivated but simply decided on merit. While the task force was doing its work, I met fellow member Clay Cochran, an icon of the rural housing movement, a large man with a goatee. He was the executive director of the Rural Housing Alliance (RHA), the then-premier rural housing organization in the country. At his request, I joined his board thinking it was imperative that HAC and RHA work in unison and not in competition.

The HAC Board hired Gordon Cavanaugh to be our executive director.

He had a deep commitment to the poor and to low-income housing. Gordon had the experience of working in a highly charged "political" job as executive director of the Philadelphia Housing Authority, and he also possessed a likeable personality which is a plus in getting strong personalities to work together. He would need the support of Congress, the Farmers Home Administration, and divergent community-based organizations, especially RHA and Clay Cochran. As a member of the RHA and HAC boards I was in a unique position to support Cavanaugh. The goateed Clay was used to being the voice of rural housing for the poor, and with his strong ego he would jealously guard his preeminent position. If he thought HAC was going to supplant the Rural Housing Alliance, he would put up roadblocks to the development of HAC, making sure the new and vibrant national rural housing organization would go nowhere. A soft and deft touch was called for. Both Cavanaugh's and my personalities were perfect for the task of consensus building. Together we convinced Clay that HAC was not a substitute for RHA and would be a needed additional resource for the rural poor. To his credit he bought our entreaties. Gordon fulfilled and surpassed all of our expectations in the job. I learned a lesson that would come in handy in the future: be patient and respect the views of others in winning them to your side.

My evenhandedness, directness, and commitment to developing practical solutions for helping the poor led to my being trusted by both organizations, RHA and HAC.

In the early '70s I visited two of our housing projects to celebrate their completion. The two visits produced in me diametrically opposite emotions: depression on the one hand and exaltation on the other. I experienced these contradictory emotions many times in my efforts to assist the poor.

The HAC Project was located on the Oglala Sioux Pine Ridge Reservation in South Dakota, and the RHA Project took place in a small community in the rural mountains, a two-hour drive outside San Juan, Puerto Rico.

The Pine Ridge Reservation had been the scene of the Wounded Knee Massacre perpetrated by US Army Troops in 1890, and eighty-three years later, in 1973, it was again the scene of violence between the US Government and tribe members involving the American Indian Movement (AIM) and the FBI that left two agents dead.

It was the most desolate place of all the reservations, slums, and barrios I had visited. The last business that employed any sizable number of Reservation Indians (it made all types of fishing flies) had just relocated to Taiwan. The hopelessness that I saw in the vacant and hung-over eyes of the men was accentuated by the bitter wind that blew down from Canada over the barren hills. The level of drunkenness among them was astronomical. The Reservation, when measured by data of social and economic indicators (meaning health, substance abuse, education, employment, housing) was at the bottom. Although it was obvious that we had done nothing to alter the underlying conditions, at least we had provided protection from the biting cold, put nonleaking roofs over people's heads, and installed indoor bathrooms.

Was spending money on housing for a limited number of Reservation Indians—without impacting their dire financial situation—a waste of resources? There is no simple answer to this question. On the one hand, one can argue (along with the French philosopher and novelist Albert Camus), that anything lowering suffering is worthwhile. On the other hand, given the limited financial resources, spending such funds on things that do not alter poor people's fundamental economic condition is a waste of these limited resources. The debate cannot be resolved here. It would require another book to do it justice. I know that cynicism arises when efforts fail to materially change the condition of the poor, but having realistic goals was essential for "staying in the game."

Only when our plane took off from Rapid City and we flew level with the majesty of the presidential faces of Mount Rushmore did my feelings of depression lift ever so slightly.

The trip to Puerto Rico was the exact opposite. We took a two-hour bus ride into the mountains to attend the opening ceremony of the houses RHA had funded. When we arrived the mood was joyous. The families who would occupy the houses personally thanked each board member. Spanish, English, and Spanish translation flowed. The little square of the village was beautifully decorated with colorful streamers. There were tables loaded with food; music filled the air, and lots of rum was consumed. You could touch the joy of the people in the village. I felt that it was a special privilege to be able to make this day happen for the rural poor of Puerto Rico, and it gave me energy to continue the fight.

BECOMING THE HOUSING LAW PROJECT DIRECTOR

The '70s were a time when alliances between whites and blacks for economic and racial justice frayed. Many blacks did not trust the motivation and efforts of white people. They wanted blacks deciding strategy for blacks—in my view, a reasonable position to hold. At the same time, Jews who had been an integral part of the civil rights and antipoverty movements were now tarred with the brush of other whites who were suspected of predatory business practices at the expense of black communities. For some there was no place for whites in their movement, even as advisors. In times of tension, nuance disappears and demagoguery prevails. It is a relatively simple matter for unscrupulous black community leaders to use this tension to scapegoat whites for their own political purposes.

One such situation arose at a National Tenant Organization conference. Ken Phillips, the founding director of the Law Project, who had hired me, made a presentation to the tenant leaders from all around the country, outlining our efforts to assist tenants and community leaders nationwide by filing lawsuits and winning statutory and administrative changes favorable to them. After his speech, a few black NTO members attacked him as just another "plantation boss" who was not really helping them. Prejudice ignores facts. As the conference proceeded, their voices steamrolled into many. Unlike the head of the San Francisco Tenants Union who had defended me, Jesse Gray deserted Ken. Anthony Henry, who was black and the first NTO executive director, whispered to me that for internal "political" reasons, Gray would not protect him. Ken's basic human dignity be dammed! He added that Ken should not take it personally, but the safest way for Gray to remain in power was to support the anti-white feelings in the room, adopting the black-white divide. This divide was growing stronger in the black community.

Ken could not see the situation for what it was—a political stunt aimed at Gray's keeping the power. Politics can sometimes be raw, and you need to develop a thick skin to the games that can be played at your expense. He felt betrayed to the core and resigned. Ken was a product of money, an upper-class neighborhood, and the San Francisco private school system. He did not possess the personal toughness of someone from a diversified public school system who had learned how to maneuver on the streets of the Bronx. For me, it was simply politics, but as I said to Anthony Henry, it was a nasty thing to do.

A few months later, at the request of Mike Heyman, the chairman of the NHLP Board, I took Ken's place as director. Ken deserves a lot of credit for getting the Law Project on its feet.

NIXON AND THE BACKUP CENTERS

A five-month acute danger period for the specialized backup centers, such as the Housing Law Project, was the time Howie Phillips was acting director of the Office of Equal Opportunity (OLEO). This was the agency charged with implementing President Johnson's anti-poverty program. In January 1973, Phillips was tasked (or so he thought) by President Nixon to dismantle Johnson's Great Society programs, including the legal services. He was the '70s equivalent of Texas Senator Ted Cruz, a prominent conservative purist who saw the world in moral black-and-white terms. He also was a Jew who had converted to become a Christian fundamentalist. I never saw him smile.

His appointment in January 1973 to the post caused an enormous outcry in Congress and the legal community. Several months thereafter, a meeting in DC was called for the backup centers, the local Legal Services offices, NLADA, and others to discuss strategy for dealing with Phillips' administrative actions.

I met with my NHLP chairman, Professor Mike Heyman, to advise him of the present state of affairs and get his strategic input. When I said we might have to sue Phillips, he immediately authorized me to do so. I replied that only the University of California Regents had that authority to sue Phillips and OLEO. He said, "Let me worry about that," and repeated that I had a green light to sue Phillips. Most people in his position would have walked away from potential political trouble. Not Mike; he stood tall.

As it turned out, I never had to sue Phillips. As a result of a lawsuit filed by Congressional Democrats, a federal judge declared Phillip's actions to break up the OLEO programs null and void. The judge also held that since he was never confirmed by the Senate, he could no longer continue to be acting director (acting director was a short-term, temporary appointment, and he had already exceeded the allowable length of time in office). Five months after his appointment he resigned when President Nixon did not, as promised, veto funding for the Great Society programs. In 1974 he left the Republican Party and founded the Conservative Caucus. He ran three times for president on the Conservative Party ticket and lost each time.

Mike Heyman went on to be chancellor of the University of California, and secretary of the Smithsonian Institution (1994–1999). On my trips to DC I loved visiting him in the secretary's turret office—in the "nation's attic."

Phillips' extreme, no-compromise attacks on the Legal Services elicited strong support for the program from bar groups, especially the American Bar Association (ABA). This support allowed Congressional Democrats in 1974 to pass the Legal Services Corporation Act. Legal Services lawyers were now governed by an independent government agency run by a board, nominated by the president, and approved by the Congress. A president could no longer directly end the program on his own.

Although the passage of the act made it more difficult to end Legal Services for the poor, it did not stop the Nixon and Ford White Houses from their efforts to curtail the efficacy of Legal Services lawyers. In my view, "law reform" survived only because the Nixon White House was consumed with defending him against impeachment, and Ford, too, had too many other issues on his plate. Jimmy Carter's winning the Presidential election in 1976 saved the backup centers and "law reform" representation for the immediate future. It brought me a great sigh of relief and would give me the freedom, in good conscience, to move on from the Law Project. We were no longer at "death's door."

GOING FOR BIG FUNDING

The turbulent political time of the '70s taught me that we could no longer rely on funding exclusively from the federal government. As director of the NHLP, I decided in 1973 that we needed to approach the large foundations.

John Simon was the head of the liberal Taconic Foundation founded by Audrey and Steve Currier. Audrey Currier was an heir to the Mellon fortune and the daughter of Ailsa Mellon Bruce, the sister of Paul Mellon. He was at the time one of the eight richest people in the US.

A light plane on which the Curriers were traveling had disappeared between San Juan, Puerto Rico, and the Virgin Islands. Their bodies were never found. They had named John Simon, their lawyer at a top Wall Street law firm and a Yale Law School graduate, as executor of their will and guardian of their three children.

I had known John for a long time. Our paths had crossed many times at conferences where we were both speakers. I called him and explained that I did not want Taconic dollars, but rather his advice on how to approach the big boys, meaning the Ford and Rockefeller Brothers Foundations. He suggested I come visit him the following weekend at the two-thousand-acre Currier Estate in the hunt country of Virginia, near Middleburg. I accepted his invitation and told him I would like Dave Madway, head of the economic development side of the project, and Arnold Sternberg from my DC office to join me. He said he would send a car for us.

Madway and I flew to DC and stayed at the Washington Hilton. Right on time the following morning, the doors to a Cadillac limousine were opened by a liveried, light-skinned black chauffeur, and the three of us got in for the several-hour drive to the Currier Estate.

It seemed to take twenty minutes to get from the front gates of the estate to the house. As we entered the living room to greet John, I elbowed Madway to point out that the Utrillos and Picassos on the walls did not have thumbtacks in their corners to hold them up, as ours did in college. They were real.

We had lunch on the patio overlooking the hills of the estate. John's wife joined us and summoned a black maid to serve us by ringing a bell. I noticed several head of cattle roaming the hills and asked John, "Why cattle?" He said, rather than having to mow the grass, it was cheaper to have the cattle do the job.

The incongruity of discussing the issue of how to best help the poor and access foundation money to do so was not lost on us. But John provided a blueprint with the names of key foundation officials who would prove invaluable to our securing several grants. These grants would be vital to the Law Project's ability to continue its law reform efforts. Moreover, they would not be subject to any possible federal restrictions.

Before we left, John asked if we wanted to see the tack room and a restored carriage of Queen Victoria they had bought from the Rockefellers. Dave and Arnold hesitated; I shouted, yes, thank you! Susanne, my horsewoman wife, would not have forgiven me if we had not taken John up on his offer. The tack "room" was bigger and better than my own house. This stand-alone structure was made entirely of mahogany wood. John told us they would sometimes hook up the carriage to the horses and drive around the estate. I could imagine them rolling over the two thousand-acre estate in the royal-crested carriage, shouting "Off with your head" as they approached one of the cattle. What a fantastic ending to a dreamlike day for three children of Jewish immigrants.

Thanks to John's advice, we received funding from both the Ford and the Rockefeller Foundations. At the time it was a welcomed safety net.

My resignation from the NHLP became effective in January 1977, the same month Jimmy Carter was inaugurated. Of course, the former was not as newsworthy as the latter. I felt worn out by the political and budget battles. In general, executive directors do not last as long as staff attorneys who stay energized, maybe due to their direct contact with different clients and areas of the law. For me, the political and budget battles were repetitive and had become intellectually boring. I learned with time that I enjoyed the challenge of starting an endeavor rather than the day-to-day management of an organization. I also did not wish to become a cynic like some of my brethren. It was time for a new challenge.

In 2007, the MacArthur Foundation awarded the Law Project its prestigious Creative and Effective Institutions Award (the institution-version of its Genius Grant) that came with a check for half a million dollars. The award cited the beginning of the Law Project and its almost forty years of excellence in assisting the poor. It was satisfying to know I had played a role in its successful history. Today, almost fifty years after I became a founding member, the National Housing Law Project still continues its good work.

CHAPTER 10

DENIAL IS THE ROOMMATE OF ADDICTION—PART I

A s my professional career moved forward in high gear, I continued to ignore the many signs that my alcoholism was blossoming.

The first time I got drunk, I was seventeen years old and in my first year of college. I celebrated the end of the first semester with two new CCNY friends, DiStefano and Balcerak, at the men's club of DiStefano's father. The Sicilian club occupied a storefront on Montrose Avenue in the Bushwick section of Brooklyn. It was a replica of clubs that could be found all over southern Italy: one large room with fake marble-top tables, wooden chairs, and a kitchen behind a closed door in the rear. The walls were decorated with faded photo scenes of Sicily. The men were playing cards and checkers while drinking their new batch of homemade red wine out of small water glasses. They had the muscular bodies of hard-working laborers you didn't want to get into a fight with.

Happy to see DiStefano, the club welcomed us in, clearly proud that DiStefano was the first in his family to go to college. So was Balcerak, and I was the second in mine. We were known as the "Three Musketeers" among our fellow-students.

Although I was nervous at first, the smiles on the faces of the men allowed me to relax and tell them I had come all the way from the Bronx to taste their famous red wine. From the first glass, the full-bodied taste was delicious. My friends and I ate the pretzels, nuts, and pizza set out on the tables and fell into the slow drinking pace of the men. I enjoyed the increasing lightness of body and mind. The "Grapes of the Gods" made me feel like a man among men and on top of the world.

After two hours at the club, instead of going home with a mild buzz on, I followed my friends to DiStefano's family apartment where we continued celebrating. Wanting more and not knowing when to stop is a central part of my story. This time the wine was store-bought, and I was no longer participating in an Italian-American cultural experience. We were now simply three young men getting drunk together, releasing the tensions of our first semester. We traded "war stories" and laughed about our calculus professor who insisted that I was the Italian and DiStefano the Jew. No further food was consumed. I began to drink faster while my friends continued to sip. When I left an hour later for the subway station, I had no idea how intoxicated I was. On the long ride home to the Bronx I vomited many times. I now was the bum I usually tried to avoid in the subway.

This embarrassing experience did not scare me off. As time passed, the negative fallout receded from my consciousness, and I only remembered the fun part. I later discovered I had a "drinking trigger gene" that overwhelmed my rational thinking after one drink. For a long time, however, this didn't stop me either.

Over the next thirty years, my drinking career went from fun to mostly fun and some trouble, to more trouble, to finally mostly trouble. I was never a "low-bottom," "bowery bum," "dumpster-diving," or "grocery cart-pushing" alcoholic. I never consciously drank to get drunk or to be in blackout. Until the last year of my drinking, a year of serious trouble, I did not drink every day and could stop for periods of time, making it easy to deny I had a problem with alcohol. Although I never went to prison for killing someone in a bar fight or while driving drunk, I paid a heavy price: loss of a marriage and family, economic distress, loss of self-esteem and, deep humiliation.

Drinking gave me a feeling of freedom, aliveness, a sense of being in touch with my artistic and silly, carefree side. When I "had a few," I was quick, and my shyness was forgotten. I did not feel insecure any more. I even thought I was smart, charming, good-looking, and felt I could access the inner world of a poet or actor. A full range of emotions suddenly, as if by magic, became available to me that otherwise seemed blocked. I loved the feeling of losing my inhibitions and being totally alive. Dancing gave me a similar feeling. Whether I was a kid chosen to audition for tap dancing on a TV program called *The Children's Hour*, dancing the Lindy on a NYC predecessor to *The Dick Clark Show*, or gliding around a dance floor in New Orleans to Cajun rhythms, I always felt at one with the music and in a state of freedom and joy. But after several glasses of wine or a few drinks, I was Fred Astaire floating over the dance floor, doing a one- or two-step with Ginger Rogers in my arms. I was Fred Astaire at a supper club in Mexico City, dancing and drinking martinis and oozing his "top-hat-and-tails" sophistication. I was not merely the one- dimensional, rational, and analytical man I appeared to be without the "help" of a drink. When sober, I felt unable to be free and creative to the same degree. I have often asked myself why? Was it fear of being judged? Doubting that people would be on my wavelength and appreciate me? After years of 12-Step work, I am still not certain why; I just know now that I can access these feelings of being alive, witty, and silly without booze or marijuana.

As I said, in the beginning, drinking was fun and filled with jokes, pranks, and hijinks. While attending the University of Chicago Law School, after a few drinks I would climb up the side of my dorm to the second floor window of my Mormon friend Dave and, with a flashlight pointing to my face, state in otherworldly tones, "David, this is God speaking." I would make "angels" in the snow, break out into a tap dance, or imitate Ezio Pinza, belting off-key songs from *South Pacific*.

One night my friend Frank and I had a few drinks and a hamburger at the famous University of Chicago institution, Jimmy's Woodlawn Tap. Always ready to "spice up life," I challenged him to a race home in our cars. Frank was winning, but as we approached a stop sign he stopped; I didn't. A policeman in his patrol car across the street was waiting for just such a fool and turned on his flashing lights and siren. He had me follow him to the police station to pay a fine. I did not have enough money on me, so I called Frank and asked him to go to my place and get the "Coffee Hour" money from my job providing students and faculty with coffee every weekday in the main lounge of the law school. The money was on my dresser, divided by coin types in individual coffee-stained Styrofoam cups.

Frank arrived and put the four dirty coffee cups on the desk of the sergeant in charge. The sergeant barely concealed a smile as we started to count out the pennies, nickels, dimes, and quarters necessary to pay my fine. By this time word was out in the station about these crazy university law students with Styrofoam coffee cups filled with pennies. Some of the cops broke into laughter when they saw the sergeant's desk. The columns of coins were a sight to see. We were their evening entertainment.

After a night of drinking with another law school friend, Mack, we set out at 1:00 a.m. to ride his motorbike on the Outer Drive highway along Lake Michigan. When we reached 70 miles per hour, with me looking over my shoulder for cops, Mack launched into a couple of wheelies. With his strong arms, balance, and overall skills he managed to steady the bike that dangerously wobbled as he returned the front wheel back to terra firma. The next wheelies were executed with ever more daring. All I thought was how happy I was that Mack was in charge. Several cars blew their horns as we zoomed past them. As luck had it, we didn't end our ride at a hospital or morgue. But our alcoholic bravado wasn't over yet. Mack thought it would be fun to show me a slum apartment he had lived in while he was part of Martin Luther King's drive to help the poor of Chicago. It was a neighborhood run by black gangs—not a good place to visit for outsiders, especially whites, at any time of day. It was pure insanity at 2:00 a.m. Again our luck held, and Mack revved the engine as we sped off.

One evening, after a few drinks, Mack and I wound up at a party. I was having a good time and refused to leave. But he was adamant. He picked me up, carried me to the car, and dumped me in the back seat. Before he could get behind the wheel, I opened the door and headed back to the party. He picked me up again, and again put me in the back seat, but this time he pushed the door button down. Somehow it didn't occur to this full-scholarship law student at one of the top schools in the country that locking the door wouldn't do the trick. Of course I simply pulled the button up and left the car again. We were doing a great imitation of Abbot and Costello or the Keystone Cops!

Another night of comedy ended very late one evening at a bar on our way back to the law school dorms. We hoped to pick up women and had prepared ourselves. As soon as Mack spotted two women at the bar, he left me at our table and started his Irish charm pitch. His pitch included the line that I was a poet who had published in the *Atlantic Monthly*. It was the wrong line for this bar. The women had no idea what the *Atlantic Monthly* was. Moreover, they knew in a second that Mack had had too much to drink. When he turned around to point out his famous poet friend, I was asleep with my head on the table. Although in retrospect we both thought we were pathetic, the next day we found the evening hilarious.

At this time of my life I was not very introspective. My youthful exploits did not make me think I was reckless or insensitive to the feelings of others. The exploits were fun or funny to me. I was self-centered and convinced I wasn't causing anybody (including myself) any harm.

There was a period when I was the guy people relied on to drive them home after a party because I usually did not over drink.

When my first wife Linda and I went with another couple to visit Pamplona, Spain in 1963, I was the designated driver. The reason for the trip was my intent to run with the bulls in the street at the San Fermin festival. After a day and evening of drinking wine in the streets and at the bullfight, enjoying the traditional one-liter Spanish bota bag (wineskin), we continued to party through the night with some newly found local student friends. The streets were packed with drunk and noisy party revelers of many nationalities and ages, all drinking wine. The Falange (President Franco's personal police) noticed our raucous group and gave our Spanish friends a hard time about their public drinking and intoxicated condition, threatening to arrest them. Fueled with the bravery and stupidity of booze, we foreigners protested loudly that they should leave our friends alone. The Falange stopped their haranguing and told us all to move on and go home. Our new friends were saved from a night in jail, and pure luck saved us from following them there. I tried to find a place to park our small Simca in order to safely go to sleep (there were no vacant hotel rooms in Pamplona) and found a place in what I believed was a public park. When we awoke in the morning (sadly too late for me to run with the bulls) I discovered that I had parked on the front lawn of someone's house. Maybe it was not such a good idea to rely on me as the "safe drinking" driver. In those days no one abstained from drinking before driving; one simply tried to drink less. Ironically I was the only person in the car who had developed a full-blown drinking problem. The others left the occasional alcohol excesses of youth behind.

My "mostly fun and some trouble" drinking period started in the late sixties, during my first tour in Washington D.C., as a young lawyer (between ages twenty-seven and thirty) in the Civil Rights Division of the Justice Department.

One of the signs that trouble is brewing with alcohol is a strong negative personality shift. When I drank too much I could become verbally aggressive, insensitive, the master of the put-down, and sometimes I could turn downright nasty. Not a big surprise for someone with lawyer training and having grown up on the streets of the Bronx. The irony was that the man who could be attractive, charming, and witty with a glass or two of wine turned into a person no one wanted to be around after a few more glasses. Although I was never physically abusive, I was a milder version of Dr. Jekyll and Mr. Hyde.

My insecurity also led me to exaggerating a story or outright lying in order to look good or powerful. I remember telling people how I parachuted out of an airplane. Anyone who knew me knew that I had a fear of heights and would never jump from an airplane. But my son had done it, so I knew the drill. I could not admit to myself or in public that I wasn't the brightest, the best athlete, the best anything. I thought people would only like, respect, and accept me if I was at the top of any pyramid. I was not comfortable being an ordinary man doing the best he could.

My "Mr. Hyde" personality took hold when my youthful two-year marriage to my first wife Linda ended. A week after we separated, having had a number of post-work cocktails, I knocked on the apartment door of her female ex-boss with the intent of an amorous night. There was no reason, except booze, to think this was even a possibility. With annoyance, she immediately made this clear, and with embarrassment I left just as immediately. When I awoke the next morning, I felt mortified. A sober Al could see his action as a shameful act to get back at Linda. The drunken Al guy couldn't care less about the feelings of Linda's boss, or Linda herself. My self-worth suffered greatly from this acting out. A glass or two of wine the next evening, however, started the process of pushing the shame from my conscious mind. I said to myself, "Oh well, we all do stupid things." Within a few days I no longer felt the effects of that evening on my self-esteem. Only later in my 12-Step Program did I recognize the shame and insecurity I had fostered and continued to hold onto.

In this era, the two-martini-lunch was still in vogue in Washington, DC. After the split-up with Linda, I started to partake in the two-martini ritual. One martini and everything about my life was fine. By the second everything was funny. In reality it was not. I buried the hurt and pain of my failed marriage—in fact Linda had joined "our friend" Phil in Minneapolis and planned to marry him once our divorce became final. Thirty years later, when we met at a longtime friend's funeral, she told me that the change in my personality when I was drinking had ruined our marriage for her.

My lunches by now were lasting two and a half hours. Unlike my boss, I could not function with any alacrity, much less at top speed, after lunch. If I came back to work I was simply useless. I didn't recognize that I was in a state of depression and that alcohol increased this condition. Although in retrospect I accepted that my work writing memos, legislation, and briefs suffered during this period, at the time I never thought about it. Maybe I assumed I would get a pass, as a number of my colleagues were aware of my divorce situation. There was a yearlong period, in fact, while I was on assignment in Mississippi, Tennessee, and California, when I did not drink to excess and performed my work at a high level.

It was only when I started to look for work on the West Coast, in 1968, that I came to know someone in the chain of command above me had been unhappy with my performance. I never discovered who that was. The person never said a word to me, but had made a negative comment to a prospective employer who wanted to hire me. None of my friends ever commented on my sorry state during this six-month period. I learned that people don't tell you about the effects of your drinking on your work and personality. They are either self-absorbed, not observant, do not wish to look at their own drinking, or just don't care enough to get involved. Although I lost a job opportunity because of this, I lucked out and was not prevented from another, even better one. Thus I did not have to face the impact of my drinking on the job. I chalked it up to a superior who simply didn't like me. Denial is central to the story.

Most alcoholics in recovery instantly relate to and understand the powerful role of denial in their life. Nonrecognition of the growing negative consequences of excessive drinking is common to alcoholics. We may have different factual stories, but we have many core realities in common. The prose may be different, but the drama of our drinking lives is very similar.

This is how denial works, even in the light of clear and continuing evidence of the problem. First, the deep feelings of shame and embarrassment after a negative incident lead to our suppressing the incident. We do not wish to face reality. As time goes by, the incident literally vanishes from our memory. As my 12-Step Program states, alcohol is "cunning, baffling, and powerful." Though it is unbelievable to a non-alcoholic, many alcoholics do not admit to themselves the toxic causal relationship between their drinking and the disastrous consequences befalling them. Soon after a two-month stay in the hospital from a drunken motorcycle accident that literally ripped the skin off the front of his chest, a man in the program returned to his motorcycle and to drinking. Another man relapsed after twenty years of sobriety after drunkenly crashing his car over a cliff and killing his young woman passenger. I met many people in the program who did not immediately stop drinking even after they lost their jobs, houses and families.

My denial was facilitated by the fact that for most of my drinking career my major serious incidents were far apart and not overwhelming in their fallout. In addition, my denial was fueled by my fear that not drinking meant losing the ability to enjoy life. I read this sentence now and think what a sad statement it is. But thirty years ago it was a deeply felt truth. No wine with dinner, no martini (the end of sophistication), no Scotch, no after-dinner drink? How would I take the edge off after a hard day?. How would I overcome my initial shyness at parties? How would I be quick and smart with repartee? And how could I accept to publicly admit that I had a problem I could not handle, letting everyone see that I was not drinking and therefore was a weak man? I used to be the guy who said, "How can you trust a man who does not drink?" Think of something you cannot live without: sugar, chocolate, lemon, bacon, bread, sex, and listen to the stories you tell yourself in order not to give it up. You may start to understand denial's powerful hold on the psyche.

During my two-martini lunches in DC, my longtime SNCC friend Chuck McDew, a second buddy, Reggie, and I went to a late-night party after attending another gathering that night. I began a conversation with another guest. As was my want then, especially when drinking, I reacted to his superior, aggressive manner by deciding it was my duty to take him on and verbally destroy him. While I was engaged in this activity with my hands in my pockets and enjoying myself, he suddenly hauled off and hit me in the jaw. I fell to the floor where he proceeded to kick me until McDew and Reggie pulled him off. The next thing I remember was the two of them holding the man by his feet out the fifth-floor window, asking me if they should drop him. Luckily I responded no. Of course I had too many drinks to pick up the signals that the man was in a state of anger over something that had nothing to do with me. His wife and her lover were both at the party. He probably wanted to hit them, but I would do.

As McDew, Reggie, and I were leaving the building, the man took a swing at McDew. This was a big mistake. McDew responded, and the man spent the rest of the night in the hospital. We could not go home in case the man had made a complaint to the police. The three of us slept at McDew's girlfriend's house. The situation was a very sorry state of affairs for McDew and me, a Department of Justice lawyer and an "officer of the court." Spending time with McDew led to many unwise decisions and troublesome situations. Nevertheless I followed his lead and avoided taking stock of the possible consequences. The fact that I was lonely and upset after the split with my first wife, Linda, colored my judgment.

McDew had a jealous streak. When a male coworker was showing too much interest in the girlfriend he planned to marry, McDew decided to scare him off. He wanted Reggie and me to be present in case he needed added muscle to make his point. We were supposed to stuff a banana in our pockets to give the impression we were carrying guns. Of course, aside from being downright ludicrous, it was a potentially dangerous move. What if the ruse worked, and in response to thinking we had guns, the man pulled out a knife or gun? Although in the end we did not join McDew, the whole incident was a clear case of stupid and dangerous alcoholic thinking.

Shortly before McDew got married, we both had a fling with two black secretaries in the Civil Rights Division. This was another perilous misjudgment on my part. Even then, in1967, it could have severely impacted my career if this indiscretion had become public. The mere fact that I was their boss was enough to make the relationship inappropriate. I was in my late twenties and continued on my merry path, ignoring red flags. The negative consequences had not yet risen to the point where I had no choice but to pay attention.

Having met Susanne in April 1968 during one of my Civil Rights Division trips to the SF Bay Area, I decided to leave the woman (Corinna) I had been living with over the past year in DC, and quit the Justice Department. In October, 1968, I joined Susanne in her apartment in San Francisco. In January 1969, we moved into a house in Oakland near the Berkeley border when I started my new job at the National Housing Law Project at the University of California. We married in April 1970 after she became pregnant (it was planned). I was present at both Annik's birth in December of 1970 and Noel's birth in September of 1973. We used the Lamaze natural childbirth method. Nothing in my life has been more exciting or beautiful than witnessing the birth of my children.

The next ten years (1968–1978) went by in a treacherous calm, but there still were too many nights of being argumentative and dismissive of others. My need to contradict and take the other side in any political or other argument made me the poster boy for why folks don't like lawyers. I thought I was just being logical and analytical. People during this time might comment to Susanne about my arrogant and combative personality. They did not say anything to me. Many of my friends never saw the truly obnoxious Al, but the negative drip-drip of my alcoholic behavior had a deep effect on Susanne. One illustrative incident during this period was when, during an argument, I slammed the bedroom door with such force that the embedded floor-length mirror fell to the floor in pieces. Luckily, both children were under four and slept through the night. I did not get the connection to my father and the crashing glass when I was five. I went on dismissing Susanne's concerns. I thought I was a normal drinker and she was overreacting because her father had been (and was) a nasty alcoholic. My brother and a number of friends reassured me that I was not an alcoholic. I could go on as before, ignoring that little by little I was destroying Susanne's love for me.

During this period Susanne and I still had lots of fun together. We often traveled abroad, and all Suzanne's birthdays were spent exploring different parts of California. We had many dinner parties with great folks and varied conversation, and both of us had good work—Susanne was busy as an artist, and I as a lawyer in legal services. We had a family. Along with the upsets there was laughter in the house.

As I said earlier, I neither drank every single day nor drank to excess each time I did drink. Without giving it much thought, I was able not to drink for days or weeks at a time. Therefore it was easy to forget my bad feelings and the disturbing consequences that sometimes resulted from drinking to excess. Toward the end of this period, Susanne and I argued about the number of nights I would regret the next morning. I was so sure that she was exaggerating that I volunteered to place an x-mark on the calendar after each of these nights. I believed it would average out to about six times a year. Imagine my horror when it turned out to be several times a month. I say horror not so much because it showed me my problem, but rather because it threatened my drinking. The mind is a trickster, ready to alter reality at any time to accommodate our desires.

As a result of the "truth telling" calendar, I followed the path of many alcoholics: I tried to control my excessive drinking by giving up hard liquor. To give up martinis was to give up my fantasy that I was the sophisticated Fred Astaire at the bar of the Twin Towers restaurant overlooking the lights of New York City. It meant no more Armagnac (never met a bottle I did not have to finish in one seating) which was so much smoother than cognac. And no more Scotch on ice, or neat without soda or water to dilute its effect. And no more tequila straight with lime and salt, conjuring up enjoyable times at the famous Las Brisas Hotel overlooking Acapulco Bay, where Susanne and I had our own swimming pool and fresh rose petals placed in the water every day. At night we would join our newly met jet-set friends to dance and drink at the two famous supper clubs high atop the mountain. The booze fueled lively conversation and laughter. We formed friendships, including one that continues to this day—some forty years later.

A therapist in DC said we had a symbiotic relationship. Susanne allowed me to drink and she could enjoy her nighttime cocktail or wine. We both smoked pot together.

I now had to limit myself to a maximum of two glasses of wine when I drank. Of course those would be the two biggest glasses I could find. When this didn't work, I drank only Champagne. And when this proved problematic (most parties did not serve the bubbly) I brought my own bottle of Champagne to parties. But time and again I broke my own self-imposed limitations. I finally gave up liquor in all forms and replaced it with marijuana. I must point out that I made the change to satisfy Susanne, not myself. For whatever reasons I did not have the same negative personality changes on pot, even when I overdid it. I have an addictive personality, and overdoing it—from chocolate chip cookies, or apple pie to booze or pot—was part of me.

I will return to my alcoholism during and after my time in the Carter administration. Needless to say, things did not get better. But first, more on my role in the administration.

95

CHAPTER 11

THE CARTER ADMINISTRATION

In 1977, months after Pat Harris was confirmed as Secretary of Housing and Urban Development (HUD), I became one of three finalists for the job of San Francisco Regional Director of HUD. The director oversaw the activities of HUD in California and a number of other western states. This was a political, non-civil-service appointment. It was an important and big job. I went down a psychologically typical path in my thinking about the position. A number of people with whom I talked had the same experience in seeking a high-level political appointment. We all started out thinking, "I am well respected, have proven my worth—they would be lucky to get me." By the end of the process we would all be ready to "sell our eldest child" to get the job.

The job of regional director was not simply a choice on merits, but involved obtaining important political constituent backing. Among others, the American Federation of Labor Unions (AFL-CIO) and the Episcopal Church of San Francisco sent letters to the secretary endorsing my candidacy. Getting these endorsements took time, effort, and involved networking among my contacts in DC and San Francisco.

Secretary Pat Harris invited me to DC for an interview. She was the first black woman to hold a cabinet position. Previously, she had been our first black woman Ambassador and a board member of IBM and Chase Manhattan Bank. She had graduated first in her class from George Washington Law School.

HOUSING AND URBAN DEVELOPMENT

I flew into DC from San Francisco with excitement about my possibilities. I felt confident in my record of achievement and had no doubt that I would be effective in the job. The morning after I landed I took a cab to the mammoth HUD building. On my way to the secretary's office for the interview, I was greeted by the executive assistant of Larry Simon, the assistant secretary of Housing/FHA Commissioner, who said Larry would appreciate my stopping by at his office after my interview with Harris. I had known Larry for a number of years in his capacity as an important member of the Homebuilders Association. He had been a successful and prominent builder of a thousand homes on Staten Island.

Harris's office, in the tradition of cabinet members, was very large, with many pictures of family and congressmen on her desk and walls. The requisite government-issued pictures of President Carter and Vice President Mondale hung on the wall behind her desk. When she rose to shake my hand, I saw in her brown eyes a steel will that belied her petite stature. She greeted me without warmth and seemed to be uninvolved during the interview. When I left her office I was perplexed by her disinterest in me and felt there was no chance of my becoming the regional director. As requested, I went to Larry's office afterward.

In sharp contrast, Larry, who was a large man, greeted me with warmth and a big smile. His executive assistant and other members of his inner circle joined the conversation. Unlike Pat Harris, Larry did not return to his desk; we all sat in close proximity on the two couches in his office. This created an informal feeling that was in stark contrast to the Harris interview. He said that if my good friend Marilyn Melkonian did not accept his already made offer, he wanted me to consider being a standby for the position of deputy for Housing. I was flattered and interested. My annoyance at spending money on a plane ticket for no apparent reason dissipated somewhat. During the discussion one of his assistants said the job would be at a GS-18 level (the highest level in the system). I responded that there was no monetary difference between a GS-18 and a GS-17, to which he replied, "That's true, but you will have more stripes." *Wow*, I thought, *welcome to government bureaucracy*. However, I did take note of his comment. Marilyn accepted Larry's offer, making our discussion moot.

Secretary Harris ended up appointing a college classmate to be the regional director. No wonder she had appeared to be unengaged in the interview.

I did not have any feelings of rejection or resentment about not getting the job. The positive side of trying to score a political appointment is that in the end it does not have anything to do with you personally. It usually is a political decision or, in this case, a decision based on friendship.

MORTGAGES FOR THE INNER CITY

In August 1977, I was consulting for the Hawaii Legal Aid when Bob McKinney, the chairman of the Bank Board (Federal Home Loan Bank Board), called to invite me for an interview in DC. I thought, *Here I go again.* But this time I knew the potential job was real. My friend from the Ford Foundation, Anita Miller, had recommended me to the chairman while she was being interviewed by him for a board position. Bob McKinney was charming and had a sense of humor. I laid out how I would move forward with a strategy of having the Bank Board push Savings and Loans to develop lending in the inner city. He asked what I thought were insightful questions. In addition to agreeing on an overall carrot-and-stick strategy, our personalities were compatible. I was aware that, given my reputation and long-standing relationships, I would provide him with a buffer and give him access to advocates for low-income housing groups, many of whom had opposed his appointment. He offered me the job of director of what would become the Office of Community Investment (OCI).

The office was the first attempt by any financial regulatory agency to deal with the responsibility of financial institutions for making mortgage loans without regard to race or neighborhood. I would start in October and thereafter return to Berkeley to take a three-week Christmas break from my new job to help plan the family's move east, and to say good-bye to my wife and children for a month or so. During this break I was supposed to flesh out in writing the proposed strategy I had outlined for the chairman in my interview. I asked my friend David Madway to help me write it as I was insecure at this time in my career about my writing skills. The memorandum had to impress the chairman, and as David was an excellent writer, he was my security blanket. To my knowledge, McKinney never read the memo. Was the request a test to see if I could deliver under pressure, or did the events surrounding the creation of OCI just outrun his reading time? I believe it was the former.

A "NEWBIE" IN DC

While I was looking for a place for us to rent, I stayed with my longtime friends Judy and Roger Wolf at their house on Capitol Hill. We had become friends ten years ago when they were my downstairs neighbors in DC. Roger had been in the DC Legal Services program, and Judy was Congresswoman Bella Abzug's first administrative assistant. I was present when they brought their first two sons home from the hospital. We have remained close friends for fifty-two years. Sadly, Roger died in 2018.

As I was now involved in regulating institutions in the financial sector, it was high time I started to read the Sunday business section of the *Washington Post*. To my amazement I came across an article about Chairman Bob McKinney setting up a new office in the Federal Home Loan Bank Board in order to deal with inner city housing investments and mortgages. The article went on to say McKinney would not divulge the name of the person he had chosen to head up this effort. However, "informed sources said the person was Alvin Hirshen." I thought to myself, "Welcome to Washington, DC, Alvin Hirshen."

The next day, I went to my sparkling new office in a new office building across the street from the old Executive Office building and the White House. It was ultramodern, with lots of windows and walnut trim. Only senior staff had offices; the others worked in open cubicles. The building had a courtyard that in winter was used as a skating ring. I was playing in the big leagues.

STAFFING UP

My first task was to hire a staff. As I was dealing with a new office in the Bank Board, I first had to get Office of Management and Budget approval. This approval included the overall budget, the number of people in the office, the titles of their positions, their grade levels, and the step levels within the grade levels. For example, it was possible for a GS-15 grade level to be at a step level 7. This meant that he or she would receive the same dollar salary as a GS-17 at step level 1. Money was not the reason political appointees such as myself came to work in government. Although the pay was the same, the GS-17, step level 1 was provided with a bigger office and better furniture than a GS-15, step level 5. This bit of Byzantine bureaucracy was spelled out in detail in the regulation of the General Services Administration (the people who run the buildings and decide what gets put into them).

The size of your office and the type of furniture were indicators of your perceived power position in the bureaucracy. Another was how close your office was to the head of the agency. Yes, I am talking about adults. My office was on the same floor and close to the chairman's. Thus, in the Washington game of perceived power, I had power. I told my deputy, Richard Tucker, that he should "manage the staff" while I would "manage the mirrors (perceptions)." The knowledge from my years in the Civil Rights Division and at the Law Project about how Washington, DC, worked proved useful.

In order to move forward with my program, I needed to quickly get the OMB approvals of my proposed staff positions and GS levels. This could be a tricky and time-consuming process. I enlisted a friend of ten years, Bruce Kirschenbaum, who had been the deputy director of the National Legal Aid and Defender Association (the professional association for Legal Services lawyers), to assist me. Bruce was now on the staff of Jack Watson in the White House. Jack would become the president's second, and in my view most effective, chief of staff. He became a friend and ally over my time in Washington. Remembering my conversation in Larry Simon's office, I told Bruce that for the fun of it we should see if my position could be slotted at a GS-18 level.

The White House magic worked, and OMB approved my requests, including the GS-18 slot, in record time. I would later learn that McKinney was angry with his executive assistant for allowing me to garner the last Bank Board OMB allotted GS-18 slot. He had wanted it as an enticement for his future general counsel's appointment. Nobody said a word to me about it. I only learned about his anger from his other assistant, Paul, who became a close friend and ally during my time at the Bank Board. Again I chuckled about "the ways of Washington."

We gave the new office the name Office of Community Investment (OCI). Henceforth, savings and loans would be required to invest in low-income communities by providing them with mortgages and housing construction money. My first hire was Richard Tucker as my deputy. I had known "Tuck" (or Dick) for many years while he was Gordon Cavanaugh's deputy at HAC. Tuck and I interviewed and hired applicants (who turned out to be women) for three division director positions.

Because I was starting a new office, I was in the unusual and lucky position to decide about every person who worked for me. In the federal government, you usually inherited an existing civil service staff that could be a mixed blessing. From the beginning and throughout my time as director, I had the loyalty of my OCI staff. They believed in my vision for the office and recognized my dedication and skills in implementing this vision.

None of my staff was more loyal than my permanent secretary, James. He was a gem. He had been on the staff of Senator Sparkman (one of the Southern giants who ruled the Senate) when he resigned to join the Roman Catholic priesthood, giving away all his money and assets. After he left the priesthood, at the request of a close female friend he became the guardian of her son. His ward was graduating college in 1978 and wanted to go to medical school, but James did not have the funds to support him. I was aware of a federal scholarship program that would pay for medical school if the recipient committed to practicing for five years in rural America or on an Indian reservation. His ward agreed to this requirement. I called Bruce Kirschenbaum and said, "If we can get the ward this scholarship, it may turn out to be the only sure and lasting thing we've done while in office." He agreed, and the scholarship was obtained. My secretary's ward would finish second in his graduating class at George Washington Medical School.

The Federal Home Loan Bank Board staff was overwhelmingly white male. One day I noticed a number of blacks from the mailroom and the driver corps walking into Tuck's office. Senior staff offices had glass walls, so it was easy to see who was there unless the blinds were drawn. I jokingly asked him, "What's up with all the blacks streaming into your office? Are you organizing a numbers racket?" (Of course the numbers racket is not the exclusive domain of blacks, but rather a feature prevalent in poor neighborhoods. My father's candy store in the Bronx was a place where bets were taken mainly from whites.) He asked if I was not aware? I had appointed the highest-grade level black employee in the history of the Board, and they were stopping by to congratulate him. The division directors were also the first women at their grade in their positions. I had unwittingly broken barriers. It was gratifying to know that while trying to make things better for the poor, I had initiated a small change at the Bank Board.

It was very clear to me that whatever power I had devolved directly from the chairman, but I was delighted when my friend and ally Anita Miller (the person who suggested that the chairman hire me) was confirmed as a board member six months after I started. Her support of my strategy with the chairman and the Bank Board staff was invaluable. I remembered the lesson I learned in getting HUD support for Senator Brooke's proposed legislative amendments. The bureaucracy is not a monolith. Even if the leader of an agency wants to implement change, the content and nuances of the proposed change can be affected by different points of view within the agency. The general counsel's office and others were not always on board with the changes OCI was proposing. Anita was an important voice in the debate over new regulations. I could count on her vote on regulations I was supporting. On a practical level, I should note that my legal background was a crucial asset in arguing for my positions at Bank Board meetings.

DO IT DIFFERENTLY AND HAVE SOME FUN

Before I left California for DC, I purchased forty small ceramic ice cream bars with a bite taken out of the top. They could be pinned to the lapel of a suit or a dress. I thought it would be fun to hand them out to people, and if enough people wore them, tongues would wag. I gave them to senators, congressmen, hill staff, senior government officials, and friends. All reacted differently. Some put them on (usually the younger folks), others said they would give them to their wives, but many were just perplexed. Almost all wanted to know the significance of the pin. In one case I replied, "I am sorry I cannot say—it is a symbol of a secret society." But usually, I told the truth, especially to people with whom I had to establish a good working relationship. I told them that it was just to brighten up the day. It was wonderful fun and interesting to see how people reacted to an unusual piece of jewelry. A silly pin and serious government officials did not, in the main, fit easily together. West Coast met East Coast with small success. Another interesting reaction was to a Jewish boy from the Bronx wearing fancy Western cowboy boots with his suits. I just did not want to be part of the official DC prep school look. It turned out to be an icebreaker with many people. As with the ceramic ice cream bars, the boots set me apart from the "faceless bureaucratic crowd."

EVEN IF YOU ARE TRYING TO HELP

Although I hired all my staff, Bill Whiteside was an exception. His organization, the Urban Reinvestment Task Force, oversaw locally based Neighborhood Housing Services of America that developed local partnerships with savings and loans to provide low-income housing. Bill was already part of the Federal Home Loan Bank Board. Given my mandate to have savings and loans invest in low-income communities, it made sense that the newly created Office of Community Investment would supervise his organizations. Whiteside turned out to be on the darker side of the mixed blessing of inherited staff.

The task force was within the jurisdiction of the Bank Board because of its role in creating housing units and obtaining mortgages for low-income and minority families. The chairman was uneasy about Whiteside and wanted to replace him, or at the very least have me tightly control him. He thought Whiteside had been too independent of Bank Board supervision. In addition, their personalities did not mesh. His executive assistant went so far as to suggest I use the GSA office regulations to bring Whiteside down a notch and show him who was in charge. Macho was a large part of the DC scene. In my view, this was just silly. You can be tough without being mindlessly macho. I told the assistant I would not use the GSA regulations but would simply manage Whiteside. I had no need to control him. The work the task force and housing services were doing in many neighborhoods across the country was beneficial and vital. I wanted to support the task force's efforts as they added to my vision and that of the chairman. But Whiteside had become paranoid about his tenure. He could not see that I was trying to protect him, not replace him.

I enlisted Warren and Mary Widener to make Whiteside understand that I was key in his not being fired by the chairman. Warren had been the mayor of Berkeley and had worked at the Law Project. Mary was a giant in the urban reinvestment field. They tried, but to no avail. Luckily for me and the chairman, the Congress was in the midst of transforming the task force into an independent agency to be called the Neighborhood Reinvestment Corporation, run by a board consisting of the Financial Regulatory Agencies and HUD. I convinced McKinney to support the legislation. The legislation passed in 1978, and the board hired Whiteside to run it. We had avoided a personnel fight that would have made enemies of people and organizations I needed to move my program forward. This was a win-win result.

Whiteside continued to run the program he started, and I could focus on my strategies to further involve savings and loans in their low-income communities. An old Washington personnel tactic of moving a problem person up and out had worked.

REGIONAL STAFFING

The last part of the task was to hire OCI staff in the twelve regional Federal Home Loan Banks. These Banks were similar to the Federal Reserve System Regional Banks. They provided loans to their member savings and loan institutions. At this period of time there were approximately 2,400 associations nationwide, and they originated 80 percent of the single-family mortgage market. The regional banks also supplied the funds for the Federal Home Loan Bank Board to run its operations. The chairman's power over the regional banks was based on his required approval of their budgets. Each bank had a board that picked a president to run the bank. The president had final say over hiring his own staff. This meant my new regional staff really owed their first allegiance to the president of the bank who hired him or her. Sorry to get into the weeds, but I feel it necessary to give a proper understanding of the delicate nature of my leadership issues at the regional level.

McKinney sent a letter to each of the twelve bank presidents explaining that as part of his community investment effort, I would interview their three chosen finalists for the position of community investment officer, and would have final approval of the one they chose for the position. He went on to say the regional community officers would be charged with implementing the policies and programs of OCI and the board. Bob McKinney's only leverage over the bank presidents was final approval authority over the regional banks budgets. I was faced with a tricky proposition. Withholding approval of regional banks would be a clumsy point of leverage. Finesse over hardball was called for. I had to get the bank presidents voluntarily onboard if I were to stand a chance at success.

I phoned the bank presidents, laid out a proposed agenda to interview the three candidates, and locked in the dates for my proposed visit.

My deputy director, Dick Tucker, and I flew into Cincinnati to interview the three candidates of Chuck Thiemann, the president of the Cincinnati bank. Chuck was a cigar-smoking, hard-drinking, smooth operator. During a bathroom break-in the interview, I asked the first candidate in passing why he wanted the job. He responded, "What job?" He went on to say, "Chuck asked me to come in and discuss community investment with you." Chuck Thiemann was red-faced when I mentioned in a low-key manner what his "candidate" had said. He admitted he had already chosen his community investment officer. I remarked that I highly valued honesty in my relationships. I then told him to cancel the second and third "candidate's interview" and bring in his choice. She turned out to be a very strong candidate.

Chuck became an important supporter and friend. I think he remained guilty for his charade because he went out of his way to obtain the official status of Kentucky colonel for me from the Governor of Kentucky. Watch out, Colonel Sanders! I continue to smile when I look at the certificate hanging on my office wall commissioning me as a Kentucky colonel in the state militia. A Jewish boy from the Bronx could now sip mint juleps with the horse set of Kentucky. (Of course if I had lots of money and owned a thoroughbred horse or two, I could do that anyway.)

STRATEGIES

In early 1978, OCI held a conference with over 100 participants. The diverse groups included community organizers, low-income home purchasers, realtors, for-profit and nonprofit developers, and representatives of the twelve Federal Home Loan Banks. In addition, there were representatives from insurance companies, labor, HUD, Small Business Administration, Congress, Freddie Mac, Fannie Mae (key secondary market organizations) and Wall Street as well as city mayors. All the key housing players were in attendance.

As an outcome of this conference, we gained the support and created a vital partnership between OCI and the stakeholders. With the approval of the chairman, I developed a carrot-and-stick strategy to move savings and loans in the right direction. The stick consisted of the toughest financial regulatory agency anti-discrimination regulations coupled with the Community Reinvestment Act Regulations. Senator William Proxmire of Wisconsin, chairman of the powerful Committee on Banking, Housing and Urban Affairs (he replaced the infamous Senator Joseph McCarthy) was the key person in developing and passing the Community Reinvestment Act, 1977. The act was aimed at reducing discriminatory practices against low-income neighborhoods, a practice known as redlining (drawing a redline around low-income neighborhoods where no mortgage lending would take place). One of the key parts of the act was that the Bank Board and other financial regulatory agencies had to take into account the low-income neighborhood activities of a financial institution applying for approval of any new branches, mergers, or acquisitions. I was charged by the chairman to sign off on any such application before it could come to the Bank Board for consideration. It was ironic how this requirement made me a "popular" person for visits from savings and loan institutions. Even my old friend Mickey Kantor (Clinton's secretary of commerce) paid me a lobbying visit on behalf of California Savings and Loan Association The chairman's requirement was a very valuable tool in my ability to gain cooperation from the industry. Without my approval they could not implement their business plans and therefore stood to lose large sums of money.

The carrots were the creation of a five-year, $5 billion Community Investment Fund coupled with training and technical assistance programs. Basically we had created the first public-private partnership program. Today public-private partnership programs are the *sine qua non* of community development worldwide.

The fund allowed member institutions to borrow from the regional banks at below-market rates, based on their community investment plans. Approval could be obtained for plans ranging from the institution hiring a community investment officer to a full-blown public-private partnership program. Over the five years of the program's existence, it acted as a catalyst for the construction of, and granting of mortgages to, half a million low-income housing units.

We devised and disseminated pamphlets and videos to be used in training and technical assistance programs. Some of the subjects addressed were how to access government monies and develop partnerships (including local, state governments) with the federal government, community organizations, and nonprofit as well as for-profit, low-income housing development companies.

My staff joined twenty-five bank-sponsored education sessions for its members and led seminars for small numbers of savings and loans (S&Ls) tailored to their specific needs. We worked together with many mayors to help develop partnerships with their local S&Ls. For example, along with board member Anita Miller, I met with the executive committee of the Conference of Mayors in Anchorage, Alaska, to get their support of our program. During President Carter's term, the mayors rather than the governors had the White House's ear. They were the people to go to to get things done.

The Anchorage meeting took place in a new, beautifully designed hotel owned by Wally Hickel, the former secretary of the interior of the Nixon administration. The hotel was built of wood and had large glass windows that looked out on breathtaking snow-covered mountains. It was as if I had been transferred into the middle of the glory of Alaskan nature while seated in a warm lobby or conference room. Hickel had been fired by President Nixon for his outspoken views on policies of the administration that had a negative impact on the environment and young people. The former Department of Interior secretary personally knew many of the mayors and made himself available to "schmooze" with them. He was a gregarious and charming man full of stories of his time in office.

The bonus part of meeting with the executive committee was that the host city's firefighters were available to drive us around in bright red fire department vehicles during our free time periods. This is how I got to know the layout of the city and, a short ride from downtown Anchorage, discovered the awesome deep-blue icebergs. Wow, what a treat. Until you see the blue of the icebergs in person, you cannot understand their beauty and magnificence. I had never been in a city in the United States where nature is so right at your fingertips.

During my tenure as director of the Office of Community Investment, I gave numerous speeches all over the country at national and state meetings of S&Ls. I especially remember one such conference in Louisville, Kentucky, where I met both Art Buchwald and Mohammad Ali. For years I had read Buchwald's hysterically funny political satire columns in the *Washington Post,* and now I found myself seated next to him on the plane. He was the same small, stocky man I had seen in pictures. He was the featured entertainment at the conference. I was eager to talk political satire, and he wanted advice on his investments. Nonetheless, given the length of the flights, we both won. I experienced small bursts of his wonderful wit, but in the main he was serious and focused on his financial portfolio. His performance at the conference met my every expectation. He was a delight. The next morning I saw Mohammad Ali across the hotel dining room eating breakfast with his daughter and friends. My son Noel would not have forgiven me if I had not got his autograph. I waited until he had finished eating, walked over to his table, and introduced myself, expressing my admiration for his political courage. He was as handsome a man as he appeared in pictures and on TV. His smile and graciousness put me totally at ease. He asked me what I was doing in his hometown of Louisville, and he paid attention to my answer. I felt his genuineness. I returned home with an autographed picture of Ali addressed to Noel.

I also assisted individual savings and loans to publicize their community projects. One such event was a speech for Cal Fed at the groundbreaking site of a new low-income, fifty-unit apartment project in the Valley. We took the elevator to the roof of the building located in Century City, Los Angeles. Sitting on the helipad was a four-seat bubble helicopter. To drive to the site could take hours, depending on traffic. I vividly remember my heartbeat increasing exponentially when I strapped myself in and we lifted off the roof. There was nothing below my feet on the glass floor but the far-away ground. I kept saying to myself, "Don't look down." I hate helicopters! (Once on a flight from DC to San Francisco, I sat next to one of the president's helicopter pilots who went into detail about how inherently unsafe helicopters are. He even said that was why the president's helicopter would fly at very low altitudes.) As there was extensive positive press coverage, and Cal Fed received the necessary positive publicity, the speech was considered a success. The president of Cal Fed became an ardent supporter of mine.

The strategy of carrots and sticks that I had conveyed to the chairman years earlier was being implemented at a faster pace than I reasonably could have hoped for. It was a heady and rewarding time.

THE PRESS

I cannot overemphasize the role of the press in governing at the national level. It is quantitatively different than at the local and state level. The press is truly the fourth branch of government (at this time there was no Facebook, Twitter, or other social media). Unless it is reported by the press, America is unaware of good and bad things that spring forth from our government in DC. In a Kafkaesque sense, there is no reality other than what appears in print. Thus, governmental officials and the press are engaged in a never-ending dance of manipulation. At times it is not clear who is leading. The federal official wants to demonstrate that he or she is doing good things for the public (gaining more power) while the press wants to put a spotlight on the embarrassing failures and, more importantly, the really bad things (such as lies and criminal activities) happening in DC.

An example of "unless it's in the press it doesn't exist" syndrome was a public hearing when Senator Proxmire, who had given Chairman McKinney a very tough time at his confirmation hearing, apologized to him.

He said he had been wrong; the chairman was doing an outstanding job in the community investment area. Proxmire was politically shrewd enough, however, to make the statement only after the press had left the hearing room. His apology would have entered the Congressional Record, but since it was not reported by the press it "did not exist" in the minds of the general public, and McKinney was never publicly vindicated. In Washington, politicians normally do not admit mistakes to the press.

LUNCH AT THE WHITE HOUSE

A special feather in my cap was to have an announcement at the White House of the $5 billion Community Investment Fund (discussed earlier) that the Office of Community Investment had developed. Mayors, governors, Bank Board members, Federal Loan Bank presidents, S&L executives, and community organizations were invited. An announcement at the White House gave the Community Investment Fund the president's imprimatur and would attract most of the Washington press, thereby giving it instant stature. A president's program, as opposed to a program of the Bank Board, was the difference between day and night. That stature brought with it a level of cooperation from all the players in the process. It also made the chairman and OCI appear to have political clout with the White House, a useful tool in managing the mirrors I mentioned earlier.

The story of how the announcement came about is a perfect illustration of how the federal government works, as opposed to what the press reports about how it works.

The Community Investment Fund (CIF) perfectly fit within the already announced president's Urban Policy Program (OCI helped to write it). Chairman McKinney and I recognized the positive public relations potential for the administration and us. For the administration, CIF demonstrated that the Urban Policy

Program had an immediate effect on low-income housing. It would make it easier to get all the players involved in creating low-income housing to cooperate with us. McKinney set about trying to contact Vice President Mondale and First Lady Rosalyn Carter directly. Time was of the essence, but Mondale was out of the country, and McKinney was having difficulty getting a response from the first lady.

It turned out that my mother was visiting in DC, and I had arranged with my friend Bruce Kirschenbaum (who was on Jack Watson's staff) to have a special tour of the White House and take her to lunch at the White House Mess. The White House Mess was open for lunch only to senior White House staff and their guests. It was located near the old Situation "War" Room (where plans for World War II were developed). It was called the Mess because the US Navy provided the food and wait staff. The food was not fancy, just burgers, BLTs, and salads. The tables were placed very close together.

No matter how many times I had a meeting or had lunch at the White House, I never lost my sense of awe and history when I traversed the same halls that Presidents FDR, Truman, and Kennedy had walked. I thoroughly enjoyed taking the kids, Susanne, my mother, my brother, my now-wife Julie, my Deputy Director Richard Tucker, and a few friends to lunch at the Mess. It never got old!

In the Mess you might spot the vice president or a number of the most senior staff, White House staff, senators, congressmen, mayors, governors, or senior government officials you saw on TV or read about in the paper.

My mom and I sat down with Bruce, who asked me what was going on. I said, "You guys are blowing another golden PR opportunity." I explained McKinney's efforts to reach the first lady. He told me to wait a minute as he dragged his chair over to the next table and started to talk with a gray-haired woman who was vaguely familiar. It turned out to be Anne Wexler, special assistant to the president, who was the senior woman on the White House staff with a distinguished record of accomplishment in the world of politics. I had met her in passing three months earlier at the White House announcement of President Carter's Urban Policy Paper. After a few moments, she joined Bruce as he returned to our table and asked me to fill her in. Then she suggested McKinney and I meet her in her office in three hours. We did so, and this is how it came about that the launch of the Community Investment Fund in June of 1978 was announced in the White House.

The morning after the ceremony, the *Washington Post* ran a front-page article about the fund and noted that the presidential role in its announcement was due to the close relationship McKinney had with Carter since their days together in the Naval Academy. I took a copy of the paper into McKinney's office and asked with a smile, "Should I call in a correction to the story and tell them the real reason behind the presidential announcement was that a son took his Jewish mother to lunch at the White House?" The chairman leaned back in his chair and, after a second, we both laughed out loud.

Another White House announcement ceremony I participated in was that of President Carter's Urban Policy Paper. I had worked closely with Donna Shalala (assistant secretary, HUD Policy and Development) and Bob Emory (assistant secretary, HUD Community Planning and Development) on this paper. Shalala had an impressive mind, and Bob had a wealth of experience in urban issues. It was a delight to work with both of them.

Immediately before the president would announce his Urban Policy at the White House ceremony, the invited mayors, governors, members from Congress, and businessmen and women had been gathered together in the basement of the White House. The group included a veritable list of the who's who of the Democratic Party and the American urban political scene. I knew a number of them and enjoyed entering into the conversation. After some time, many of the pros began to grumble about booze not being served. Carter had a booze-free White House.

We were then escorted from the basement to the East Wing of the White House to hear the president's speech. I stationed myself on an aisle for a better view and in hopes that my then-wife Susanne, watching the speech on TV, would spot me. After Carter finished his speech and was on his way out, to my great surprise he stopped, shook my hand, and asked; "How did I do?" In great excitement I responded, "Wonderfully, Mr. President." Of course, I would have said the same thing even if I had not liked his speech. It was not my place in this situation to grade the President of the United States. I had no idea why he stopped and asked my opinion as I had never met him before.

While Carter was giving his speech, I kept turning around toward the TV cameras for the benefit of my wife. The result was that the following month's *NAHRO Journal* had a cover page photo of the invited crowd looking at and listening to the president. That is, all but one Alvin Hirshen, who was looking at the TV cameras. An embarrassment, but hilarious!

THE BEGINNING OF THE END OF MY TIME IN WASHINGTON

At a yearly convention of a national association of the industry, chairman McKinney told a Polish joke. Dumb! The president of the association was of Polish ancestry but had anglicized his Polish name. Dumb, but rectifiable with the man in question. It wasn't something that would undermine the performance of his duties as chairman unless the Polish joke story was planted by political enemies in a *Washington Post* gossip column. Leaking to the press to intentionally harm someone is an old DC tradition. Once it is in a newspaper or on TV, what may have been a careless word or a joke heard only by a few turns into a major cause célèbre with devastating consequences. Instead of being the golden boy with close ties to the White House, McKinney became a toxic commodity. He had to spend much of his time responding to inquires over the incident. In certain states there are large Polish communities that vote. His effectiveness as chairman was over. He recognized this and resigned.

I was saddened and concerned by McKinney's resignation in May 1979. Saddened because we had developed a personal rapport, and concerned that his successor might not continue to give me his or her 100 percent support. The chairman's unqualified support was the key to OCI's success. Together we had made the Bank Board the leader in community investment among the financial regulatory agencies.

To protect OCI I decided to ask my friend, mentor, and current board member Anita Miller if we could put her name before the White House as a potential new chairman. Jay Janus, HUD undersecretary (the number two position at HUD), was her main competition for the chairmanship. She put her hat in the ring. I mobilized Bruce Kirschenbaum and his boss, Jack Watson, to back her candidacy. However, Hamilton Jordan, Carter's chief of staff, was backing Janus. It was a David-and-Goliath fight.

I received a call from McKinney's former press secretary, who was now in the White House, that Carter had signed the necessary document nominating Anita to be chairman. In my excitement I told Anita what I had learned, breaking my own rule of needing two separate sources before passing on this type of information. My glee turned to gloom when it was announced in September 1979 that Jay Janus was the new chairman. Apparently, after learning of Carter's choice, Jordan had stormed into the president's office and strongly reminded him that he had agreed to honor Jordan's choice for positions in the administration. The agreement was based on the fast-approaching election in 1980. Important political considerations had to impact the appointment process. Jay Janus's clout in the Democratic Party was much stronger than Anita Miller's. David had lost to Goliath.

Janus and his executive assistant never broached my active support of Anita for chairman, although I had no doubt that he was well aware of it and in time would want to replace me with "one of his own." I picked up a signal that this was the case when I met with his executive assistant to discuss my job performance review. My performance had not changed one iota from the time I received an outstanding review by McKinney. However, my rating now was lower, knocking me out of contention for a bonus. Ah, the ways of Washington.

Although I was annoyed, I would bide my time and continue to lead and perform. I assumed that Janus would not make an immediate move with respect to my status until after the election. It would have appeared as "payback pique" and diminish his reputation.

It was election day in November of 1980. Bruce Kirschenbaum and I had left a hotel ballroom filled with low-spirited Democratic Party volunteers and were going down in an elevator when Bob Strauss, President Carter's national campaign manager, entered and joined us on the ride to the lobby. He said that the early results in a number of states "looked good for us." Strauss was the ultimate salesman and cheerleader, and he was giving words of encouragement to the troops (even if the troops consisted of only the two of us). Of course both he and we knew Carter had lost the election to Reagan. My time in DC was drawing to a close. A political appointee comes and goes with elections. It had been a fantastic run. I enjoyed all the ego hits my position provided, but more importantly, we had put in place a number of regulations and programs that made a significant difference in the lives of minorities and low-income families.

The staff asked me what kind of send-off party I imagined. I told them we should have three. One was a low-key gathering just for the staff at one of their homes. The second, a cocktail party at the Bank Board for all the people we had worked with from the Hill, community groups, the White House, and the different federal agencies. The third was to be a black-tie affair at a friend's fabulous house in Georgetown.

The staff party was relaxed and filled with laughter and warmth. Jay Janus presided over the Bank Board party, and people from the different groups I had worked with came to say good-bye. The number of people who attended (including Jack Watson) and their kind words were heartwarming. Although I never had the same simpatico with Janus that I had with McKinney, he was gracious in his praise. McKinney flew in to join the black-tie affair. The weather cooperated, and we had the party in the large, exquisite back garden of my friend's Georgetown house. We all danced to a wonderful band.

The Bank Board paid me the honor of doing a story about me in the *Federal Home Loan Bank Board Journal.* It was a rare event for the journal to feature a Bank Board official. McKinney wrote, "Al's performance in the job was exemplary. Starting a new department in an agency is a major task, but I never heard a complaint from Al Hirshen. I believe that the Bank Board, the Federal Home Loan Bank System, and the savings and loan industry will long remember the accomplishments of Al Hirshen." Jay Janus, (now that our time together in the Administration was over) was generous and wrote, "Your accomplishments at the Bank Board during your tenure here have been monumental. [Your programs are] the most significant new direction taken by the industry over the past several years." Chuck Thiemann, Cincinnati Federal Home Loan Bank president, wrote, "The current status of the CIF program speaks highly of the significant contribution Al Hirshen has made to the well-being of our communities during his tenure at the Federal Home Loan Bank Board." Dave Dennison, the community investment officer at the New York Bank, wrote, "Al Hirshen pioneered the concept of dialogue among the multiple sectors that impact housing development and rehabilitation."

The family and I returned to California and life moved on, although it did take me a period of time to adjust to the fact that the press was not calling me for my opinion.

CHAPTER 12

DENIAL IS THE ROOMMATE OF ADDICTION—PART TWO

For about a year starting in the fall of 1998, when I joined the Carter Administration in DC, I did not drink. I only smoked pot.

Why did I think it was okay to bring pot to DC? I never seriously stopped to consider the very different legal and social attitudes toward pot smoking between Berkeley and DC. My old friends on the East Coast all smoked pot, including an assistant DA, giving me the impression we were in the majority. My mistake was brought home to me by a couple's shocked reaction to my smoking pot at my house. The man was an important Senate committee senior staffer. He and his wife were very upset because their son was a heavy pot smoker who went on to harder drugs. They had watched a loved one go downhill, starting with pot. I was lucky that they were very decent people. They could have turned me into the police or spread the word of my illegal habit in the wrong places. This incident and the general difficulty of substituting pot for booze in social situations led me to return to drinking. Susanne did not object. Going through life without altering my state of mind was impossible to entertain.

But while my drinking continued to be an irritant in my marriage, it did not affect my time as a senior official at the Federal Home Loan Bank Board in the Carter Administration in any significant way. My professional colleagues on the Hill, in the administration, or the Savings and Loan industry never saw me drink to excess. I did not repeat the two-and-a-half-hour martini lunches. Over time, the only ones who saw me drink were my senior and regional staff. But I was always available to the staff for work, whether at 11:00 p.m. at my home or on the road at a regional staff meeting at 7:00 a.m. after a night of drinking. Staff meetings would always start promptly at 7:00 a.m., even if we had been drinking together until 2:00 a.m. I used to joke about the tardiness of latecomers, telling them, "If you play hard, you need to work hard and be on time"—a motto I vigorously followed myself. Whatever my DC senior staff's real thoughts were, they kept those to themselves and continued to be protective of me. They believed in our mission and my ability to implement it. Moreover, they liked me.

Two days before the last major conference my staff and I organized for the S&L industry, I had a final luncheon meeting with my consultants. We started drinking Scotch at noon and continued drinking until we finished the planning meeting at five. When I returned to the office to get my car out of the garage, the staff offered several times to drive me home. I declined because if they drove me home, Susanne would know I was drunk, and a fight would ensue. Of course this was pure "alcoholic thinking" —as if Susanne would neither smell my Scotch breath nor notice my drunken behavior. "Alcoholic thinking" is delusional, self-serving, defensive, impulsive, grandiose, and paranoid.

In my rush to get home (because I was late for dinner), I crashed into a line of cars waiting for the light to change at an exit from Rock Creek Park. Somehow I thought the cars had started to move forward. The irritated policeman said, "I do not have the time for a sobriety test," and after moving my car to the side of the road, out of the path of rush hour traffic, he issued me a ticket for reckless driving. I had eluded the negative consequences of a DUI, but not without putting another nail in the coffin of my marriage. This incident was a portent of things to come.

Alcoholism is a progressive disease physically, spiritually, and emotionally. Hangovers get worse, guilt gets deeper, "blackouts" start to occur and happen at greater frequency. Even after a period of abstinence, it roars back with a fury. The 12-Step Program meetings and literature are replete with stories of people who, after many years of sobriety, started drinking again and immediately returned to the same place (or worse) in the progression where they had been when they quit.

"Alcoholic thinking" follows a similar progression downward. My lack of adult judgment, buttressed by my self-centeredness, got worse. I invited a fellow consultant, with whom I had partnered to sell several branches of a savings and loan, to spend the night at our house. The man was a severe alcoholic. We had dinner, and instead of wishing him good-night after a reasonable time, to the annoyance of Susanne, I decided to buddy with him and join him for some after-dinner booze. She went to bed angry. I had made another of the many small decisions that kept deepening a chasm between us. However upsetting that evening was, my excessive drinking led to even more serious trouble.

After a normal wine and dinner meeting in Santa Monica with a potential savings and loan client and his wife, I finished the meal drinking Armagnac. Way too many Armagnacs to get behind the wheel of my car and drive from Santa Monica back to my friends' house in North Hollywood. The next thing I remember was a number of concerned black women and men at a gas station in Watts, suggesting I have several cups of coffee as they filled my gas tank in the middle of the night. To this day I have no memory of how I got there. How did I make the wrong turn onto the freeway? What possessed me to take the Watts exit? I was in blackout. Watts and North Hollywood are in opposite directions from Santa Monica. It was as if I had dinner in Manhattan and drove to Brooklyn instead of driving home to the Bronx. The universe once again smiled on me because I didn't hurt or kill anyone or myself. I will be forever grateful to the people at the gas station for spotting my condition and treating me with such kindness. The next morning I woke up in shock at the reality of what had occurred, but the next night I continued to drink as before. I told myself I could control my drinking and did for many nights, until the next incident.

After attending a cocktail party at a savings and loan conference at a resort in Scottsdale, Arizona, I decided to walk back to my room to use the bathroom. The next thing I knew, a police car light was shining in my face. Apparently while in blackout, I had walked out of the resort and up a hill to a housing development where I was trying to enter a house with my room key. I was so drunk that I didn't notice the difference between a very steep hill and a flat walkway. The light shining in my eyes, coupled with the sight of a very large policeman, must have brought me back to my senses. My street savvy came to the fore, and I quickly explained to the officer that I had gotten lost and was a high US government speaker at a conference at the resort below. He simply told me to get some coffee and explained the route to get back to the resort. I thought taking his card and offering to help him get a position with the FBI explained his leniency. But maybe he simply was a kind guy who knew I was no criminal, just a garden-variety drunk.

At another savings and loan conference, this time in Southern California, I only became aware of a drunken episode weeks after it occurred. A person in the industry told me he heard that at the cocktail party at this conference I had shoved my friend and drinking buddy (the executive director of the trade association of California Savings and Loan Institutions) into the pool. I wondered why people would spread such vicious gossip. I continued to wonder even after another colleague repeated the story to me. Years later I realized I must have been in another blackout, and they were telling the truth. In hindsight, the fact that this episode happened in plain view of people in the industry whose respect I needed to be successful as a consultant made it only more devastating. It was a mystery to me why I would think pushing anyone in his business suit into a swimming pool was funny. It is the kind of childish behavior I would judge others harshly for when I was sober.

When I suffered a heart attack at forty-five, I should have realized that I was in deep trouble, and so was my relationship with Susanne. I was in a hospital built by Susanne's father in Newport Beach, in the John Wayne suite (he died in this hospital). The doctor did not want me to fly home to Oakland alone, but Susanne did not want to fly down from Oakland to accompany me home. We fought about it on the phone. Was the reason her fear of hospitals, or she was in the process of "washing her hands" of me? In retrospect I think it was a combination of both. After the call ended I had pains in my heart. The staff immediately wheeled me into a room and proceeded with an echocardiogram. My heart was okay, but the nurses were furious with Susanne. My brother reluctantly stepped in after I asked him to help. This was not the first time, but it was easier to impose on my brother than fight with Susanne.

I returned home and celebrated being alive in our backyard with two friends and a bottle of Champagne. Susanne did not join us. I even suggested, after we finished the bottle and I was in a mellow-glow state, going to the liquor store and buying another. They sensibly declined. It was not until years later that I accepted the possibility that my heart attack was connected to my drinking episodes. I chalked it up to the bad luck of heredity. Hadn't my brother, who didn't usually drink to excess, had a heart attack eight months earlier?

Not too long thereafter, I woke up to Susanne's chestnut-green eyes staring at me with disgust. Why? What I had I done this time? All I remembered from the previous night's European send-off party was laughter and the quick, witty repartee I so loved. Some of us had been trading stories from traveling together in our youth, creating a special feeling of warmth. Friends who left the party midway through the evening later commented on what good form I had been in. But later that night, I had apparently used the N-word in addressing a long-term black woman friend of ours. I had said, "N, shut up" after consuming a bottle of Ouzo that my law school friend David had brought as a nod toward our time years earlier in Greece. What made this especially shocking was that I had absolutely no recollection of the event.

As the day wore on and I was recovering from the major physical impact of the night, the all-too-familiar feelings of shame, emptiness, guilt, and anxiety over what I had done slowly came to my awareness. "Oh, no, not another blackout," I moaned. Not another situation of egregious or aggressive behavior while drunk.

I was a man who had "run" with blacks in my youth, had close black friends in my adulthood, and devoted my professional life to right the wrongs of racial prejudice. Was I a fraud—just the same as the people I had criticized all my life? Was I a racist deep down? I was shaken to the core.

I thought that in blackout I had perhaps reverted to my years in high school when my black friend Cecil Harris and his "posse" liberally used the N-word, even in addressing me. When I conjured up the party incident, I had a vague recollection of having been annoyed with our friend. There is a saying that the truth comes out when you are drunk. Maybe that was the case. After much soul-searching, however, I didn't think the truth came out that night.

The husband of our insulted friend called Susanne and told her that if our friendship was to have any chance of surviving, I had to talk to his wife immediately. She accepted my apology and my explanation, but our couples' relationship never regained its closeness.

The party turned out to be my final drunken episode and final blackout.

Looking back, I did not stop drinking because the blackouts were increasing in number and rapidity. I did it to save my marriage and keep my family together. I did not give up my denial. After the N-word episode, we went to a couple of therapy sessions where Susanne made it clear she would end the marriage if I did not stop drinking. I promised to stop, but only after we returned from our planned family trip to Europe, in August 1985. I could not imagine traveling in France, Spain, and Italy without having wine. As promised, I stopped drinking upon our return. I also stopped using pot and the occasional use of other people's offered cocaine.

At this stage in my story, you might think I skated free of any real consequences due to my drinking. You would be wrong, dear reader. Although I was for a time a "two-martini man," it is true I did not drink myself to death as Jack Lemmon did in *Days of Wine and Roses*. However, as is the case with many of the drinkers I have met in my 12-Step Program who were not low-bottom drunks, I suffered from loss of self-respect and humiliation, not to mention financial difficulties and psychological pain, even before losing my marriage.

Five years after I stopped drinking and using marijuana, in April 1990 Susanne and I sat down with Annik and Noel to tell them we were separating. I will never forget the look of bewilderment and fear on their faces. Annik was twenty years old, and Noel was seventeen. She was in college and home on spring break; he was home from his boarding school. I could hardly speak. I had seen this scene many times in the movies and on TV, but this time it was my family and real. "Is this a permanent split?" "Are you getting a divorce?" "Who will we live with on our vacations from school?" Each question tore at my heart. Although we said the split was temporary, somewhere deep inside we knew it was not. We tried over the next few years to get back together. When Susanne wanted to, I was not ready, and when I wanted to, she was not. Too much damage had occurred. In addition, now that the focus was not all about my drinking, differences between us about basic values, child-rearing, and finances came forward. The loss of my family was very difficult for me. My guilt over the kids' turmoil was big. Although they had not experienced most of my drunken episodes, they could not have escaped from the reality that their father had a drinking problem. It was the elephant in the room. Being a "two-time marriage loser" weighed on me, even though I had concluded years ago that marrying my first wife Linda had simply been a youthful mistake.

Because of my "alcoholic thinking" I lost job opportunities, and in the interim between the split and the divorce I wound up borrowing large sums of money from friends to keep up the lifestyle of the family, including Annik's college and Noel's boarding school. I was determined that the kids would not have to "pay" for our separation and my financial problems. Given the fact that I was unwilling to move elsewhere, long-term job opportunities at my level were scarce. I ended up driving a taxi in Oakland. I was known at the company as the "lawyer-taxi driver." I was determined to do whatever I had to do to stay afloat. Driving a cab was honest work and not a great embarrassment to me, but it did cause me occasionally to wonder if this would be my fate for the remainder of my life. Sleeping in friends' spare rooms to maximize my disposable income was deeply humiliating. I was determined to find a way to regain my economic and social status.

It was only after being clean and sober for five years that I joined a 12-Step Program. My kids tell me that only then did my behavior change for the better. I went because of an invitation from the woman I had just started to live with. (We call this the thirteenth step.) Another year and a half would pass before my mask of denial began to fall away. I found out I could be witty, smart, and likable without booze. Indeed, stopping drinking was the first step in allowing me to face life head-on, accepting things I could not change, and letting go of resentments. I am nowhere near perfect in doing this, but I have progressed toward this goal. I stopped drinking for Susanne, but I stayed clean and sober for myself.

CHAPTER 13

LIVING AND WORKING ABROAD

In learning about others while traveling abroad, you learn a lot about yourself. First, you learn foreign means foreign. The American way of life and seeing things is best left at home. Flexibility and acceptance are called for, as is a sense of humor. Being a fan of Beckett or Jean Genet's Theatre of the Absurd plays is helpful. Understanding a local's way of seeing things without throwing away yours is essential. You will find there are many ways to organize your life and society. Personal preference guides which one you choose. You will be changed for the better by living and working abroad.

PART 1: INCREDIBLE INDIA

It is a testament to the unique visual and emotional richness of India that twenty-nine years after working there, everything is still vivid in my mind. The sheer number of people and the extreme poverty magnify each experience. Every type of person is found in India. They cover the full color range from very dark to tan to white, and come in all shapes: not just the thin and tall Indians of travel books, but short and fat people as well. Bearded or not, hatless or wearing turbans. Women wear saris and scarves of brilliant colors in different configurations. All the religions of the world are present, not just Hindu, but Muslim, Christian, Buddhist, Jewish, and so on. Other countries may have similar religious mixes, but nowhere are they in the same numbers or as spread out through the whole country. Temples, mosques, churches, and even synagogues are everywhere.

During the month I spent in India as a consultant for USAID (United States Agency for International Development) in 1988, I worked in five cities and visited another five as a tourist. As often was the case with my USAID assignments, the weather was at its worst. In Delhi and other places of dry climate, the temperature would reach 117 degrees, and in high humidity climates such as Bombay (Mumbai), it was 103 degrees.

The purpose of the mission was to approve five local developers of moderate-income housing as recipients of financial aid from a newly created Housing Bank. The bank was to receive the USAID funding and supervise its use (creating proper accounting procedures, for example) by the five local housing development corporations.

THE CHAOS OF INDIA

When I arrived in India, the US government was concerned about new acts of terrorism in the aftermath of the 1985 Air India plane bombing. Recently, the US had released several Sikhs, who had been convicted for their role in the bombing, to the Indian authorities. The government's concern about retributive violence against US citizens and companies was wellfounded. On our first morning in Delhi, after a scheduled meeting in the Citibank building, we drove to the sprawling and enormous US embassy for a meeting with the ambassador. He told us that over the next few days there was a real chance of terrorism on the part of Sikhs aimed at Americans. We should leave Delhi as soon as possible and return after a few days. We rescheduled our appointments and immediately left for Ahmedabad. An hour later, at 12:15 p.m., a bomb went off in the lobby of the Citibank building. One person was killed and fourteen were wounded. We missed being harmed by three hours.

In Delhi, all the drivers of rickshaws (a three-wheeled, motorized taxi cart called *tuk-tuk* in Thailand) seemed to be Sikh. To counter the threats against Americans, we told them we were Canadians. In retrospect, I chuckle at our silly ruse because the Sikh drivers would never be able to discern the difference between an American and a Canadian accent.

Ahmedabad, Gujarat, is a city of approximately five million. The cotton textile center of the country, it is called the Manchester of India. Only in India will you see a city of five million people share the streets with the sacred Brahman cows. It is a testament to the power of religion that the hungry poor do not kill and eat the cows. I have a photo that captures these crowded streets, with the women's multicolored saris and pantsuits flashing brilliantly against the muddy browns and blacks of the animals and roads. I spotted a luscious outdoor fruit and vegetable market, but by the time I crossed the street to inspect the red-red tomatoes and deep-orange carrots, I was overpowered by the smell of animal feces. The odor from burning cow-dung patties that are used for cooking and fuel, or from the excrement of animals walking the streets of densely populated cities, can be unexpected and overwhelming. No fruits or vegetables for me!

Ahmedabad is also famous as the home of Gandhi. Gandhi was a Guajarati. After interviewing the CEO of the local housing development corporation, I visited Gandhi's Sabarmati Ashram, a flat dirt compound on the banks of the Sabarmati River. Its simple structures and the stillness that can be found inside (I spent several hours there) mirror the simple dignity of Gandhi himself. It is astonishing to comprehend that from such a humble place, a revolution against a leading world power was started and changed the world.

We returned to Delhi to catch up with our rescheduled appointments. I was well aware of the absurdity of having to determine the honesty and competence of the five development companies after only a two- or-three-day interchange with their executives. I was comforted, however, by the fact that the newly developed Housing Bank would have the time, procedures, and expertise to confirm or not confirm my judgment. As life would have it, my judgment proved correct, and the project was the most successful of the numerous USAID assignments I worked on over the years.

In Delhi you acutely feel the chaos and poverty of India. It is crushing. No other place in my travels has come close (Cairo being the closest). Beggars are everywhere. When your car stops at a stoplight, a woman carrying a baby in her arms appears from nowhere and knocks on your window, pantomiming food for the baby.

If you respond and open the window, within a second hundreds of children and other women with babies in their arms materialize from nowhere. In all probability the babies do not even belong to the women but are part of a sophisticated "begging gang." Most beggars are taught not to take a polite no as an answer. For me, the toughest beggars to refuse were the lepers and the men without legs on roller platforms, both tugging at my pants.

I encountered the gulf between the rich and poor in India whenever I left my five-star, air-conditioned hotel. If my taxi turned right instead of left, I would find myself in the middle of a Delhi slum with cheek-by-jowl tin-roofed wooden or cardboard shanties. The density of the shelters and population was staggering. On the other hand, I enjoyed the exotic and charming nature of India when I arrived back at the same hotel to see an elephant eating a tree just before the car-drive entrance. The sterile government buildings and boulevards of New Delhi were a sharp contrast to the teeming street life of Delhi.

People react differently to the devastating poverty of India. To emotionally survive, either you don't go, leave as fast as possible, or shut down all or part of your humanity. A friend who was on his fifth trip to India, after landing in Delhi and showering at his five-star hotel immediately drove back to the airport and flew home. The sights, sounds and smells of Delhi had simply overwhelmed him. I understood that overreacting to the misery would help no one. Nonetheless, I had to partly close down my emotional self in order to function. It was not easy to face the reality of India, but I felt it was important to look deeper and recognize that even in this wretchedness, Indians retained the human capacity for love and the desire to make life better. In my conversations, after our business meetings were finished, I saw these qualities in some of the Indian men I was interviewing. They talked glowingly about their parents and children and their aspirations for the projects they wished to build. These projects would allow moderate-income tenants or owners to live much closer to their work and allow for more family time. They also talked about the caste system, the poor, and their hopes for change.

INDIANS ARE NOT ITALIANS

Nevertheless, the impact of living daily with extreme poverty, a strict class structure, the difficulty of earning a living, and the holdover of the worst attitudes of the British aristocracy made me feel that Indians are Italians without charm. Both are aggressive in getting what they want (a minor example is cutting to the head of the line), but Italians operate with a twinkle in their eye and laughter at the "dance of life."

Three examples from Delhi will demonstrate my point. The first had to do with a taxi ride from our hotel to the shopping area of Delhi. We arranged the cost of the ride with the driver before leaving the hotel. On the way back we went through the same process, but this time the driver gave us a price 40 percent higher for the same ride. When I said we had just traversed the same distance for a 40 percent cheaper fare, he said, "Oh yes, but that was without the shopping bags you now have." I still give him points for his agility, but he did not wink or smile. An Italian would have laughed at the situation together with you. A minor rip-off is tolerable if accompanied by charm.

Another time I asked a man for directions. He offered to take us there, and I assumed he would lead us to our destination, as would be the case in Italy. Instead, he walked us to his taxi and demanded an outrageous fare to drive us one-and-a-half blocks. He acted with plain aggressive hustle and without any redeeming grace.

Last, when your flight is called at the airport, Indians will literally run you over to get to the gate and then run through you again to identify their luggage that has been set out on the tarmac before being loaded onto the plane. This procedure was put in place as a safety precaution after the 1985 Sikh-orchestrated Air India bombing. At least Italians would run you over smiling and saying, "Scusi, scusi," letting you know that it's not okay, but they can't help doing it anyway.

The airport stampede reminds me of the difficult logistics of doing business in India. First and foremost, although Indians speak English, our totally different pronunciation means we are really speaking different languages. I have no trouble understanding Brits or Aussies, but it took a while before I understood what I was being asked when someone inquired how I liked my "otel." It was my hotel I was being asked about. In time, and with great difficulty, I was able to understand 90 percent of what was said at the moment it was said. Of course, it was impossible (too insulting) to have an interpreter.

Three other factors created difficulties for me in 1988: First, although I had no trouble calling DC or Berkeley from Delhi, it was impossible to call across town. This meant there was no way to confirm appointments. You had to go to the meeting at the prearranged time and hope your counterpart would be present. Many times the meeting was delayed a full hour. Usually there was no air conditioning and no waiting room. Your choice was to stay put and swelter, or go back to the comfort of the hotel and try again later. Also, you could neither call an airline to change flights nor see if your plane from Delhi to Bombay was on time. I waited a number of times at the non-air-conditioned airport for my plane that was three or four hours late. The whole process sapped my energy and was emotionally tiresome.

Driving safely anywhere in India was a matter of luck, maybe even a miracle. I would close my eyes the minute my driver turned on the engine. The professional drivers normally were exceptionally good at avoiding other cars or people crossing the street. But to avoid a bug on the highway, they would swerve wildly in the direction of people and animals walking on the side of the road. Amazingly, neither would react in panic and flee. The highways were too narrow for large trucks and cars going in opposite directions. As the drivers of the trucks never accommodated anyone, the approaching cars had to swerve off the road to avoid head-on collisions. Would we, another person, or an animal on the side of the road be killed as the truck merrily went on his way? Only fate would answer this question.

THE TAJ MAHAL IN AGRA

Whenever I work in a country, I make time to explore and experience the street life, famous sites, and the beautiful countryside it presents. In this regard, the Taj Mahal in the town of Agra was a must-see destination.

To access the train station and descend the stairs to the platform for the train to Agra, one had to literally enter the sidewalk "houses" (without ceilings or walls) of the poor. The dwellings in front of the station went on to my right and left as far as my eye could see. Uninvited, I strode through "kitchens," "bathrooms," and "bedrooms." Women were cooking over wood and cow-dung fires; senior citizens were still in their beds, which consisted of very thin mattresses or just cardboard, and others were relieving themselves on the ground in a "bathroom" space.

While sitting in my first-class, air-conditioned train, directly across from me on another track I saw a train bound for the Punjab, with as many people sitting on top of the cars as were crammed inside. These are the cheapest (free) and most dangerous seats. Many people die each year using this mode of transportation.

The Taj Mahal lived up to its billing, although the drought that year had diminished the beauty of what once was a deep-green grass approach to the palace. I was lucky to get a tip to stay at the Sheraton hotel across the river from the Taj and see it bathed in moonlight from the window of my room. It was as advertised: very beautiful and truly romantic. I felt the deep loss and testament to love that inspired this architectural marvel.

As wonderful as the Taj was, the more amazing site for me was the UNESCO World Heritage Center of Fatehpur Sikri. The four-hundred-year-old, five-mile walled royal complex has embattlements on three sides and a vast artificial lake on the fourth. The lake is linked to the city by an elaborate water supply system. Fatehpur Sikri embraces a palace, courtyards, gazebos, and one of India's largest mosques. The complex is unique for its open spaces and gates. Each gate is grand in size, and most have elaborate carvings. The buildings and floors are made of local red sandstone. Among the seven gated entrances, Agra Gate is the most important as it was used for royal ceremonies.

Fatehpur Sikri was founded by the Mughal emperor Akaba in 1569. It was the capital of the Mughal Empire from 1571 to 1585. The Mughals ruled mainly northern India from 1526 to 1707, after Babur (a direct descendant of Genghis Khan) defeated the Muslim rulers. Emperor Akaba personally supervised the planning, design, and the work of the local artisans in the construction over a ten-year period. What fascinated me the most about the site was the inclusion of elements of Persian, Hindu, Jain, and Islamic architecture. What a fantastic place! This respect for the major religious-ethnic populations was symbolic of how the Mughals ruled.

My trip to Agra taught me two lessons. First, even though you are in a first-class car of the train, the cleanliness standards (especially with respect to dish washing and drinking water) are not the same as in some of the first-class hotels. Second, make sure your consultant contract with USAID contains a provision for use of the medical facilities at the embassy. I had to go to a private doctor and then take a long rickshaw ride to get my lab work done. The next morning I had to pick up the written report from the lab and return with it to the doctor's office. Of course, the lab and doctor's office were at opposite ends of town. A first-class train ticket had not saved me from picking up a bug from drinking my hot tea. Antibiotics stopped me from doubling over and continually running to a bathroom. Finding bathrooms I wanted to use outside of my hotel presented a major problem. Although this situation definitely had its comic elements, it was not fun. With a smile, the doctor said, "Welcome to India."

My next stop was visiting a housing development company in Bombay (Mumbai). When my taxi exited the airport around 7:00 p.m., we drove by what seemed to be fifteen square blocks of people sleeping on their beds under the sky and very close to each other. At the time I presumed that they preferred sleeping in the street because their houses were not air-conditioned. But as I write this I am still not sure if this was the reason or if they had no houses to go to.

BOMBAY AND THE GLORY OF THE RAJ

Although Bombay is a modern city and the Indian center for finance, commerce,, and entertainment, I found myself one moment side by side with a Sadhu holy man with flowering white hair and a face painted in yellow, red and white, and the next witnessing a man defecating in front of the Indian Federal Reserve Bank.

From my window in the old section of the Taj Mahal Hotel, I admired the Gateway of India that was built to commemorate the visit of King George V and Queen Mary in 1911. It is called the Taj Mahal of Bombay. Its arch-domed structure, completed in 1924, is eighty-three feet above ground at its highest point. Facing the Arabian Sea, the Gateway became the ceremonial entrance of the viceroys and governors. Since the time of Queen Victoria (1858) until independence (1947), India was under the direct control of the British Crown. This period of time is called the Raj. To me the Gateway symbolizes the over-the-top pomp and ceremony of the Raj, the British military control, and the wealth derived from India. Coupled with the British feelings of superiority, the "Indian Empire" created a negative and troubling legacy.

Bangalore (now Bengaluru) has a welcome "benevolent" climate (temperatures in the '90s) that attracted the elite of the Raj. I saw many examples of their expensive houses and gardens, demonstrating that the legacy of the Raj was still alive in Bangalore. The city was the home of the Kannada language film industry. The Kannada language has an unbroken history of over a thousand years and is spoken by over forty million Indians, yet I had never heard of it. Only in India could a language spoken by more people than those of many other countries fall off the radar.

Mysore, which is near Bangalore, houses the incredible Amba Vilas Palace (Mysore Palace). It is another example of the extreme wealth of many principalities during the Raj. The British could ignore the problem of the poor but not the status and power of the Indian princes. Amba Vilas (built from 1892 to 1912) rivals Versailles for sheer size and may surpass it for its breathtaking beauty, especially when it is lit up at night. The east (front) gate is usually opened only once a year during the Dasara festival in autumn, and then only for very, very important persons (VVIPs). You could ride elephants through the gates and arches, and they did! The building is made of fine gray marble with deep pin marble dooms. Inside you find stained glass windows and ceilings, mosaic floors embellished with semiprecious stones, and a wooden elephant howdah (frame for carrying passengers) decorated with eighty-four kilograms of gold. The glory of India's bygone days is on display in other places as well, for example in the Amber Palace in Jaipur with its phenomenal embossed, double-leaf silver doors of the Sila Devi temple. Realizing the staggering wealth that existed in India, especially when juxtaposed with the overwhelming poverty of the country, is helpful in understanding the paradoxes of present-day India.

A TRIP TO THE DESERT

The last of my interviews was with the CEO of the Madras housing development corporation. He was an example of the fact that there is always an exception to generalizations about people. Although he was a member of the upper class, he had a deep concern for affordable housing. We had a working lunch at his club that confirmed the city's reputation for top-notch food. The irony of our eating at a British-style club that he could not have entered only a short time ago was not lost on me. We all have our contradictions.

After finishing my assignment I decided to stay on in India and visit Rajasthan. Rajasthan is in the desert, and the temperature was 117 degrees, but I decided to go. To paraphrase an old saying, "Only mad dogs and Al go out in the noontime sun." I hired a car and driver for the trip. The car was a classic Indian-made Ambassador. It had beautiful lines and plenty of room. It also had a problem: the air conditioning only worked when the car was stationary. I could go nowhere and be cool, or go somewhere and sit in a pool of sweat. We set off from Delhi on my desert adventure trip. I would go to Jaipur, Puskar, and Mandawa.

Jaipur is the capital of the Rajasthan province. It is known as the "Pink City" due to its painted pink sandstone buildings. For two nights I stayed in the Rambagh Palace hotel with its beautiful gardens, joining the peacocks to roam through them. I was one of the six guests crazy enough to visit Jaipur in May. I ate all my meals in a sometimes completely empty hotel restaurant. The meals were eaten to the sound of sitar and drum music. Because of the searing heat, I only left my room in the early morning and late afternoon. Jaipur was a wonder to behold. The women's clothing, made of deep and rich hues of red, pink, gold, and blue, was beautiful set against their ebony-colored skin. Their large, intricately designed silver and metal jewelry was a perfect addition. The juxtaposition of the colorful women with the browns of the desert hills and the light pinks of the buildings was marvelous.

It was 117 degrees in the early afternoon when I reached my hotel in Puskar, one of the top ten Hindu religious sites in the world. It is also the site of a famous Camel Festival that attracts many thousands of visitors every year. It is the home of the only major Brahma temple in India. Brahma is the Hindu God who created the world. The temple is close to a sacred lake, and my hotel suite overlooked the lake. The only other guests in the hotel were three young German hippies. After a shower, I set forth on a fifteen-minute walk to visit the temple. With every step, the calm of the lake setting gave way to the chaos of hordes of beggars and trinket sellers, none of whom would take no for an answer. It was an annoying, nonspiritual, mood-changing experience.

Once I entered the temple, the beggars were replaced by numerous aggressive monkeys swinging on tree branches from one part of the temple to another and running at me for food. In spite of this further irritating experience, the noise of the aggressive beggars and monkeys seemed to disappear for a short period of time, and I was left with a magical, mystical feeling brought on by the sight of the beautifully carved stone statues adorned with orange carnation garlands and the trees with numerous tangled vines within the temple. But soon the monkeys rudely returned to my consciousness, and I had to run the same gauntlet of beggars and trinket sellers back to the hotel. When I sat in my room I closed my eyes to conjure up the brief feelings of wonder I'd had in the temple. One minute of true peace was worth thirty minutes of hassle. I experienced this jarring juxtaposition again and again in India.

Around sunset I was sitting in the outdoor roof restaurant overlooking the sacred lake when the Hindu version of the Muslim call to prayer exploded over the loudspeaker. As I listened to the chanting and watched people enter the sacred lake, suddenly a thousand white-wing bats flew over my head. The sound was deafening, as if I was about to be run over by a very loud train. All I could think was "Holy moly Gunga Din" (I saw the faces of Cary Grant and Douglas Fairbanks, Jr. in the movie of the same name). Ah India! A phrase I repeated often.

That night I awoke every two hours in a bed of sweat, and a cold shower allowed me to sleep for another two hours. The temperature had fallen to 103 degrees.

The next morning I set off for what should have been a three-hour ride to Mandawa, which was even deeper in the desert. After a six-hour non-air-conditioned ride that consisted of taking the wrong turn over and over again in the 117-degree heat, I arrived in Mandawa. The town is referred to as an "open art gallery." It is dotted with fascinating mansions (havelis) that have lavishly frescoed walls outside and inside. There are numerous painted mammoth-elephants in blue or brown, with dignitaries seated on top in a "chair" in gold, red, and green. Different geometric design patterns of blue and white show up everywhere. Many of the frescoes, however, were badly in need of repair.

After the horrible night I spent in Pukar, I vowed not to repeat the experience. I would only stay in Mandawa if my room was air-conditioned. The manager said it was not, but he would supply fans. I was not having it. I told my driver we were returning to Delhi. He pleaded with me to stay in Mandawa, as he said he was too tired from the six-hour drive he'd just completed. I asserted myself and off we went to Delhi. But as the gods would have it, when we were about to hook up with the road to Delhi we were met by a blinding sand storm. We had no choice but to return to Mandawa.

The manager was delighted to see me again. He offered me the large Maharaja suite and positioned large fans around my bed. After a shower, I returned to the lobby where the manager proposed a tour of the hotel. It was empty except for a guest couple I never saw. As we started, the electricity failed and all the lights in the hotel went out. The manager, who was resourceful, continued the tour with his flashlight illuminating our way. When we were outside the walls of the main hotel, the electricity returned to reveal a charming garden. The manager asked me where and when I would like to have dinner. I said, "If possible, right here and now in the garden?" He said, "Of course," clapped his hands, and a table and chair appeared from nowhere with a turban-clad waiter standing at the ready. As I sat down he clapped his hands again, and an exquisite young woman appeared and began to dance to the music of the sitar, played, as it turned out, by her father. Under a canopy of a million stars, with a waiter serving me in a garden, with the fortress wall of the hotel as a backdrop, I had my five-star dinner and watched a beautiful young woman dancing. I was Maharajah Al for a few hours.

On our way back from Mandawa to Delhi, we stopped at a railroad crossing where the gates were down, but people on foot and bicycle went around and under the gates and crossed the tracks. After waiting twenty minutes, I was getting impatient to be on our way, when suddenly the gates lifted. No train ever passed. Again, ah India!

Friends tell me that getting around and the logistics of doing business in India have much improved since 1988. They also tell me that the overwhelming poverty and class distinctions I encountered remain, but so do the magical experiences I discovered in India.

PART II: ALBANIA: THE LAND OF CONCRETE MACHINE GUN PILLBOXES

Near the end of 1994 I flew into Tirana, Albania, to begin an intermittent USAID consulting contract for fifteen months. My task was to help the government develop a housing/infrastructure strategy. I was among the first of a handful of US consultants in Albania, employed by PADCO, a DC-based international consulting company. At that time, the runway at Tirana airport was made of very large octagonal concrete blocks, which fitted together unevenly. It felt as if I was landing on an old-fashioned NYC bathroom tile runway. You never knew if you would puncture a tire and/or skid off the dilapidated runway. Each time it was a spooky, bumpy experience. The pilot told me Tirana was his trickiest landing challenge. It was just one example of the effect of years of isolation and economic distress brought about by the long, harsh dictatorship of Enver Hoxha (1944–1985).

As we were driving from the airport through the bucolic countryside of grapevines and farmland, I noticed machinegun "pill box" bunkers everywhere, and many sharp, knife-like stakes attached to posts in the grape and farm fields. My driver said they were placed there by Hoxha to repel a NATO and American paratroop invasion. The whitewashed pillboxes were small in size, maybe three feet high, and set on a foot-high bunker base. It was never clear to me how a person could fit inside them to fire a machinegun. Some 700,000 bunkers were placed throughout Albania. It is estimated that the amount of concrete used to build them is three times the amount used for the Maginot Line in France, after World War I. My guess is Hoxha knew no such invasion was planned, but it was a good propaganda device to heighten fears, consolidate his power, and control the population. In time they would become a photo opportunity for tourists and, in Tirana, an art object painted in vivid rainbow colors.

I came and went every two or three weeks for over fifteen months, and the Hotel Tirana (back then the only decent hotel in town) was my home away from home. The hotel was relatively new, with clean, nice rooms and a restaurant just off the modern lobby with swatches of red, black, and yellow colors. The staff always greeted me with a warm smile. As time went by, I got to know about their families and their dreams for the future. The hotel faced Skanderbeg Square with the National Museum and the very large, eighteenth century Et'hem Bey Mosque that contains famous frescoes rarely seen in Islamic art as they are representative, depicting waterfalls and birds. A four-lane boulevard with a grass divider began on the opposite side of the square and ended in the Parkui Madah (Grand Park), where residents fished in the artificial lakes. I regularly jogged from the hotel along the boulevard into the trails of the park. Depending on the season, I would be greeted with a view of either green or snowcapped mountains that framed the city. The trick was to enter the square without being hit by a bicycle going at full speed against the traffic and the traffic lights.

On the verdant park side of the boulevard, kiosks were lined up one after another, all selling the same small items such as batteries, cigarettes, magazines, and newspapers. How the owners eked out an income selling the same things was a marvel to me. The friendly owners who spoke English told me it was a second or third source of income for them. They said, "Every few lek (Albanian currency) contribute to our survival," and I added, "in the poorest country of Europe." (The yearly per capita income has ranged from a low of $1,243 in the 1980s to a high of $4,541 in 2015).

Albania and its capital, Tirana, were my favorite places to work in Eastern Europe and the former Soviet Union (except for Prague and Budapest). The sense of hopefulness, self-motivation, lightness, and irony of the Albanians stood in sharp contrast to the dour melancholy and heaviness I experienced in the Ukraine and Russia (even though I found their love of poetry, ballet, and the arts attractive). Their optimism was remarkable given the harsh repression and economic difficulties they suffered under the long reign of Hoxha. Maybe, on the other hand, it was the ending of this harsh repression that was underpinning their optimism.

Until his death in 1985, Hoxha ran Albania with an iron fist (the successor authoritarian government unraveled in 1992.) When he found that being a Stalinist Marxist was not "pure" enough, he switched allegiance to Communist China and became a Mao Marxist. He then rejected Mao Marxism as too revisionist. In reality, he was a thug who stole from and subjugated his people, killing or imprisoning any opposition. Although Albanians were historically capitalistic smugglers and made a good living, they lost their sense of cunning under the yoke of Hoxha. Albanians told this joke about wealth: "How do you find the richest man in Albania? Roll a quarter down the street and see who picks it up."

Two stories exemplify the fear and tension under his rule. The first is about a man who was forty-five years old when I met him. He had recently been freed from prison and told me the following story.

"When I was nineteen I accompanied my father, an Albanian-born American citizen, on a trip to his place of birth to visit his family. But the Albanian authorities did not recognize our American passports and refused us an exit stamp. The American government was powerless to help. (We see the same governmental impotence today in many hostage situations.) Six months after the exit rejection, I was waiting in a very long line for food when I foolishly shouted out, "This wouldn't happen in America!" I was promptly arrested, stood trial

for statements against the state, was convicted, and sentenced to prison where I remained for twenty-five years. While I was in prison, my father died."

His story left me speechless.

The second story took place in the office of the executive assistant to the president, Sali Berisha. We were ten minutes into our conversation when he spontaneously started laughing. I was puzzled and began to feel uncomfortable. I asked him why he was laughing. He said, "I just now fully understand that I am sitting in the former Russian embassy talking to an American. Just a short time ago, if I had mentioned the word American, I would have been jailed." His statement sadly confirmed the released prisoner's story.

As is often the case in the immediate aftermath of the downfall of a dictatorship, things go from nothing is allowed to everything goes. It takes a while to form an acceptable and reasonable new government. You start out in the "Wild West," where laws do not necessarily govern. Whatever you can get away with becomes the underlying psychology of people's actions. Imagine a situation where there is no recorded land title. For forty-eight years, the state owned all the land. How do you reestablish proof of private ownership, especially after the destruction of World War II? USAID had a team of experts attempting to do the nearly impossible. In the meantime, you might as well take back land you claim had been rightfully yours!

On the way in from the airport I saw new villas that had been built on reclaimed land. The "owners" had rigged an electricity line from the main grid to their houses. The loss of income to the utility and its effect on price and availability for others was not their concern. Many of these folks were recently released prisoners, and it was politically impossible at that time to remove them from the land or make them pay for electricity. The same political reality made it impossible for the government to evict the victims of Hoxha's tyranny from squatting in partially built apartments.

The challenge for me was to develop a strategy that would bring the rule of law to the country and at the same time meet the urgent needs of the people. The only way to do this was to have a jointly developed government/citizen action plan. My task was to help put the pieces together and provide solutions that worked elsewhere and could be modified for the reality of Albania. I worked closely with the government and interested citizens. It was a great adventure and a way to get to know Albanians close up.

I knew you could not impose a program developed in DC without local input: you would be doomed to failure. A telling example was the World Bank's Emergency Housing Program in Albania. It happened during the era of President Reagan, and therefore "home ownership" was the buzzword. Home ownership was the objective, whether or not it fit the realities on the ground. There were many unfinished multifamily units from Hoxha's time. The World Bank decided that these existing mostly two-story apartments should be built out to their original five-story plan. I was told that the World Bank economists in DC had not checked the existing structures to determine if there were sufficient water and sewer infrastructure hookups to support the expansion. In addition, the rebar sticking out of the support columns had long ago rusted and would not support additional floors of construction. The economist program planners apparently did not have sufficient construction experience to understand that their plan, if implemented, would have resulted in an unsafe slum. (I experienced this lack of practical, "in the field" experience in other World Bank projects I worked on). Moreover, the former political prisoner-squatters could not afford rent, much less home ownership. It was not hard to understand why the deputy minister, who was also the minister of Housing, was using the World Bank funds for other useful purposes. This was another example of Albanian ingenuity and political savvy. He knew the bank would not challenge him. The head of the World Bank office in Albania asked me to talk to the deputy prime minister about this misallocation of funds. I had developed a very good relationship with the minister, having arranged for and accompanied him on a trip to Washington, DC, to meet with the secretary of HUD and senior USAID officials. I declined because it was not wise to risk my rapport with the deputy prime minister over an issue that was not part of my assignment.

I also had a close association with the executive assistant to the prime minister. The PM had been a senior official during the Communist era, which was not uncommon in other former Communist countries where I worked. These close connections would be essential if there was to be any chance of moving ahead in a reasonable time.

The executive assistant to the president arranged a meeting with President Sali Berisha. The president paid me a compliment (I was told) by having the meeting in his intimate inner office. The office was small, with just enough space for his desk and a few chairs. There were no pictures or paintings on the walls. The only decoration was a flagpole with the Albanian flag behind his desk. The meeting consisted of President Berisha, his executive assistant, the American Ambassador Joseph Lake, PADCO's chief of party (the person who resided in Tirana full time and was in charge of PADCO's international consultant activities in the country, including me), and myself.

Berisha was a charming and handsome six-foot-tall man with shiny, deep-black hair. I was flabbergasted when I was told that I could not invite the woman I had hired as my assistant to join the meeting because there were no small-sized chairs available. I felt very badly about excluding her from the meeting. I was reminded of Shakespeare's line in Richard III: "A horse! A horse! My kingdom for a horse!" In this case it would read: "A chair! A chair! My kingdom for a chair!"

My invitation to meet with the president had set off alarm buttons in the State Department. Who was this guy Hirshen? What was he going to talk about? Would he ruin our bilateral relations with Albania for years to come? It was highly unusual to have a meeting between a USAID consultant and the president of a foreign country, especially a country so strategically important to the US. (Albania was a linchpin for our Balkan policy.) But on our walk to the office, Ambassador Joseph Lake said to me, "This is your meeting. I will observe." He was true to his word. He recognized that there was nothing to fear from me. After the meeting with the president, the State Department followed suit.

After the meeting I learned from Berisha's executive assistant that the president sent a memo (it copied almost word for word my proposed strategy) instructing the relevant ministers and departments to fully cooperate with me and to implement the strategy. I was pleased that the president had understood and agreed with my plans for development. With his backing, and that of the relevant ministers, there was a better than 70 percent chance of its implementation, which is not always the case in international development consulting.

Tirana had been spared the horror of the massive, inhuman concrete block housing found elsewhere in the former Soviet Union thanks to Khrushchev. Most of the apartments and office buildings were low-rise (five to six levels). Some were even painted in yellow and blue to enliven the city. There were scattered villas. Although a number of buildings were in need of rehabilitation, the architecture of the city was on a "human scale" and pleasant to walk around. However, large piles of garbage stacked behind the buildings, with rats scooting to and fro, greatly diminished this pleasure. I am told this eyesore has now been eliminated.

There was one notable grand villa neighborhood called Biloku (The Block). It was where Hoxha and his *politburo* lived. During his reign, this area was restricted to ordinary Albanians. After the downfall of the tyrants, everyday Albanians took a special delight in strolling through the area. On Sundays, many families were seen looking at the extravagant villas, the fathers pointing out Hoxha's villa to their children. As in other former Communist countries (like Slovakia, where the old city center was in stark contrast to the massive concrete blocks of Khrushchev housing), you had a pleasant or unpleasant visual experience in Tirana depending on how wide your "camera lens" was set. Visual and other contradictions were par for the course.

I experienced this on a weekend trip from Tirana to Sarandë, on the southern coast of Albania opposite Corfu. I hired a Mercedes and driver to get me there. We headed west to the Ionian Sea port city of Durrës and then traveled south through the Durrës Basin and its oil-producing fields and refineries. The streams in the area were not a mixture of oil and water, but simply running oil. The oil stench was overwhelming. I wondered what the cancer rate was in the population. Some of the most polluted places in the world I have seen were in former Communist countries, not in the citadels of capitalism. Slogans are not matched by deeds. We left the Basin, heading southwest through a big mountain range with occasional ancient castles, and returned to the Ionian Sea, north of Sarandë.

At that time Albanian drivers had relatively little experience as only the elite could afford and were allowed to own cars before liberation. My driver did not hesitate. Without checking for oncoming traffic, he moved into the oncoming lane on hairpin curves of a very narrow highway. My anxiety was heightened by the lack of any guardrails and the thousand-foot drop-offs. Telling the driver to be more careful would have been a waste of words. I just shut my eyes and hoped for the best.

We were driving a "brand new" rehabilitated 1980s-era Mercedes. I would see many of these cars in Albania, compliments of the Albanian and Italian Mafias. Albania has more Mercedes per capita than any other country. The owners could not take those stolen cars out of Albania, as an old Albanian joke illustrates: "What do you call an Albanian in a car? A thief." If an Albanian wanted to legitimately buy a genuinely new Mercedes at the factory in Germany, he had to bring the car to

Albania by a circuitous route to avoid being held up and having the car stolen on the Autobahn or Autostrada. Folks at the factory would tip off the Italian-Albanian joint venture Mafias that a car was on its way. Albanians added a new dimension to car buying, unknown in the US. As I said, Albanians were creative.

As we approached Sarandë, the dark luster of citrus and the pale green of olive trees descended to the shore toward the deep-blue, shimmering Ionian Sea. The view was especially enthralling after the oil fields of the Durrës Basin. I stopped and walked on the golden sand beach framed by sea and mountains. I also spent some time in a cove surrounded by natural caves dug into the white chalky "Cliffs of Dover" bluffs. To find empty, pristine beaches and coves anywhere in Europe is a miracle. The next morning I drove ten miles south of Sarandë to the exquisite ruins of Butrint, a UNESCO World Heritage Site. The site has been inhabited since 50,000 B.C., both as a Greek colony and a Roman city. The place is remarkably preserved, with marvelous Byzantine mosaic floors, ancient columns, walls, and parts of buildings, all on the edge of the deep blue sea.

Upon my return to Tirana, I discussed with the authorities that this rare area needed to be protected. An intelligent, environmentally wise development plan was needed, but my advice was not fully heeded. Nevertheless, the Albanian Riviera is still a place where you can find beauty and solitude at a reasonable price.

Unlike the other former Communist countries I worked in, the combination of fresh fish (thanks to the lakes and ocean) and pasta (thanks to the Italians who ruled Albania for many years) combined to make dining enjoyable. The restaurants were small and could be found on the first floor of small villas. They were clean, and the owners and staff were attentive even when I visited without Albanian dignitaries.

I had lined up the political and strategy ducks for our jointly developed housing/infrastructure program and was looking forward to returning to Albania to assist in its implementation. I was especially excited at the prospect of joining the executive assistant to the prime minister on one of their military helicopters and flying to a mountain resort to fish the lakes for the highly regarded freshwater Koran fish, hike the mountains, and visit the ancient castles that dotted the landscape. However, as often can be the case in third-world international development, events beyond your control can make a mockery of your best efforts. Chaos and violence erupted as a result of a Berisha-supported Ponzi scheme that had a widespread, devastating economic impact. Personnel of the US embassy and USAID had to be helicoptered to safety. My step-by-step development over fifteen months of the necessary foundational building blocks for success was destroyed in a few weeks. This was not the first time my efforts would not bear fruit because of circumstances beyond my control. I had learned these reality lessons the hard way in other third-world countries, from the Maldives to Russia, Moldova, and Jamaica. Thus, I was steeled for such unforeseen events, but I was heartbroken for the people of Albania. Sadly, I would not return to Albania, but the people remain in my heart. I still hope events will allow me to fish the lakes, walk the mountains, and see the progress they have made in the last twenty years.

PART III: UKRAINE: THE LAND OF BROWN AND DANK

In December 1995, when the Dayton Accord ended the war in the former Yugoslavia (Bosnia, Serbia, and Croatia), USAID was instructed by the Bush administration to render aid to these new countries. In its usual infinite wisdom, Congress did not appropriate additional funds for the task. USAID had to cobble together the money from existing programs. Ukraine was one of these existing programs that suffered the consequences: the full-time American consultants were removed from three of the four cities where the aid program operated.

Ukraine's loss was my gain. Congress's parsimony and shortsightedness created a consultant job for me, based on my prior work for the international consulting company PADCO (who ran the in-country program). I would fly in for short-term stays over almost a two-year period, to directly supervise the Ukrainian personnel in the USAID programs in Kiev, Odessa, and Kharkov, and also to oversee the one PADCO consultant who remained full time in Lviv.

The USAID program was designed to help the Ukrainians transfer ownership of existing apartments from the government to private condominiums, which meant that private housing maintenance and management companies had to be created.

This may have seemed a good idea to the Washington planners who wanted to push the latest Reagan administration theory of the benefits of home ownership. Once again I was witnessing a politically motivated housing theory being applied to a situation where the facts on the ground made it unworkable. Unlike in America, there were no laws spelling out the rights and duties of homeowners. Prior attempts to pass such laws had been unsuccessful, and without them any new "owner" was in a legal never-never land. Moreover, the government had not supplied the necessary funds to repair big-ticket items such as roofs and boilers. New owners would be saddled with expenses they could not afford. They rightly thought this made no sense. Ukrainians felt that if they lived on the first floor, why should they be responsible for the condition of the roof or elevator? And why should someone on an upper floor be responsible for a common area like the lobby?

I had the false assumption that people in a Communist country would easily understand that they had to share responsibility for parts of a building they owned in common. It did not occur to them that the value of their apartment was based, in no small part, on the condition of the building as a whole. After so many years of looking only after themselves and suspecting their neighbors were government spies, it was difficult for them to accept that they needed to work together to preserve the value of their apartment building. Because the government had not funded the repairs of big-ticket items (roofs, boilers, elevators), it made no sense for the tenants to become owners. They would much rather make do and remain renters. There was no incentive to change their status.

KIEV

Upon arriving in Ukraine, my first task was to choose a hotel. That choice was based on whether a hotel had its own working hot water system. You had no choice with respect to heating because the government-operated, citywide heating systems that the hotels relied on would break down or were programmed to start or discontinue on a certain date, no matter how far below freezing the outside temperature was. You could always go to sleep in your long johns underneath all your clothes, and with many blankets on top to deal with the cold, but a cold shower was too uncivilized for my taste.

My hotel in Kiev was the typical brown and dank place that is a staple in the countries of the former Soviet Union. Breakfast was served in small dining rooms on four different floors. Once I found the floor with the babushka women servers who were the most hospitable and efficient, I was all set for my breakfast of brown-bread toast, a fried egg or cheese, and coffee. It was not unusual for me to be offered vodka at breakfast by one of my fellow guests, served from their private bottle. Ukraine, like Russia, was and still is a country of alcoholics. A World Health Organization survey found it had six times the level of alcohol abuse of Germany. Twenty percent of Ukrainian men have alcohol and drug disorders. In 2007, the deaths of 40 percent of men and 22 percent of women were alcohol related. My fellow guests would look perplexed when I said *nyet* to their breakfast offer.

The hotel contained offices on the lower floors, one of which was occupied by one of the Ukrainian mobs. As I took the elevator to my room on the eighth floor, I often shared it with a mob boss and his armed bodyguards. The about five-foot-seven-inch boss would be dressed in very expensive-looking suits. His muscular bodyguards, dressed in less expensive suits, would tower above him. When we rode together in the elevator, the following "movie" would play out in my head: the doors would open as the mob boss reached his floor, and several men with machine guns would start shooting all of us inside the elevator. It would be a vivid example of wrong time, wrong place.

One day as I was leaving the hotel, I noticed the boss getting into his armored Mercedes, with his bodyguards behind him in their Suburban. Only fifty feet from the hotel entrance, both cars screeched to a halt. The boss got out of his car as his bodyguards surrounded him with their Uzis at the ready. Simultaneously, a car going in the opposite direction also screeched to a halt. A smartly dressed man got out carrying an attaché case. He proceeded to open the case and retrieve a file of papers. He handed the boss a pen and waited for him to sign the papers. Then everyone got back into their cars and drove away. I stood motionless in the street, my heart racing.

The presence and influence of the mob in Ukraine, as in Russia, in this post-Soviet time cannot be overstated. One example was the VVIP service at the airport. One could pay a fee and go to a separate building to avoid the hassle of the crowds at the passport exit control. On one occasion the building was closed. In broad daylight there had been a mob hit over a soured business deal. The hit took place on the tarmac between the VVIP building and the stairs to board the plane. On my next flight from Kiev, the VVIP building was reopened. Life and the mob went on.

A young Ukrainian who headed our Odessa office (he had been a major in a

Soviet military intelligence unit) one day told me that an Odessa mob boss wanted to talk to me. I thought it wise to meet with him. It turned out that he wanted advice about how to make condos out of several apartment buildings the mob owned. Thinking it was "the better part of valor," I said we would assist him. Lucky for us, he never returned.

On one of my trips to Odessa I stayed at a decaying, elegant hotel facing the Black Sea. I had a suite well within the limited USAID hotel budget. It was winter and very cold and gray. I got into bed wearing thermal underwear, a sweater, and a coat, and I had three blankets on top of me. Just as I was getting warm, the phone rang. Enjoying the warmth, I delayed getting out of bed to answer the phone in the living room area of the suite. By the time I picked up, I was too late to catch the caller. I got back under the covers. Again, just as I was getting warm, the phone rang. This time I rose rapidly, cursing out loud. A female voice asked if I "would like a young woman?" I told her I only liked older women, and not to call again. As I was back under the blankets and about to fall asleep, I heard a knock at the door of the room next to mine. It was "the young woman" who had found a willing client. The women of Ukraine are famous for their beauty and, for many, their role as prostitutes throughout Western Europe as well as the former Soviet Union. Similar to room service, their services were offered openly at all the hotels I stayed at in the Ukraine.

Odessa, the third-largest city in the Ukraine, was filled with beautiful but decaying architecture. It was the home of Pushkin, who was revered in Ukraine and especially in Odessa. In his honor, the old cobblestones on the intersection where he lived have been left in place.

BEING A JEW IN UKRAINE

Odessa had a "Jew Street" that once housed the vibrant Brodsky Synagogue. Streets were named for their inhabitants, thus there also was a "Greek Street," a "Bulgarian Street," and so on. Looking out on the Black Sea from "Jew Street," I felt, for one of the few times in my life, that no matter how I viewed myself, I was always a "Jew" to certain people. As my brother would remind me, "No matter how I defined myself, to Hitler and the Soviets I would be a Jew." At its peak, soon after the Russian Revolution, more than 40 percent of Odessa's population was Jewish. World War II, the Holocaust, Soviet repression, and an exodus after the fall of Communism in the 1990s reduced the population to 3 percent.

The black water of the Black Sea that seemingly went on and on touched an emotional nerve and made me feel how trapped the people on "Jew Street" must have felt. Between the vast sea and the armies of the neighboring countries who wished do to them harm, there was no escape. In 1941, 50,000 Odessa Jews were massacred by Romanian troops.

I had a similar feeling when I visited the Babi Yar Memorial in Kiev. More than 150,000 people were killed here, Jews, Roma, Communists, and Soviet prisoners of war. The soldiers machine-gunned the prisoners and poured lye over them before the next group was brought to the site. What I saw was a very wide and deep indentation in the ground where grass had grown over the screams and bodies of the victims. In 1941, 33,771 Jews were murdered here by the Nazis (with assistance of the Ukranian fascists) in a single operation.

If my mother and father's families had not emigrated to America twenty-seven years earlier, I might have been one of the victims.

There still was a synagogue in Kiev. I asked an Austrian-Jewish colleague to join me in visiting it on the Sabbath. It would be the first time he had entered a shul. (A number of Austrian Jews celebrated Christmas rather than Hanukkah.) The original synagogue was a very large building in the center of the city. It had long ago been mostly converted to a children's theater. We walked around the first and second floors but could not find the synagogue. Finally, in the basement I spotted several men in their tallis and tefillin. They invited us in. The congregation consisted of seventy-five people who fitted into a small room. As in my youth, the men and woman sat separately. To my surprise, there were a large number of young people in the congregation. After fifteen minutes my friend and I had experienced enough and left. A smile came to my face as I remembered the deal I once made with my rabbi in preparation for my bar mitzvah—I would go on playing ball with the boys on the block instead of coming to Hebrew school to learn Hebrew and Jewish history, if I promised to study my havtorah from the recording he gave me. I kept my word, and my "reading" was a success.

A WEDDING IN ODESSA—BOOZE AND WAR

The wedding of the Ukrainian head of our office in Odessa cemented two things for me: a) the role of booze in this society, and b) the absurdity of war in almost all circumstances.

The night before the wedding, the groom hosted a big party on a German ship docked offshore (a way to avoid paying taxes). The chef was French. A new world was coming to Ukraine.

At our table was a close friend of the groom who had served with the groom as a colonel in the Soviet Army intelligence. They had figured out ways (including in Vietnam) to either kill or defeat the Americans. Now the colonel was a senior executive with Mars Bars. I repeat, a senior executive with Mars Bars! I told him I wanted to take him on a tour of the world to talk to young men about the futility of wars of ideological differences, because in the end both sides will work for Mars Bars.

The next day, the wedding party lasted a typical eight hours. The groom's father, who was younger than I and spoke no English, repeatedly shouted across the room: "Al, vodka?" To which I would respond, "Nyet." Next, he shouted, "Al, wine or Al, beer?" Again I responded, "Nyet." Finally, toward the end of the eight hours he shouted, "Al, Cognac?" I think he was trying to be hospitable to the "important guest." He could not imagine someone not drinking at a wedding. The same could happen in America, but after the second no, the American might get, "Al does not drink." For a man not to drink is unthinkable in Ukraine. Drinking is an essential form of male bonding.

Another example of male bonding was the request of a Ukrainian staff member that we buy several bottles of vodka to drink on the train from Kiev to Odessa. He wanted to bond with me, but could only do it if he was drunk. The elaborate custom of toasts at a business dinner is not really an opportunity to honor the guest, but rather an acceptable opportunity to get drunk. After one such occasion for a visiting senior USAID woman official, the manager of our Kiev office got blotto—very drunk with slurred words, staggering, aggressive behavior, and ending in a blackout that left him no memory of the night's events. He turned up the next day badly beaten in a fight he got into on his way home. At the same occasion, many of the Ukrainians who floridly toasted an important visitor privately told me how they hated her. The toasts were a complete charade. Americans also can be insincere in their toasts of a dignitary, but they normally don't use the occasion to get blotto.

TRAVEL IN UKRAINE

A word about traveling by planes and/or trains is warranted. I would not travel by plane within Ukraine during the winter. Maintenance of the aircrafts was always an issue, but especially in winter. However, it was safer to fly Ukrainian than Russian-made aircraft.

I once took a flight from Odessa to Kiev. I flew on a twenty-five-seat Russian-made jet (no choice). The inside of the plane was in miserable shape, with torn upholstery covered with tape and chairs that were broken and either didn't recline or reclined on their own accord.

As I looked out the window I saw several men in suits looking at the plane. One of them had a screwdriver in hand. I imagined them saying, "I do not give a damn, we need the money, we fly." After a thirty-minute delay, the plane took off without incident. An hour later we landed safely in Kiev. After waiting twenty minutes, the door and stairs at the tail end of the plane had neither opened nor unfolded. Finally, the pilot walked from the cockpit to the back of the plane and proceeded to kick the door open, whereupon the stairs unfolded, allowing us to exit.

The trains presented their own problems. First, they were very slow because of the track beds; a trip that should have taken three hours took thirteen hours. The train chugged along at a top speed of thirty miles an hour. Second, in winter there was no thermostat to control the heat in your compartment. You were traveling in a sauna. To survive, you had to strip down to your underwear. Third, some Ukrainians had come up with the scam of injecting a gas that put the occupants of a compartment to sleep in order to rob them of their suitcases and valuables. The perpetrators enlisted the aid of the women train employees who had the keys to each compartment. Friends I knew had their valuables stolen in this manner on a train between Moscow and St. Petersburg. I was given a tip for how to prevent this from happening: you had to buy Bix candy. This small, Japanese-made white candy came in a plastic dispenser that was the perfect size to be jammed into the inside key mechanism and prevent anyone from opening the door from the outside. The only problem to this perfect solution was when you had to go to the bathroom and leave the compartment unlocked. No choice: the hell with it. I was not robbed on my several trips to Odessa.

LVIV AND KHARKOV

Lviv is a small city in the western part of the country, near the border with Poland. In the fifteenth century, the Polish king resided there. It is still today the epicenter of Ukrainian nationalism. If you speak Russian, no one will respond.

The Market Square (Rynok Square) in the center of the old part of the city is charming, especially in the summer. The square consists of the towered city hall and forty-four renovated buildings dating from the fifteenth century, among them wonderful examples of Renaissance-style construction. Rynok is a UNESCO World Heritage Site. I would sit in a café and have a coffee and pastry in the early evening, listen to live music, and watch the water dancing from the four large statutes of Greek motive (Diana, Neptune, Amphitrite, and Adonis) in the receding light. However, in the winter when the streets turn to ice, walking turns into dangerous "ice skating" without skates. On the stairs and entrance to the city hall (where I needed to go for meetings), I frequently witnessed people crashing to earth as they tried to enter the building. I managed with great effort and care to avoid this trap.

Again, the treatment of Jews is an ever-present reality just below the surface. My Ukrainian colleagues would tell me about government jobs unavailable to Jews. In 1936, 32 percent of the population was Jewish. As in Kiev and Odessa, most were killed in the intervening years. It is ironic to learn that Lviv was the home of Sholem Aleichem, the famous Yiddish playwright and author.

Kharkov, a city of 1.5 million in the eastern part of Ukraine, was the ugly, heavily polluted industrial capital of the Ukraine. Almost 50 percent of its population were and are Russian speaking. The USAID program here was the slowest in implementation. The officials I met with clearly did not want to be there. It would be an understatement to say these former Soviet officials were not willing to modify their old bureaucratic ways and look to the future. Early on, it became clear to me that the meeting would only be perfunctory, and moving the program forward would at best be difficult. The cold eyes of the officials made me feel as if I was in an American movie with evil Soviet Union officials who were about to decide my fate.

NICE GUY CHUMP

In May of 1997, I planned to fly from Kiev for a five-day trip to Odessa and to Kharkov for the first and last time, return to Kiev for a day of work, and then catch an evening flight to London. There I would meet my wife Julie and start a vacation trip around the west of England. Before boarding the flight to Odessa, I asked my driver to safekeep a large suitcase filled with clothes for the vacation. There was no point to lugging it to Odessa and Kharkov. He would simply pick me up at the airport with the suitcase, drive me to work, and then back to the airport for the trip to London. At the time this seemed efficient and simple. Afraid not!

When I arrived back in Kiev, my driver had a startling announcement: my large suitcase had been stolen from the trunk of his car as he was in line to get gas. What followed is a tale of how "nice guys" get screwed.

His uncle, who worked in our Kiev office, and several other Ukrainian employees of PADCO asked me to swallow the loss of what amounted to $600 of clothes. They all said I could afford it better than my driver. I did not accept their argument. Yes, I could afford the loss better than he (the loss of my favorite worn leather Bombardier jacket was very upsetting). But although the amount of money involved would not break me, I was not, as they assumed, a rich man to whom the amount of money in question was of no matter. Equally important, how could he not notice that the trunk was open while he waited for gas? I never believed his story. All these years later I still believe he was part of the heist.

Nevertheless, as a compromise and to lessen the immediate financial burden on him, I agreed to have him pay $300 then and $300 in a month, on my next trip to Kiev. Since members of his family worked at our Kiev office, I thought he would not embarrass them. Wrong! They continued to think I could bear the loss of money much more easily than he, and they were in no way embarrassed by his nonpayment of the second tranche. The driver just disappeared, and that was that. When it comes to money, people in third-world countries just see it differently than we do. This is a reality, and in their place, I probably would take the same position.

DIFFERENT PERCEPTIONS

Another case of different perceptions had to do with the embezzlement of $55,000 by our office manager in Kiev. It turned out he had been slowly siphoning off funds over a yearlong period of time. When his theft first came to light it was in the $15,000 range, and I advised Washington PADCO to immediately fire him. Because this embezzlement involved USAID funds, Washington PADCO thought the Ukrainian government would assist in the recovery, and until this occurred it would be better not to fire the office manager (OM). I disagreed, but to no avail. I did not have any faith in the Ukrainian government because I knew the OM was protected by the mob. When he was drunk, he would tell me about his connections. Sadly, I was right. He accelerated his embezzling until he was finally fired. The negotiations with the OM and Ukrainian government for repayment went nowhere. PADCO and USAID were out $55,000, and even though the Ukrainian government was receiving substantial financial assistance from the US government, it felt no obligation to assist in recovering the funds.

In Ukraine, where the mob's influence was and is rampant, normal Western expectations were misplaced.

A Ukrainian version of truth reigned at a restaurant in Kiev that promised Chernobyl-free vegetables. They never explained how this was possible. On the one hand, it showed recognition of the problems that existed after the accident at Chernobyl (a fire and explosion at a nuclear fuel plant gave off tons of radioactive fallout that drifted northwest as far as Norway). On the other hand, an official map in the government offices in Kiev showed that the radiation fallout from Chernobyl stopped on the east side of Kiev and started again on the west side of the city. Miraculously, it just skipped over the city. Eat your vegetables! Be happy, don't worry! Communist logic and its distorted view of reality die hard. Of course, this phenomenon is not limited to former Communist countries.

The best part of working in the "nada land" of Ukraine was the charming sight of elderly couples dancing to live music in the large underground caverns beneath the boulevard intersections.

To keep traffic moving on the six- or eight-lane main boulevards, one had to cross the boulevard by descending and then ascending flights of stairs. In this underground world people sold all kinds of goods and performing magic and music. I close my eyes and still see the men's gray-white hair sticking out from underneath their fur hats, and the women in fur coats and heels expertly whirling around to waltz tunes as the weather above ground was below freezing. Life presents moments to smile even in the "land of brown and dank."

PART IV: JORDAN: WORK AND ADVENTURE

In 2014 my friend and former law professor, Ken Dam, recommended me to the Financial Services Volunteer Corporation (FSVC) for a short-term assignment. Ken was on the board of the FSVC and had been a deputy secretary of State and Treasury in two separate Republican administrations.

I was delighted when I was chosen as a volunteer co-chair for a five-day seminar in Amman, Jordan. It was sponsored by the State Department, and the topic was "Accessing Budgets for NGOs (non-governmental organizations)." Many countries do not provide for citizen participation in the governmental budget process. As part of its democracy program, the State Department provides assistance to NGOs in developing avenues for citizen participation in the governmental budget process.

When I was living in Indonesia nine years earlier, I visited Jordan with my client, the governor of Riau Province, Indonesia. We planned to meet with senior Jordanian officials of the Aqaba Free Trade Zone. He was coming from Yemen and I from Jakarta. This allowed me to arrive two days early, hire a car and driver to go from Amman to Aqaba, and on the way stop for a day at the more than two-thousand-year-old city of Petra, a combined man- and nature-made wonder.

Since my first visit, I had been going on to Julie about how incredible Petra was and how much I wanted her to see it. Now the universe had presented us with an opportunity to do so.

We flew into Amman where we would spend the night before proceeding the next morning by car to Petra for three days, and then on to Wadi Rum and the land of Lawrence of Arabia. Four days later we would return to Amman, and I would begin my task as co-chair of the seminar.

As we drove from the airport to our hotel in the dimming light and listened to the call to prayers from the mosques, I felt the magical feeling of this ancient city, founded in 7250 BC. Originally built on seven hills, Amman now had spread to nineteen. The hills provided an open expansiveness for the dense population. There was not the feeling of cheek-to-jowl apartment houses you find elsewhere in many less-developed countries. The dry, hot air combined with the brown hills to let you know you were in the desert.

The next morning we met for breakfast with Danyelle, the young, highly capable, and vivacious Christian Lebanese woman who ran the FSVC program in Jordan. She was a gem. She helped to ensure that the program we developed would be useful to the attendees, which meant it had to address the realities on the ground in Jordan. In addition, she acted as a liaison between the co-chairs, a Turkish professor and me.

She also kindly assisted Julie and me in putting our vacation together before work began. She organized our cars and drivers and found our guide in Petra as well as a local company for our three-day camel trek out of Wadi Rum into the desert of the Valley of the Moon. Her local connections were invaluable in getting the best and most trustworthy people. This was especially important in finding the right trekking outfit in Wadi Rum.

After breakfast she accompanied us to meet the driver to Petra in the lobby of the hotel. He was a short man in his mid-fifties with a paunch. His English was excellent. At the last minute, I asked for a change in our route to Petra. A friend had advised me to forego the quicker Kings Highway for the route that hugs the Dead Sea. (The Dead Sea is not a sea but a lake in the Negev desert.) Danyelle renegotiated the price of the trip with him, and off we went. My friend's advice turned into a great tip.

The Dead Sea, in the Jordan Rift Valley, conjures up the Bible, Genesis, and King David. It is here that the angels told Lot to take his family and leave Sodom (Gomorrah too) and not look back. His wife, as we all know, did not follow instructions and was turned into a pillar of salt. We saw the cream-colored "pillar of salt" standing alone on top of a hill that was framed by the purple and gray mountains behind it.

Aristotle wrote about the Dead Sea's healing waters, and Herod built the first health resort here. The mud around the it is highly valued for beauty products. Julie bought a few jars for her friends and herself. I tried them too but without seeing a noticeable improvement to my face.

We saw a cluster of reinforced concrete hotels built on the edge of the sea that were not very inviting to us. Instead, our driver parked the car on the side of the road, and we found a path down to a place where we could put our feet in the water and then wash them clean of salt with bottled water. Wow—Aristotle and us! The Dead Sea has 34.2 percent salinity, by far the most in the world. The salt is so prevalent that no fish swim there. The Dead Sea is also at the lowest elevation on earth.

Driving along the Jordanian road you see the hills of Israel on the far side—a visual reminder of how intertwined geography and history are between Arabs and Jews.

We left the road just north of Aqaba and headed left over the barren, brown-gray and purple mountains to Wadi Musa (Valley of Moses), the village that sprung up around Petra.

We met our young, fast-talking and knowledgeable Bedouin guide, Olga (he was given his Russian mother's first name), in the lobby of the Petra Moon Hotel. Over the next three days we would have a lot of fun with him, as both he and I loved repartee. I had chosen the hotel because it was a very short walk to Petra. A huge bonus was the helpful and sweet staff. We experienced the famous Bedouin-Arab hospitality at its best.

Even though the gates to Petra were closing in an hour and a half, we decided it was worth the daily fee to get going.

I won't give a detailed tour and explanation of this ancient Nabataean capital city. (To do so would require a pamphlet or book of its own. Many have been written.) I will talk about what particularly struck Julie and me as we walked the paths of history in this fantastic UNESCO World Heritage Site.

After paying our fee and walking past the dam, we entered the Siq (gorge). The dam helps prevent flooding in the Siq. Not many years ago tourists and guides drowned in a flash flood that ripped through the gorge. My guide on my first visit had told me he was lucky to escape the waters.

When we were a couple of hundred feet into the very narrow Siq and looked up at the walls (as high as 246 feet) of contrasting, layered red, yellow, and green-gray rocks, we were stunned. The seemingly liquid rock "flowing" down the face of the walls was breathtaking, as was the occasional bush with pink flowers growing out of bluish rock walls. I had the same sense of awe that I experienced the first time I saw them and was delighted that Julie felt the same. After walking for about seventeen minutes, we gained our first glimpse of a part of the magnificent Treasury Building—a tease, but two minutes later we stood in front of this 1320 foot-high architectural marvel carved from red sandstone. As if the crew of *Indiana Jones and the Last Crusade* (the movie that brought fame to this building) had returned for a reshoot, two camels with multicolored rugs over their saddles were stationed in front of the building. A definite "Kodak moment." The sun was going down, and it was time to leave before getting locked in.

We would walk through the Siq two more times, and my amazement was not diminished. On our second day we entered the site immediately after the gates opened, in the cool of the morning. After revisiting the Treasury, we continued walking up to the Hellenistic and Greek ruins and saw fantastic fifth- and sixth-century mosaics in the remains of a Byzantine church. Looking at the carved temples, tombs, and purple-red mountains along either side of our dirt path, I had the feeling I was in the Utah Mountains, but with incredible ancient architecture and culture as an added enchantment. Along the way Julie spotted (the eye of a potter) shards of ancient earthenware ceramics off the main path, closer to the soaring mountains. She was blown away by how finely thrown they were with perfect finger marks of the potter still visible.

We returned to the hotel for an early lunch before meeting our guide, who would drive us nine miles north to Al Beida—"Little Petra." It was here that the ancient caravans stopped to rest and resupply their water. Its location made the inhabitants rich. Again, we walked by carved temples and tombs and a preserved village from the Neolithic era. A two-hour mountain hike then took us back into Petra at the site of a spectacularly carved building called the Monastery. On our hike in this isolated landscape, we came upon a Bedouin woman with a pink silk headscarf selling mint tea to the odd tourist who came her way. People earn what they can, where they can. We had tremendous views of the Jordanian part of the Great Rift Valley that is thought to run from Mozambique to Lebanon. It was exhilarating to walk where Moses's brother is said to have tread. From the Monastery we descended the 750 steps to the floor of Petra. A young man who was a member of an Israeli tour handed me an energy bar. Maybe I looked old and tired. Counting our morning excursion, we had been walking and hiking for seven hours and were ready to return to the hotel. For fun, Julie decided to ride a horse the short distance to the exit. Julie loves horses.

She and her young Bedouin horse handler were laughing together as they galloped off on a sandy side road.

That night, Olga arranged with the chef of the Petra Moon to cook the Jordanian national dish, Mansaf ("large dish"). It consists of big chunks of lamb cooked in yoghurt with many aromatic spices, poured over rice and topped with more yoghurt and almonds. Mansaf is served with doughy flat bread and eaten with your hands. The dish was way more than the two of us could eat. We asked the chef, who came to check on how we liked the meal, to make sure that the ample, delicious remainder be shared with the staff. He was pleased by how much we genuinely loved his cooking.

We chose to eat our dinner on the rooftop restaurant of the hotel, with views of the lights of Wadi Musa and the darkening, disappearing mountain of Jabal Haroun (named for Moses's brother Aaron, who is allegedly buried there). It was wonderfully romantic.

The next morning we were supposed to hike to the top of the highest mountain in Petra for its spectacular views. However, we were both too stiff and sore for such an endeavor. Our guide quickly altered plans and hired two donkeys to take us up a different mountain where we would look down on the 8,500-seat Roman amphitheaters and the Treasury. This ride proved to be more heart-stimulating than we had bargained for. The donkeys had to negotiate numerous ancient steps that had become very slippery by the wear of time. As we ascended, Julie's donkey kept sliding and nudging mine toward the edge of the mountain path. There was no guardrail to prevent me from falling to my death many hundreds of feet below. My heart continued to pound until we stopped at the top. It was worth it as the views were stunning. The ride down was also heart-stopping because the donkeys could slip and fall at any time. I have since learned about the cruelty of many owners working with animals, but our guide was selective about who he hired. The handler did not hit the donkeys, and they were in far better shape than most of the donkeys I saw on the Monastery steps.

We returned to the hotel, said our good-byes, and met our new driver for the ride to Wadi Rum. He was a very sweet man in his sixties, but his English was not as good as our previous driver's.

Along the way we stopped for a cold drink, and he asked if we wanted to try smoking a hookah—a Turkish water pipe. We both said yes. When we entered the shop Julie inquired if the pipe would contain hashish. He nervously replied, "Don't mention that word—forbidden." We tried the pipe, but it was tobacco, not hashish. I could do without the strong taste.

As we reached the outskirts of Wadi Rum the driver asked if it was okay to pick up a child and her mother he had spotted ahead, walking on the side of the road, and give them a lift into the village. We responded, "Of course!" Community and kindness are essential parts of the Bedouin culture.

The small village of Wadi Rum is itself not picturesque, although the setting is. The endless red sand that surrounds it leads to a massive gray and red mountain border at a short distance. Our driver found the small wood and sand-constructed building with a flat roof that housed our tour company. The office of the company, Jordan Nomads, was a small room in the front with a desk and chairs. We met the young Bedouin owner, signed the necessary papers, and took a walk around the village as they prepared for our three-day camel trek. The town was gritty and had a school and many pickup trucks. Mohammed, who was in his early thirties, was one of our two guides. He was in charge of logistics (food, tent, etc.). He drove us in his truck to the outskirts of the village where we met our second guide, Saleh, and his camels. He was an older man in his early sixties, with a great smile. Saleh seemed to treat his camels well as they appeared fit, healthy (no deadly camel spiders to be seen) and relatively mild-mannered. He spoke no English.

Saleh maneuvered our camels down on their knees for us to mount. Once mounted, as the camels rose we held on to the front knob of the saddle for dear life as it felt as if we were being catapulted into space over the head of the animals. Then, with a violent jerk we were thrown against the back of the rug-covered wooden saddles that provided minimum padding. We repeated this painful process numerous times in the next three days. By the end of the journey we almost had it down.

We set off into the desert, Julie on a female camel that had recently given birth, with the nursing calf following behind and tethered to her mom, and Saleh holding the reins to both our camels. The calf's hair was lighter in color than the mother's and not as weathered and prickly. Several times a day, after we had dismounted we watched the calf suckle milk. Other times they would lie down together. And some-times, as is the case with all "kids" (animal and human), Saleh would have to go after the calf when it wandered too far from us. The camels would need to drink from a desert spring only once over our three-day journey.

Three hours later we arrived at the camp set up by Mohammed. He had staked our small blue pop-up tent into the sandy ground. Two thin mats and sleeping bags had been placed in the tent. Saleh slept outside under the stars and Mohammed in the bed of his truck. Mohammed moved our camp in his truck to new sites, brought fresh food, water, and soft drinks, and packed our next day's lunch. I loved watching him gather twigs to expertly start a fire and cook our basic dinner. When we arrived in camp, he would always provide us with hot tea in a glass.

On different days we rested near a Bedouin encampment, had tea at a tourist "café" next to Lawrence of Arabia's alleged house, and walked around the famous Rock Bridge Arch. (The latter two had too many tourists for our taste.) During our daytime treks we spotted several luxury Bedouin-type tent hotels and, in the distance, vans and SUVs jammed with tourists, all visiting the Valley of the Moon. But most of the time we were alone with Saleh and the camels in the silence of the desert. At night we especially felt the stillness and vastness of the desert under a canopy of "zillions" of stars. I continually pinched myself to make sure I was not in a dream. After a day of riding, however, pain kept me in reality. Even though we had breaks every two and a half hours, at the end of each day we thought we would never walk again.

I marveled at Lawrence of Arabia, who was able to ride for more than twenty-four hours without a break. His tolerance for pain was legendary. On one such occasion he was leading a march from Wadi Rum over this vast desert to launch a surprise attack on Aqaba. Although I loved looking toward Aqaba and remembering the dramatic moment in the movie *Lawrence of Arabia* when actor Peter O'Toole signaled the start of the march, I am no Lawrence.

The slowness of our pace allowed us to soak up the beauty of the contrasting landscape. There were massive red, ochre, and greenish-gray mesas and mountains of sandstone and granite. Pale-green clumps of bushes dotted the scene. They provided wood for the fire and food for the camels. Desert mushrooms and strange pineapple-like plants poked up out of the sand. Amazingly, there were also clusters of small red, white, and yellow spring flowers sprinkled across the desert floor. Purple thistle flowers were their sometime neighbors. The gigantic red sand dunes were fun to climb, and we spent time with a few of the over 20,000 petroglyphs to be found in this desert, some of them dating back some 12,000 years. The pictures drawn on the rocks showed camels, people, and a strange writing that reminded me of what I had seen in Egypt. Julie and I played archeologists as we exchanged theories in deciphering the meaning of what we "read" on the rock walls.

While being in the desert on camels was a spectacular experience, what made the three days unforgettable was our guide, Saleh. We communicated without being able to converse. Julie and I had never laughed as much as we did over these three days. To begin with, he gave us Arab names—Ali and Azhara (flower). As we trod along he would sing Bedouin songs. In between he would say, Ali, okay? I responded: Ali okay. He then would say, Azhara, okay? Julie responded, Azhara okay. Then Julie and I would say in unison, Saleh, okay? Then we would all laugh together. As time went on, I tried to sing his Bedouin songs with him. Again we would all laugh at my attempt. This is what is so fantastic about traveling to different places and cultures: experiencing the ties that bring us together. We all love to laugh.

Only once did we see Saleh get apprehensive. It was when we came across a herd of wild camels at a short distance. He took stern control of our camels, walking them away from the wild herd. He kept repeating the English word *fight*. We later learned he was afraid the wild camels from the herd would attack ours.

On our last morning after a very early breakfast of yoghurt, biscuits, and instant coffee, Mohammed drove us back to Wadi Rum where we met our third car and driver. Saleh had left after dinner the night before to prepare his other camels for another trek. We took the Kings Highway for the fastest way back so I would not be late for an 11:30 a.m. planning meeting with Danyelle and my co-chair, Turkish Professor H. Hakan Yilmaz.

Along the highway we were stopped at an army checkpoint. The soldiers said they were looking for terrorists who had been spotted in the area. We were quickly on our way. This is life in the Mideast and elsewhere. Another example of the political reality was the road entrance to the wonderful Kempinski—our hotel in Amman. After zigzagging down the hotel entrance road created by reinforced concrete dividers (strategically placed to slow down oncoming cars) we were met by a Jordanian army vehicle, armored and with a heavy caliber machine gun mounted on top. Julie and I were used to this kind of scene from my working in Kuwait and our living in Indonesia. These two experiences brought me very quickly out of my meditative state of mind into the present and the task that was in front of me.

At our 11:30 planning meeting we reviewed our roles and the agenda for the seminar, giving us a better understanding of the background and wants of the forty NGO attendees. During the seminar, Hakan laid out what he had learned from his hands-on experience with budgets and citizen participation in the Turkish government, and I added the relevant best practices from countries around the world that were similarly situated. (My World Bank and IMF friends had been very helpful in providing me with this information). As it turned out, I was also able to amplify what Hakan was saying by making his iffy English descriptions more understandable. We were lucky to have state-of-the-art simultaneous English/Arab/English translation at the seminar.

After about an hour and a half we were joined by the well connected, dynamic Palestinian woman who headed FSVC's local partner NGO that had sourced the attendees.

As one of the 1.9 million Palestinians in Jordan (more than half of the population), she exemplified a major political problem for Jordan. How would they be integrated into the fabric of Jordanian society? Palestinians were the majority in Amman and Zargra, the two largest cities, and 337,000 of them lived in ten official refugee camps. On the northeast border there were also camps for Syrian refugees that provided a further social-economic stress on Jordan.

The very large Palestinian population in Jordan had caused the native Bedouin population, descendants of the Hashemite Kingdom, to be a minority in their "own country." (It is complicated, as parts of Jordan were part of ancient Palestine.) There was a simmering tension between the two populations. The Bedouin minority protected their political dominance by limiting Palestinian advancement in the Jordanian civil service and army, which in turn created difficulties for a harmonious society.

The Arab Spring threatened to upend the delicate balance and the power of the king. He instituted baby-step democracy initiatives, including an advisory parliament. Fear of violence, the king's democracy initiatives, and funding from the World Bank, IMF, the United States, and other funders calmed the waters. These outside sources provided over 50 percent of the Jordanian budget. The king had his own budget, the size of which was unknown, and used it to support various projects and groups in the kingdom. Our "Accessing Budgets" seminar did not address the king's budget.

The seminar was a tiny step of support from our State Department for citizen involvement in the political budget policy decisions of the country. It was viewed as important enough for a government official, who was the director of the Budget Department, and a well-respected reformist legislator to attend.

The discussions at the seminar were lively. The participants had a wide range of sophistication and experience. The challenge for me was to include them all in the discussions. We developed a wonderful esprit de corps.

Julie joined us during our buffet luncheon breaks. The participants welcomed her warmly, and a few days before the seminar ended, as she was leaving to return to her job, she commented on how warm, hospitable, and intelligent the participants were.

After I returned home, Danyelle emailed me that based on conversations and the questionnaire filled out by the participants, the seminar was a great success. She added that it laid the framework for a second successful seminar that took place two weeks later. I was delighted and gratified. Julie and I agreed on what a phenomenal place Jordan and its people are.

PART V: NINE YEARS IN INDONESIA

I lived and worked in Indonesia for nine years. It was an astonishing and rewarding experience. Because of the length of time I spent in the country, I will tell about the four distinct periods of my stay and go into particular and unique experiences and political or social observations in separate chapters.

For more than a year I had been trying to find work, either in the San Francisco Bay Area or short-term international assignments, that would allow my wife Julie and me to continue living in Petaluma. (I previously had short-term assignments in Russia, Ukraine, Albania, and Slovakia, to name a few.) It wasn't working out! For the first time I opened up to the idea of living and working abroad. When I mentioned to Julie the possibility of a full-time assignment in Poland in late 1997, she was less than enthusiastic. She hates cold weather and understandably did not want to live through a tough Polish winter. My descriptions of working in the former Soviet Union and Eastern European countries did not help either. Soon thereafter, in early 1998, Duane Kissick, CEO of PADCO (I had worked for him in Ukraine and Albania) mentioned a possible long-term assignment in Indonesia. I responded in the negative, assuming Indonesia would be even more problematic for Julie than Poland. I broke a rule of being a lawyer and a good husband: never assume. But when he mentioned Indonesia again, rather than assuming what Julie felt ... surprise, surprise, I asked her. Julie said she wasn't opposed to the idea, and even was intrigued.

In July, Kissick called again to say he had talked with Bill Gelman, head of the USAID Regional Housing and Urban Development Office (RHUDO) in Jakarta. Apparently Gelman had heard about me from his Washington, DC, boss, Peter Kim. (Kim and I had a long friendship stemming from my time in the Carter administration.) Gelman was interested in talking to me about a long-term assignment in the Jakarta RHUDO. We set up a conference call for the next day with Gelman, and he spontaneously offered me the job of RHUDO Indonesian Liaison. My task would be to help develop public-private partnership strategies and programs for the Indonesian National Planning Agency (BAPPANAS).

On September 6, 1998, I flew off to Jakarta. Julie was not yet ready to pull up stakes. First, she wanted me to test the water. How real was this opportunity? Would it last? I would return home in October, report to her what I discovered, and then decide about our move. She would come out for two weeks in mid-January 1999 to get a feel for the place. I was excited about the possibilities and did not share her fears about the unknowns of living in a third-world country, nor her worries that the job might not last. I was never afraid of change or risk (except for heights), and was always open to a new adventure. "Think positive and watch your back" could be a motto of mine. It turned out that Julie was correct to worry about the tenure of my USAID-RHUDO consulting job, but it nevertheless was the right decision to move to Indonesia. On the financial front, I left the Bay Area $60,000 in debt and returned nine years later a millionaire. Just as importantly, Indonesia provided us with the privilege of seeing from the inside how another society worked at every level, politically, socially, and in the realm of religion. We also visited much of its breathtaking landscapes and sites. But I am getting ahead of myself.

THE BEGINNING YEARS

As the palm trees that engulf the Jakarta airport rushed up to meet my plane, all I could think was, "How fabulous!"

From my simple hotel I walked to the US embassy complex where the USAID building was housed. The fifteen-minute walk was my introduction to Jakarta:

polluted, hot, and humid, no sidewalks in most places, small shops open to the street selling everything from cigarettes to cans of motor oil. Numerous outdoor food stalls where chicken, rabbit, and goat satay was being cooked on wood fires further polluted the air. Crowds of people were walking, riding their motorbikes or bicycles, working, eating, and shopping. It was exhilarating!

The embassy, one of our largest at the time, was a sprawling complex of buildings and gardens. It was located on a large thoroughfare next to Merdeka Square, a park with an obelisk, the Indonesian National Monument of Independence, at its center. In addition to USAID, the ambassador and foreign service officials as well as Consular Services were housed in different buildings on the vast embassy grounds. I had a short introductory meeting with my new boss Bill Gelman, who had offered me the RHUDO job over our phone call. He was a pudgy man who seemed somewhat distracted at the time and turned out to be an anxious and difficult person.

Bill explained that later in the week he would introduce me to the USAID mission director and, at a regular staff meeting, to the ambassador. Next, we would have to meet the senior official in the Ministry of Foreign Affairs who approved all foreign consultants working in Indonesia. Her approval was key to starting my job. He showed me to my temporary office and told me that the next day I needed to attend an embassy security briefing.

My security briefing was standard (stay aware of your surroundings, notice what looks out of place, and register with the embassy). There was one eye-opener that proved very useful in understanding how to operate in Indonesia or any third-world country: if you are a passenger in a taxi that gets into an accident with another vehicle, don't stick around. Leave the area immediately. The crowd that will inevitably form will blame you. They will "reason" that without your being in the cab there would be no accident. The second bit of advice that was useful was to take only one specific name-brand taxi. Their drivers had been vetted. There had been a number of incidents with foreigners being driven to a quiet place and robbed.

Security at the embassy changed dramatically over the nine years I lived and worked in Indonesia. Traffic on the six-lane road in front of the embassy was reconfigured to a two-lane, one-way road, and concrete blocks were installed at the curb to prevent car bombers from having a direct run into the building complex. Bomb blast fences were installed as well. These changes slowly took place after the bombings in

Bali (October 2002 and October 2005) and at the Marriott Hotel in Jakarta (August 5, 2003 and July 17, 2009. See "Terrorism" subchapter below.) When I arrived in September 1998, there was a two-step process for entry to the embassy grounds. First you checked in with the Indonesian guards to verify you had an appointment (once I had my USAID consultant credentials, I skipped this step). Second, you went through bag and cell phone screening at an enclosed Marine guard station. The guard would again check that you had an appointment, and after verification buzzed you through, keeping your passport and cell phone. Cell phones could ignite a bomb. At that time, once you were buzzed through you had access to the entire complex. This would change. After the bombings, you had to be accompanied by someone from the office of the person you were visiting, and you could not roam the facility on your own. Even when I had meetings with the ambassador, although I could pre-arrange to bring my car onto the embassy grounds, I still had to clear three separate guarded gate checkpoints and have the undercarriage and engine checked for bombs. My driver could drop me off in front of the building where the ambassador was housed, but his secretary or a Foreign Services official had to accompany me to his office. No roaming!

Even before the increased security was in place, demonstrations in front of the embassy could cause heart palpitations. On Julie's first trip to Jakarta, after a car tour of the area around Merdeka Square, the Archeological Museum, and the presidential palace, I told her I had to go back to the embassy to get some files to work on at home. During this period you could park your car a block away from the embassy under a highway. I left her in the car with my English-speaking driver, Suparno, planning to pick up the files and be back in ten minutes. The best laid plans ... A demonstration was forming outside of the embassy when I entered, and by the time I reached my office the embassy was in lockdown. No one could enter or leave the complex. In the meantime a phalanx of riot police dressed in full battle mode was approaching our car on their way to the embassy. Julie and I were both trapped. My cell phone was at the Marine's entry guard post so I could not call our driver. Julie did not yet have an Indonesian phone. After fifteen minutes of explaining my situation I prevailed upon an Indonesian guard I knew well to let me out through a rear door of the complex. By the time I reached our car, Julie was in tears and very frightened. Welcome to Jakarta, my brave wife! She did not say, "I don't want to live here. I am leaving for the Bay Area tonight."

After the security briefing I met with the USAID Mission Director Terry

Myers. Terry was a wiry-built man with a red-tinged beard who exuded energy. He had started his job in August, one month before I did. We had many USAID friends in common. In time, we developed not only a close and solid professional relationship, but a friendship as well. Our friendship was cemented during a mandatory USAID personnel and family evacuation due to terror threats against Americans in Indonesia. These evacuations took a big toll on families. Kids' schooling was interrupted, and the uncertainty of family reunification increased the stress on parents and spouses exponentially as time passed from days to months without a decision. The USAID mission director was deemed essential to the operation of the embassy, but his family was not. Thus he stayed and they left. Because Julie was not in the country at the time, Terry and I spent many nights together for dinner or going to the movies. Our conversations became more personal, and our friendship deepened.

To support Terry, when I was no longer a USAID consultant I became the chairman of the USAID committee of the American Chamber of Commerce in Indonesia, a private sector organization. Over my years as chair, our friendship allowed us to develop a unique relationship between USAID and the private sector companies in Indonesia. This relationship would become a worldwide model.

In November 1998, I went apartment hunting with the help of a fellow USAID consultant. After looking at several apartments, I chose an apartment complex, Eksekutif Menteng, as my home base because it had been built in the middle of a kampung (a small neighborhood), unlike the sterile Hilton Hotel apartments that had been built far away from the tumult of the streets. I love the action of the streets and wanted to be part of Jakarta life. Across the street, past a large square, "wet" and flower markets were always teeming with Indonesian residents from all over Jakarta. The "wet" market had very narrow passages with fish set on ice, chicken, goat, beef, and lamb in various stages of butchery, and tons of flies swirling about. There was no refrigeration; therefore we bought our chicken, meat, and fish at an upscale market in the basement of the Hyatt Hotel complex, a five-minute drive from our apartment. Here we were introduced to the gourmet delights of salmon from Tasmania and Australis Barramundi (sea bass). In another part of the "wet" market, the orange of carrots and the green of string beans and lettuce sat next to the hairy red rambutan, the purple mangosteen, light green pomelos, and orange-yellow mangos.

In season, all the markets were saturated with the overwhelming, soured-cheese smell of the durian fruit. When you ate it, you didn't want it touching your clothes. We never got to love this favorite Indonesian fruit. The "wet" market was flanked by the food stalls with their smells and ever-present smoke wafting into the air. I loved this market from the start, but it took Julie a while to follow suit. At first I had to accompany her, but once she mastered the language and got used to the crowds (in Indonesia the crowds had a hum as there was no shouting) and the sound of the ever-present motorbikes, she would go off to shop with the anticipation of enjoying the scene. The flower market was a joy to behold with its symphony of colors. Julie was surprised to see bunches of blue hydrangeas among a sea of bouquets and potted tropical flowers such as ginger, tuberose, Plumeria and Hibiscus. She learned from the "flower ladies" that the Blue Hydrangeas grew in the mountains of Java, and we would get to see them on our trips into these mountains. Intrigued by these reminders of home, Julie regularly bought flowers of all sorts for the apartment.

One block in the opposite direction from the apartment, we discovered the antiques street. Although the time had passed when you could buy great antiques in these shops, Julie and I could spend hours looking for unusual gifts for friends or objects to decorate our apartment.

We loved going for our Sunday walk through the treelined streets admiring the fancy villas several blocks away from the Eksekutif Menteng. Julie is a birder and would take her binoculars ("bins") with her on these walks. One time we walked past the army guards and the car-blocking gate up the street where Suharto and his family stilled lived. Julie spotted some birds in the trees around Suharto's villa and trained her "bins" on them, when all of a sudden, from nowhere several soldiers came running at us screaming something in Indonesian. It turned out they simply did not want binoculars pointing at the ex-president's residence. The incident went from scary to funny the farther we walked away from the "Suharto Street." Needless to say, bird watching on that street was abandoned.

The young Indonesian front desk and gym staff at the Eksekutif Menteng were sweet and helpful (including on occasion going to the drug store for us). They made our stay there very pleasant and easy. We used to joke around with them and laugh a lot. However, the time I remember best and most clearly was joining them on the roof of the apartment building to watch Chinatown burn up. It was the second time arsonists had started fires during the November 1998 riots. We watched in silence and shock. The next week I went to Chinatown and saw the devastation of burned-out businesses and buildings. The effect of this bigotry is etched in my memory forever, as is the fear that many Chinese-Indonesians I knew still felt months after the riots. Many Indonesians justified the torching of Chinatown by saying the Dutch and Suharto favored the Chinese and made them rich. However, the majority of businesses and buildings belonged to hard-working, middle-class Chinese-Indonesians. The people I talked with did not get that based on their logic, they should have burned down buildings and businesses belonging to the Dutch and the Suharto clan and its backers. Bigotry and reason are not handmaidens. But bigotry and terrorism are.

TERRORISM

I had just returned from the San Francisco Bay Area and was sitting at my desk at Ernst & Young, on the thirty-second floor of the Stock Exchange building in Jakarta, when my office shook from what felt like a truck falling on the ceiling. The high-tech announcement system blared out that this was an emergency, not a test, and we should descend to the street using the stairs and not the elevators. I did not know what had happened, but after a few minutes, I obeyed the repeated warning and started down the staircase to the street. The stairwell was filled with young Indonesians in a high state of anxiety. As I went down I kept repeating in a loud but calm voice, "Stay calm, don't run, don't push." Indonesia is the source of the phrase "running amok." Whatever the cause of our evacuation, being trampled in a stampede was a real possibility.

It turned out that a large bomb had exploded in the parking area of the basement. It caused severe damage and killed a number of drivers who used to congregate in the waiting area there. This was my first encounter with terrorism. When I reached the exit, many of the Indonesians who worked in the Stock Exchange building were talking on their cell phones a few feet from the structure, heedless of the distinct possibility that another bomb could detonate. The cell phone service was inundated, and I could not get through to my driver, Suparno, who usually waited in the place where the bomb had gone off.

With great joy and relief I spotted Suparno twenty minutes later outside. I gave him a big hug. It turned out that he had just returned to the building. I had asked him to take my luggage from my trip to my apartment and hang up my suit and dress trousers. This request may have saved his life. The world moves in mysterious ways.

I was in the United States when the first Bali bombings took place, in 2002. I returned to our house in Bali a week later and drove one hour to visit the bombsite. I was stunned by the size and ferocity of the bomb. It had opened an enormous hole in the ground, reminding me of pictures I had seen from World War II and the damage done by bombs dropped from airplanes. That a second bomb was detonated aimed at people who had escaped or were coming to the site to help was particularly depressing. I just sat down on the side of the road and stared at the craters. Could I emotionally understand the mentality of the terrorists who caused so much death and destruction? I could not come close! Intellectually I could grasp how someone could commit this act, but I could not understand how he or she thought it furthered his or her goal. History shows that societies unite against terrorism (even at the cost of freedom). As is often the case, most of the people killed or injured by the Bali and Stock Exchange building bombings were Indonesian-Muslim taxi and private-car drivers.

The August 5, 2003 and July 17, 2009 bombings in Jakarta ironically took place at the Marriott Hotel—a US embassy certified "safe" hotel.

With its restaurants, the Marriott was a meeting place for foreigners. I frequently had lunch or breakfast meetings there. It had very large, curved glass windows that allowed for views of the street scene and the high-rise buildings of Jakarta. There was a fabulous buffet with jumbo prawns, smoked salmon, roast beef, and numerous salads among the many offerings. In addition, a separate dessert buffet was also spectacular. You could imagine being in any upscale Western city. The main restaurant's entrance and top half was situated directly next to a curved car entranceway, while the bottom half, down five steps, was adjacent to the street. Suparno and I were on our way to the airport when we heard an explosion. "Bomb," we said in unison. It turned out to be the Marriott. My good friend Jim Castle and his wife were having lunch there when the bomb exploded. Luckily, their table was situated behind the mammoth columns that held up the ceiling, hundreds of feet away from the glass windows. The columns absorbed much of the blast. My friends survived with minor cuts. Others were not so lucky and were killed or severely injured.

After the bombings, life in Jakarta changed. The entrances to hotels and office buildings were reconfigured with cement barriers so that cars had to zigzag at a very slow pace toward the entrance. Cement barriers were also set up to provide at least a hundred-foot barrier between windows and the street. Army personnel with heavy caliber weapons were on duty at the driveway where your car stopped in front of doors to the building. Security staff conducted bomb searches under the carriage and in the engine area of car. Metal detectors were placed at the entrances, and handbags and briefcases were opened and hand searched.

In retrospect, what was weird about these drastic changes was how quickly they became an accepted and normal part of our life in Jakarta. By now, these drastic changes are the new normal at most airports in the world.

Although we had left Indonesia, I was back in Jakarta in July 2009, working on my ferry project for Riau Islands Province, when the second Marriott bomb went off. The bomb was placed in a small breakfast room where one of the regular business seminars sponsored by my friend Jim Castle's company was taking place. The terrorist had taken a room the night before, and the bomb material had been smuggled to his room by a florist. The terrorist panicked and did not place the bomb deeply inside the room. This lessened the impact dramatically and determined whether you died, were injured, or escaped unharmed.

A number of my friends were hurt in this bombing. Visiting them in the hospital changed how I reacted to terrorist acts. Previously, I had only paid attention to the number of the dead and had not given much thought to the injured. To me they had simply survived. I never considered how their injuries might cause them endless pain and change their lives.

The day after the bombing, as I walked past a number of patients in their beds in the crowed hallway, I thought my friends needed to get to Singapore for medical treatment ASAP, given the poor quality and haphazard nature of medical care in Indonesia. When I entered the room of my Canadian friend Andy Cobham, he was chatting with the nurses and his Indonesian wife, who was sitting in a chair a few feet from the bottom of the bed. He gave me a big hello. It turned out the screws that had been packed into the bomb were imbedded in his left ankle and lower leg. He was mostly concerned that his injury would affect his ability to play golf. Funny what we worry about after a traumatic injury.

While I was visiting Andy the next day, a friend of his who had also been injured in the bombing and had just been discharged from the hospital stopped by to see how he was doing. He said with a smile, "I brought you these bolts, which they took from my leg. I think they go perfectly with your screws." Tough men's humor!

Another friend had less to laugh about. He had been medevaced to Singapore and then on to the US. His time in Indonesia was over. He had severe lung/breathing issues brought on by the blast. I was shocked and saddened to hear the news. This ex-Green Beret was famous for rediscovering the Grasberg mine in Papua in the 1960s, while hanging from a helicopter. He surely could not be brought down by anything, I thought. I was upset as well to hear that Jim Castle's young Dutch assistant had lost both his legs to the bomb. In a flash his life had changed. He had a long road to travel before he could get around again on his own.

After four days we finally convinced Andy to go to Singapore for more treatment. It turned out it was the right move. The doctors in Jakarta had missed several screws that were still embedded in his ankle.

It was lucky that Jim Castle, who had no outward injuries and felt "just fine," also went to Singapore for further examination. Jim had been at the head of the table, farthest from the bomb. The doctors there discovered several blood clots caused by the blast. He suffered severe guilt that his assistant and many of his friends were not as lucky as he.

It turned out that after treatment in Singapore and physical therapy, Andy was able to play golf again, albeit in discomfort and sometimes pain.

I now always pay equal attention to the injured and the dead, and I remember to be grateful that I walked away from the Jakarta Stock Exchange bombing unscathed.

BUILDING A HOME ON BALI

In early 2001 I was sitting in my Ernst & Young office on the thirty-second floor of the Jakarta Stock Exchange Building, when two of my partners and an associate walked in and asked if I was interested in buying land in Bali. I immediately responded, "Yes!" I had been to the island many times in the past few years and had fallen in love with the landscape, people, ceremonies, and magic of the island. My wife Julie had spent three- and six-month interludes in Indonesia to see if she would be comfortable living there. During these visits we had taken repeated trips to Bali, and I knew she felt the same way I did.

I had not thought of buying land on Bali, but I jumped at the opportunity.

Don't we all want a piece of paradise, whether it is Bali or Tuscany? On the practical side, I told myself, "If things don't work out, we can always sell the land."

As I had some free time on the weekends (Julie had not yet moved to Indonesia), I would join our associate, Indra, in scoping out possible properties. A friend of Indra's, who worked for a Balinese architect, would source the properties for me to check out.

Over the next month we visited many properties until we found "the one." It was a twenty-minute drive from Ubud (the cultural capital of Bali), up the Payangan mountain road. You had to pass through the town of Payangan, turn left, descend into "jungle," then cross a river and drive up the other side of the ravine to just outside the village of Susut. The land was 1.8 hectares (4.45 acres) of stunning terraced rice fields and views of the neighboring mountains. I had found quintessential Bali. There were no other foreigners around Susut. I met with the owner and told him we were very interested in buying his land and that my partners, Jos and Simon, would visit him the next weekend.

Jos and Simon saw the land, agreed that this was it, and successfully took over the negotiations with the owner. I called Julie in Petaluma, California, and told her she now owned a piece of paradise.

Julie and I still laugh about her look when she descended into the "jungle" for the first time. It was a look of "What has he gotten us into?" As it turned out, I had "gotten us into" a great thing. As a lover of nature she very quickly was at one with this enchanting place of terraced rice fields, mountains, colorful ceremonies, and the warmth of the villagers. While visiting the house on weekends (my work had me traveling the world or staying in Jakarta during the work week while Julie lived in Bali full time), I sometimes went alone for a walk up our mountain road and was met by female villagers all wanting to know, "Where is Ibu?" Ibu is a respectful name in Indonesian meaning mother or female of high standing. I was Bapak (father or sir). After living in the Bali house for a few years, Julie said she did not know if she would have been able to survive apartment living in Jakarta. Although she got to love the cultural richness of the city, to be happy she needed to touch the earth.

Buying land in Bali is a tricky enterprise for foreigners. Since you cannot legally own title under your own name, you are dependent on others and a legal system that is stacked against you (either due to corruption or because you are not

Indonesian). You can buy the land using an Indonesian nominee or by forming an investment structure. After consultation with a number of my Indonesian lawyer friends, I realized that the more I tried to protect myself in legal documents, the more it would appear that a foreigner was illegally owning the land, in what American lawyers would call fee simple. Although I incorporated some of their protection advice in the legal documents, as a lawyer I knew in the end I was totally dependent on the honesty of my nominee, my E&Y partner Jos. I had worked closely and socialized with him over a two-year period. He was the reason I was at E&Y. He had been the COO at the Jakarta Initiative where I worked under him. When he left for E&Y he asked me to join him there. My trust panned out! Over the time we were in Indonesia I heard numerous stories of betrayals. One horror story exemplified that you needed to proceed with eyes wide open. An American tourist was hooked up with a landowner by her driver, and although she had only known him for two weeks, she used the driver as her nominee to buy the land. His Balinese sweetness and charm overcame prudent caution. After she returned to Bali a few months later, she found her driver living in a makeshift house on the land. When she protested he threatened to call the police and have her jailed. She had no legal recourse. To go to court would have proved costly and futile. She had no document showing he was her nominee. Her infatuation with Bali and her driver left her out $20,000.

The next steps were to find an architect and contractor. I interviewed two architects. One was an American and the other was Balinese—the man for whom Indra's friend worked. It was no contest. The American was distrustful of the Balinese, grandiose and very expensive. We did not want an American house design dropped onto a rice field in Bali. We also did not want a house version of a five-star hotel. The Balinese architect, Ketut Siandana, had a spiritual side that was simpatico to mine. We talked about the spiritual teacher Thich Nhat Hanh, meditation, and the parables of the Tao. After visiting several of his projects, I saw how his spiritual side informed his aesthetic of relating to the earth. Although some of his projects were fancier than we wanted, they still had elements that were "at one with the rice fields." It turned out that hiring a Balinese would be very helpful in getting necessary governmental approvals.

After agreeing to contract terms with Ketut, I asked him to recommend and arrange meetings with three prospective contractors. I also requested comparative bids on several construction materials and fixtures. Two of the contracts had slick brochures and a well-developed sales pitch. The third, Cayadi, a high caste Balinese, had neither. He was a tall, thin man with a regal demeanor who was straightforward, sincere, experienced, and who had worked in the past with Ketut. My gut told me he was honest and could be trusted. Moreover, it turned out that the bids on building supplies were not for the same items. It was a case of comparing the cost of apples and oranges, so I was left only with my intuition as a guide, and I never regretted my choice. Cayadi and his wife became friends. He went far beyond the usual services of a contractor. He took care of us. Cayadi's high caste gave him instant status with the villagers. He knew the local customs that helped ensure a smooth working relationship with the village elders. I watched him negotiate fees for many items, starting with the right to build, in a soft and calm voice. He hired many villagers for the construction phase, to ensure cooperation. Laba, our closest neighbor, would head up the staff. We also hired a gardener and an assistant gardener, a full-time driver and two night guards. This was our way of establishing good relations with the village. We were at first annoyed and then laughed about paying the guards to sleep in a room we built for them under the main house. Cayadi, with his soft and calm manner, was also vital in getting prompt assistance and approvals from other government units (such as water and electricity).

Cayadi's manner, status, and knowledge of the ways of Bali helped us avoid the pitfalls that had befallen other friends in the construction of their homes. One friend had his entrance road blocked and construction halted for three months until he succumbed to the additional "taxes" demanded by the villagers. I would add that because we were the first foreigners to build in the Susut area, the villagers still had the sweetness of rural Bali folks and had not yet been corrupted by viewing foreigners as "cash cows." We avoided the outrageous fees demanded by villagers that our friends had been charged at the beginning of construction and again once the house was built. In a few instances, there had been threats of burning the house down. This is the dark side of "spiritual Bali." I should note that these cases normally involved non-Balinese architects and contractors. As is the case anywhere, living in Bali is different from visiting as a tourist.

It took a while for Ketut to grasp that we did not want the typical over-the-top Westerners' house that to us looked like an upscale Villa Hotel. I had told him on several occasions that we wanted simple "Bali Rural." But it was not until Julie reviewed the detailed drawings and said no to this and yes to that that he finally understood what we were after. For example, Julie conveyed that we could run the ten seconds it would take to go from the main house to our separately housed bedroom; we did not need a covered walkway. If it was really pouring, we could use an umbrella. We wanted to be at one with nature. This would include a frog symphony at night, an occasional centipede and snake, but luckily few mosquitoes (we were too high in elevation). When there was a major rainstorm with high winds, the thunder was so loud it rattled your teeth, and the lightening was so close that we became apprehensive. On these occasions (four times a year) we had to use a squeegee to get rid of the accumulated water in the open-air dining and living spaces. The bamboo shades provided no protection as they just blew open in the wind.

We chose thatched grass (alang-alang) roofs to capture the essence of Bali, even though we knew they would have to be replaced every five to seven years. It turned out that getting good quality alang-alang was not a simple matter. Bali had used up its supply of quality alang-alang, and the replacement crops were of a lesser quality. But Ketut and Cayadi were able to source it from the neighboring island of Lombok. They were also able to find top-grade coconut and hardwoods at unextravagant prices. The former were used as support posts in the main house. We used locally made toilets and fixtures, as the cost of imports from Australia was exorbitant.

The compound had three separate buildings: the main house, our bedroom house, and Julie's studio. All three buildings appeared to the eye as different-size traditional Bali houses. There was a plunge pool next to our bedroom and, near the bottom of the property, a much larger pool for swimming. Julie used this pool most days, and it was fun to sit together in the plunge pool and watch the sunset. The main structure was based on the Balinese pavilion (bale) structure with two pyramidal roofs and an open-air living and dining space. I had Ketut visit our friend Frank Morgan's "Wantilan Lama," an old-style-house in Sanur, to give him a sense of what we wanted. Our main structure had a large guest bedroom, a kitchen, and a wooden spiral staircase that led to an office/library and makeshift sleeping area (great for guests with teenage kids). The bedrooms had outdoor showers and bathtubs. We wouldn't do the latter again because it was impossible to keep the tubs clean from falling leaves and flowers.

We only air-conditioned three rooms: the two bedrooms and the upstairs office/ library (to preserve documents). It turned out we only used ours a couple of days during the year as the ceiling fan worked just fine. At seven hundred feet of elevation, it usually was not so hot. In fact, many nights in the winter we wore sweaters. The floors of the main structure and our bedroom were made of color-infused aggregate concrete in terracotta and pale jade.

The main structure bordered a terraced rice field on one side and looked out across the valley to the mountains from another.

On the same level, twenty feet away from the main house, our separate bedroom house had its own indoor and outdoor shower and johns. Continuing down rock stairs on the way to the lower pool, a third structure operated as Julie's art studio and, if needed, a third bedroom. It also had its own bathroom facility.

We entered the property from the parking area through a carved double door, painted turquoise, gold, and green, that was set in a wide column of gray aggregate concrete and yellow sandstone. Along the perimeter of the house, next to the rice field, we built a symbolic three-foot wall. The wall was not designed to keep people out, but rather to demarcate our land and let villagers know it was private. If people wanted to enter our compound to steal our belongings, we knew no wall would be a guarantee against it. Protecting our home on all sides with high walls would have felt needlessly unfriendly to the villagers. I would have made a different decision if we were in Sanur or any of the other tourist areas. We allowed the villagers to farm the top part of the land for vegetables and bananas. We felt that good, warm relations were key, and this approach worked. We landscaped the front with trees and flowering bushes to give us privacy.

Upon entering the compound you walked on large concrete squares set in a lotus pond and down rock stairs to the main house and our bedroom house on the right. There were flowering plants of red, yellow, and pink on either side of the path. Julie had designed the landscaping of plants and trees (among them, Hibiscus and especially Plumeria that we so loved in Hawaii) with the Balinese owner of a nursery who replaced any items he supplied if they did not take. Some of the flowering plants did not. We replanted, and they still did not take. It turned out these plants would have thrived close to the ocean but not at our seven-hundred-foot elevation. Another landscaping friend of our architect explained this dilemma and helped Julie pick plants that would flourish in our garden. Between the main house and the plunge

177

pool we planted several banana trees. Every Bronx boy ought to own banana trees! They tasted fantastic and spoiled us forever for their store-bought cousins.

After we signed off on the drawings, the process of building commenced. First, we had to wait a month for the terraced ground, which were former rice fields, to dry out. Then the foundation work started. As Julie was back in California during this period, I made a point of flying from Jakarta to visit the site a number of times. On my first visit I was blown away by the number of people working on the foundations for the houses, building the rock staircases, and redoing the terracing of the different levels. Women were carrying the bricks that would form the inner walls of each structure, in baskets on their heads. It could have been the construction of the Pyramids. In California, a maximum of eight workers would usually build a house; I was looking at close to fifty. Luckily for us, the cost of buying land and of construction in Bali was about 10 percent of what you would have to pay in California.

The crew first prepared very long, reinforced concrete columns to be sunk deep into the earth. The foundations of our three structures would then sit on these pillars. Both Ketut and Cayadi made a point of sinking the columns deeper than normal because the structures were being built on formerly wet rice fields. During this time I first realized that our compound was being terraced down from a parking area toward the jungle that filled the bottom of our land. When he visited us, my architect brother marveled at the construction techniques. After the foundations were finished and construction of the three buildings started, Julie, who had returned from California, moved into our friend Frank Morgan's "Wantilan Lama" house in Sanur in order to visit the site every day. Julie spoke rudimentary Indonesian, and Cayadi was available to translate when needed. I would join her on weekends when I was not out of the country on business. This was one of Frank's many gracious acts to assist us. On her ninety-minute round trips to the site she would stop along the way to look at furniture and other items for the house. Her artistic eye created a magical interior. She would not be rushed into buying but instead took her time to find "just the right things."

When I visited the site during this time, I marveled at the workmanship of the artisans as they squatted on the floor of the main structure carving and painting the doors to the bedrooms and the entrance to the compound. The bedroom's double doors contained intricate patterned carvings that conjured up nature. The carvings were painted gold (a favorite Balinese color), and the remainder of door was painted in shades of blue, green, and deep mauves. We used the same artisans to build two extra-large hardwood canopy beds for ourselves and the guest bedroom. The beds were so large and heavy they were built directly inside each bedroom.

Unlike in America, revisions to the construction plans did not require costly change orders. Cayadi made the necessary alterations without hesitation and with a smile. Two examples are worth noting. The first had to do with our bedroom's outdoor shower. The showerhead was affixed to a ten-foot-tall by three-foot-wide freestanding column. We had requested an opening in the column to let us gaze at the mountains in the distance as we showered. The workers forgot our request and built a solid column. Cayadi fixed the mistake right away, and we got our viewing space. The other example was a massive, ornate Balinese gargoyle relief that was constructed over the door to the guest bedroom. When Julie first saw it, she let out a deep sigh. Without hesitation, the relief was removed at no additional cost.

The construction of our home was completed in an amazing five months. In the US it would have taken a year or more. In Bali, before you can take up residence in your newly built home, a *melaspas* ceremony must be held. No Balinese would enter a new home without it. The ceremony assures the balance and spiritual harmony that will make your house safe.

Once again, acting beyond the scope of our contract, Cayadi took care of the matter and organized the ceremony. Given his status as high cast, he secured a high priest from Denpasar to perform a ceremony that duly impressed the villagers.

For four days, the house was readied. Every structure's roof and major posts were decorated with black and white squares of fabric called *poleng*. The bold pattern symbolizes a major component of the Balinese system of belief. Out of unity comes duality—black and white, positive and negative, gods and goddesses, life and death. It is essential to maintain a proper balance between these opposing forces to maintain spiritual harmony. Woven palm leaf decorations (*penjor*) were placed everywhere, including two very high festivity poles at the entrance to the compound. Also at the entrance, tables were built for drinks and food for our expat guests and the whole village of approximately two hundred. Our little bamboo bale (a gazebo-type open-air platform with four posts and a grass roof) in the parking area, built as a comfortable waiting place for our guests' drivers, was used as the perfect staging area for the dancers. A place for the sixty-man gamelan "orchestra" (including many from our village) with their intricately carved gold and red instruments was set up next to it, and a carpet was laid for the dancers to perform.

A large bale was constructed in front of the entrance to the compound for what turned out to be a mammoth amount of offerings. There were little squares of woven banana leaves holding flowers, grains of rice and complex portions of fruit, cakes, and roast chicken for the gods. Offerings were also placed at the doorways of the three buildings, the plunge pool, and the four corners of our property. We employed the wife, grandmother, and sister of our head of staff to craft most of these offerings, which took them many hours to prepare. The grandmother would continue to make and place daily offerings around the compound all the time we lived in the house. Women from the village also brought their own offerings that were placed on the bale in front of the doors to our complex.

The villagers listened to the gamelan and consumed the drink and food we had provided, while Julie and I changed into proper traditional Balinese attire. She wore a lace blouse (*kebaya*), a sarong and a scarf-sash (*selendang*) around her waist. I wore the traditional Bali hat (*udeng*), a sarong with a scarf-sash around my waist, and a dark-blue short-sleeve shirt. Laba, our head of staff, would always check that we were put together properly. This was a must do in order to respectfully greet the gods.

Julie and I conducted house tours for friends (including one of my partners and his wife) accompanied by the perfume of incense and the high priest's soft chanting, punctuated by bell ringing. Because it was the time of a full moon and therefore an auspicious day for ceremonies, the priest had a full schedule and had to get on with it. Ketut told us when it was time for our part in the ceremony. We knelt before the priest who held a stick of incense in one hand while he sprinkled us with holy water from the other. For each prayer we took a flower from an offering tray and held it clasped in our hands above our heads, Balinese style. Our architect, Ketut, was seated next to us and explained some of what was going on. Both Julie and I offered our own prayers for life in our new home. Before long, and after another ritual of walking around a mound of offerings three times, the ceremony was over.

It was time for us to join our guests in the parking lot. We arrived to the sounds of laughter and the *topeng* performance that was a favorite of the villagers, especially the children. Topeng means mask, and the performance is a sort of play dealing with Balinese history and current events. It is danced by two or three men who are constantly changing masks with the appearance of each new character. There was so much genuine pleasure and rapt attention to the performance that it was hard to believe the villagers had seen it many times before. Earlier, we had watched the young *legong* dancers in their richly colored costumes of gold and magenta leaving Julie's studio building and walking through the garden to perform on the makeshift stage. Their rhythmic sequence of brisk, tense movements with their necks snapping from side to side and eyes flashing was spellbinding.

After eating a late lunch and chatting with our guests, a long and special day drew to a close. We were now alone in our amazing home, which we named Villa Sorga (Balinese for Paradise). One adventure had come to a close; but living in our new home in Bali would be a whole new one.

RELIGION

Religion is woven into every fabric of Indonesian life, both public and private. Unlike in the United States of America, there is no separation of mosque, temple, and state. Every government conference, seminar, or large meeting starts with a prayer. There is no provision in Indonesia for nonreligious civil marriages, and to get married both parties must be of the same religion. Every day at five in the morning, the speakers from the mosques blast the call to prayers. Muslims make up 88 percent of the population, with Christians at 10 percent and Hindus on Bali accounting for 2 percent. While the Australians I worked with at Ernst & Young constantly griped about being awakened by the sound, I liked the rhythm and comfort of the calls. At 11:30 a.m. each workday and in the late afternoon I would watch the staff, with a prayer rug under one arm, go off to pray in rooms provided for this function in the office building. Water for the ritual cleansing before prayer would also be provided.

The family and community aspects of practicing Islam are especially highlighted during Ramadan (the fasting month) and the holiday of Idul Fitri that celebrates the end of Ramadan. Unlike the one-day Jewish holiday of Yom Kipper, Muslims fast for a whole month from sunrise to sunset without food or water. Each evening of Ramadan, the fast is broken with friends and families. All the major hotels in Jakarta have a daily fast-ending buffet. During Idul Fitri, senior government officials (meaning governors and ministers) open their official government residences to the public to meet their constituents from all walks of life and share food with them. It is important for foreigners to remember not to invite officials for a business lunch during this period.

As the country with the largest population of Muslims in the world, the majority of Indonesians practice a tolerant version of Islam, but 10 percent practice an extreme version and 2 percent are violent extremists. These 2 percent, with assistance from outside forces, were responsible for the deadly bombings in Bali and Jakarta discussed earlier. To keep the peace and avoid confrontation with extremists, the Province of Aceh has instituted strict Sharia law. I witnessed how the delicate balance between Christians and Muslims could be manipulated for political purposes with violent consequences. During Christmastime in Jakarta and elsewhere, the army was out in force to protect churches and practitioners from the violent threats of Muslim extremists. After the bombings in Bali, the Hindu clergy joined with local government to hold many peaceful religious ceremonies to cleanse the atmosphere from any negative spiritual forces that may have led to the bombings. Particular attention was paid to Balinese youth who threatened a violent response against Muslims they thought had caused the bombings. The joining together of religious, governmental, and community leaders in Bali, all preaching a spiritual message of cleansing and love, prevented further violence.

My friend Ali Alitas, a former minister of foreign affairs, helped me understand the reality of what was behind religious or political unrest. He was a person viewed with respect by the international diplomatic community—he might have been the Secretary-General of the UN if it weren't for the Indonesian military's use of violence against the citizens of East Timor. He told me to "follow the money," not the words of politicians. Religious unrest, nationalism, and political positions were usually about which segment of the elite would get the financial spoils.

I remembered his words when I was on a plane to Ambon to meet with the governor of the province. Seated in front of me was the national head of police. His deputy was seated next to me. He explained that they were going to Ambon to preside over a memorial ceremony for two national police who were killed in a battle over a successful robbery of an "armory" on the far side of the island (I would go there the next day to inspect agricultural operations that might attract foreign investment).

These killings were a continuing aftermath of the violence that had gripped the island earlier, after the fall of Suharto. The governor's assistant told me the violence was far worse than when the Dutch ruled the island. Ambon is famous for nutmeg. In the eighteenth, nineteenth, and early twentieth centuries, nutmeg was more valuable in Europe than gold. The Dutch traded New York to the English for control over Ambon. For centuries they ruled the island with an iron fist, and anyone caught with nutmeg seed was immediately put to death. This brutality returned in force when the Dutch tried to reclaim Ambon after World War II.

As I traveled around the island I saw evidence of the assistant's startling assessment. For centuries, Christians and Muslims had lived peacefully together. Now, I could see a burned-out church on the same block as a burned-out mosque. Whole neighborhoods of Muslims and Christians were gone, burned to the ground. The proximity of the two enraged populations made the destruction complete. By the time I visited Ambon, 3,000 people had been killed. The media reported the violence as simply Christian versus Muslim, but if you dug deeper and went behind the curtain of the Shadow Play, Ali Alitas's advice to "follow the money" was edifying.

The governor's assistant and others confirmed that the violence did not start as a religious war on its own accord. After the fall of Suharto, many of his closest supporters in business, government, and the army wanted to ferment unrest and chaos so the population would call for a strong hand and return them to power. Behind the Shadow Play curtain, extremist Muslims from Java were funded to travel to Ambon and cause unrest. General Wiranto (the head of the army) and other senior officials publicly admitted that outside provocateurs caused the initial outbreak of violence. The army and the police (who were accused of favoring the Christians) were pitted against each other. The hotel where I stayed bore the machine gun holes of a fight between the two factions. The Dutch ambassador who had been staying at the hotel luckily escaped injury.

A few deaths quickly exploded into religious warfare. When their children and family are killed in large numbers, people forget the origins of the violence and it takes on a life of its own. Luckily, the major Muslim organizations (Nahdlatul Ulam and Muhammadiyah) and the Catholic and Protestant leaders preached tolerance and nonviolence. President Gus Dur, who also preached calm, did send several thousand troops to Ambon. But most importantly, he refused to declare martial law, understanding the importance of civilian control to the burgeoning democracy.

The Suharto supporters and the army tried to regain power by igniting religious chaos in Ambon in hopes it would spread to two-thirds of the Indonesian people who live on Java and Sumatra, and that the population would call for their reinstatement to power to restore order. But the use of payments to Muslim extremists, politicians, and the "rent a crowd" poor (given the poverty in Indonesia it was easy to pay to have a group demonstrate for any cause) proved unsuccessful. The Indonesian people who lived on Java and Sumatra did not take the bait.

Many people have asked me, "How was it for a Jewish boy to live in an overwhelmingly Muslim country?" Although I did not wear a Star of David on my chest, I never felt I had to deny my origins. In my dealings with a cross section of Indonesians I was not made to feel uncomfortable because of my heritage nor did I hear anti-Semitic jokes or conversation. But to be clear eyed—there must be a reason that most of the Indonesian Jewish population had shrunk to almost nothing. The only surviving Indonesian Jewish community was in Surabaya. It had enough men to form a *minyan* (ten bar mitzvahed men necessary to hold a religious service) but the minyan disappeared in my first year in Indonesia. The expat community in Jakarta would utilize the services of the Surabaya rabbi for the high holiday services. Thereafter, they brought in a rabbi from the US for a few years until it proved too expensive.

There were no formal ties between Israel and Indonesia, and they did not have a local embassy. However, quiet trade and security contacts were ongoing. Only single-entry group tourism and business visas were issued. Large segments of the population were very unhappy about Israel's treatment of the Palestinians, and they could easily be manipulated for political purposes. Although there were a number of anti-US and Israeli demonstrations in front of the US embassy, I witnessed no anti-Semitic behavior toward expat Jews.

Indeed, a Brooklyn Jewish man I knew well became very rich while living and doing business in Indonesia. He represented companies such as Monsanto in their quest for government approvals. A friend who had both Israeli and British passports ran the Indonesian office of a large Israeli agricultural company under a British registry. He was a consultant to General Wiranto in his palm oil business. General Wiranto was aware my friend was an Israeli working for an Israeli company. As I said, quiet trade and business with Jews and Israelis was permissible.

An incident after the devastation of the tsunami that hit Aceh Province demonstrates how this kind of "quiet business" works. Israel had received permission from the top Indonesian military brass to send a planeload of medical supplies to assist in the recovery effort. The large garrison of Indonesian military personnel who were stationed on Aceh was severely impacted. Many thousands and their families lost their homes and were killed or injured. The military never released exact numbers because of the desire to keep the size of the military presence on the island secret. The plane was to land in Batam (because of its long runways and proximity to Aceh). As the local official overseeing the operation, Governor Ismeth Abdullah (to whom I was a senior advisor) was informed of the flight. The plane had no identifying markings. It was "flying under the radar," and as it approached Batam the Israeli military pilot radioed the tower for permission to land. The tower requested that he identify himself. He replied that the chief of the Armed Forces had okayed his landing and the tower should contact him immediately. Acting as an intermediary, Ismeth confirmed to the tower that the plane had been given permission to land. The plane did so and was quickly unloaded. The medical equipment was delivered to Aceh by the Indonesian military. The next morning there was a short article in the Batam newspaper claiming an Israeli airplane had landed there. The governor and the military downplayed the story, and there were no political repercussions. As Ismeth said to me, "Neither religion nor politics should affect humanitarian assistance." It did not hurt that the medical supplies went to assist the military.

The practice of the Hindu religion in Bali also permeates daily life, from the making and placing of offerings around your property (See "Building a House on Bali") to the ever-present temple celebrations and funerals. Most religious functions are community-wide. Our driver told us he could not drive us on certain afternoons because he had to help the other men from his village in cooking a meal for a ceremony or participate in the washing of a dead body. Julie and I joined in the home viewing of a dead person as an act of respect to his family. We never lost our sense of awe and wonder watching the colorful processions of the ladies of our village or other villages with offerings piled high on their heads. From a young age, girls are taught to strengthen their neck muscles so they can carry these offerings great distances to temple ceremonies.

When we attended ceremonies in our village of Susut and elsewhere, Laba, our head staff man, would always make sure we were dressed properly, especially wearing the required sash. At these ceremonies the villagers would always respectfully greet Ibu Julie and Bapak Al (mother and father). Unlike in the churches and cathedrals of Christianity, the temple ceremonies on Bali were relaxed affairs with children and dogs running around.

The celebration of Nyepi (Day of Silence) epitomizes the Balinese devotion to their religion. Nyepi is the Hindu New Year on the Balinese calendar. On the day before the New Year there is great excitement everywhere on Bali. People have finished building their Ogoh-Ogoh, twenty-five- and thirty-foot-tall demonic sculptures made from chicken wire covered with painted cloth, paper-mache, and Styrofoam. They are works of art, and the demons portrayed run the full gamut of scary creatures. The night before Nyepi, a hellish noise is made by the beating of pots and pans, and torches made of dried coconut leaves are used to scare off evil spirits and to purify the elements. The Ogoh-Ogoh seen in Bali's largest city, Denpasar, are the most artistically impressive, but Julie and I preferred being in our village of Susut that night. There was a charm to banging the pots and pans alongside our neighbors and to worrying together about a potential disastrous outcome as the teenagers raced through the village with sparks from the torches flying everywhere.

The next day there is complete silence! Everyone stays in his or her home without cooking or using electricity. These rules are enforced everywhere—even in the tourist hotels—by the "Nyepi police." The Bali airport is closed for the day. As I said, the Balinese take their religion seriously, even to the point of possible loss of tourist dollars. Julie and I loved this day of quiet meditation.

CUSTOM

A number of Indonesian customs relating to class can be counterproductive and/or contradictory.

When Salah Djasit, governor of Riau Province, hired me he provided me with two assistants from his office; they were supposed to follow up with his staff on what was decided in the governor's meetings with me. I was aware that the assistants regularly saw the governor during the day. Because I knew the governor's time was valuable, I did not call him directly on many issues but rather called one of the assistants and asked him to relay my message to Saleh. When I noticed in my meetings with the governor that he was not aware of what I had discussed with his assistants, I asked him if my messages had reached him. He said they had not. While he had no problem getting messages that way, he hinted that the assistants might not be comfortable relaying them. The senior assistant admitted to me, "I cannot tell the governor anything without being asked." I suggested, "Just say Al said or asked." He said he could not do that either. There was no way to change custom even though Saleh was open to it. Initiative was not a hallmark of how staff in Indonesia operated. It was a total top-down system. I was simply forced to talk to the governor directly to report on any important issues or if I needed his assistance. Inefficient, but unavoidable.

Another example of custom getting in the way of good business practice was when Western companies made proposals to Ismeth Abdullah, the governor of Riau Islands Province, and after a month still had no response. The CEO of the companies then called me, irritated, and asked what was going on. It usually turned out that the proposal was on Ismeth's desk and he had not yet gotten to it. I would convey that fact to the company, and they would relax and not feel offended. In the West it would be smart business practice to let a company know where in the pipeline their proposal was. However, custom did not allow Ismeth's staff to convey this same information for fear of making the boss look bad. It therefore became my job to tell a Western company "how things worked in Indonesia" and ease communication by playing the messenger for them.

I once told Saleh, "It's amazing that when I walk next to you, doors open without my breaking stride." Of course, when I walked alone I did not have the staff that assured this magical trick. His staff even carried his sunglasses so that he would not be burdened with the task.

Flying from Batam to Jakarta with Ismeth was always an eye-opener. The first time, I started to get anxious the closer we got to the scheduled departure time. "No way are we going to make it," I thought. Little did I know that we would be met by airport staff and driven directly to the plane. The plane leaving Batam always waits for the governor!

In contrast to the special treatment the governor enjoyed, when business was done and the Governor was hanging out with the staff, it was as if they were comrades having fun together. One time, Ismeth took the staff with him and his wife on a cruise down the Danube. Jokes, ribbing, and laughter were the order of the day. The same was true of Saleh and the staff as they watched the World Cup together. The governor won the betting pool—it was not fixed!

An Indonesian wedding party was not a simple family affair. Two thousand of the groom's parents' closest "friends" would be invited. The richer the father and the higher his status, the larger and more ostentatious the party. A wedding was a business-political affair. If the president showed up, your place in society was cemented. In order to shake hands with the lucky couple and their parents, I often waited in line for over an hour. It was an important sign of respect to be in attendance. I enjoyed these events because the food was fantastic, and I could network after standing in the greeting line.

Ostentation and love of singing combined at a party that Cano, chairman of the board of Biminatara, threw. The purpose of the party was to get the people who ran the subsidiaries together with the Bimintara board and senior staff to bring them even closer. The party was held in the penthouse apartment of the Hyatt that was majority-owned by Cano. The apartment's huge balcony had a fantastic view of Jakarta, and the bathroom fixtures were gold plated.

Indonesians are very musical, and singing is part of Indonesian culture. Maybe it is their only public show of emotion allowed by custom. At political rallies, candidates are called upon to sing. Analysts said the beautiful voice of President Yudhoyono's (commonly referred to by his initials, SBY) helped him win the election. When he released an album after his victory, General Wironto and other generals followed suit. I have seen tears running down the faces of many ruthless businessmen, murderous generals, and corrupt ministers as they sang a love ballad. At Cano's party, no one refused his command to sing. When it was my turn, I explained he would not wish to hear my voice, but I would be happy to do a tap dance instead. He consented, and my short performance was greeted with applause from the crowd and approval from Cano. Thank you to my childhood tap-dance teachers.

CULTURE

Culture is an anthropologist's paradise. Yogyakarta, on the island of Java, and Bali are two shining examples.

Yogyakarta is the old capital of Java and is the home of the Ramayana Ballet, the Shadow Play, the Javanese Gamelan, the Prambanan (a complex of fifteenth-century Hindu temples), and the art of batik. Nearby is the ninth-century Borobudur, the largest Buddhist temple in the world. It is a noted pilgrimage site for Buddhists.

Early in our time in Indonesia, Julie and I were lucky to watch the Ramayana Ballet perform on an outdoor stage with the Prambanan Hindu Temples as a backdrop. The cast of two hundred dancers is the largest in the world and brings to life a visualization through classical Indonesian ballet of this epic Hindu love story ("Ramayana"). The men wear a large black-and-white checkered cloth around their waists (*saput poleng*) that symbolizes the Balinese philosophy of balance and harmony. The temples are typical of Hindu architecture, with numerous spires reaching to the heavens. Of the eight major temples (there are many more minor temples spread throughout the complex), Shiva's is the largest at 154 feet tall and 112 feet wide. The color contrast of the blue-green and yellow costumed barefoot dancers with the black volcanic temples added to the beauty of the scene.

We also watched the sunrise over the jungle at the massive Borobudur. A central dome tops the temple, and there are nine stacked levels leading toward the dome. On each level, Buddha statues sit inside small dome-like structures, the *stūpas*—seventy-two in all, with 2,672 relief panels attached to the walls of the platforms. It was stunning to see the juxtaposition of the saffron-clothed monks against the brown-black volcanic rock of the stūpas. Julie and I had fun talking with the visiting students who wished to practice their English with us. We returned to these temples many times to show them off to our guests.

Gamelan is a thousand-year-old rhythmic style of music popular on Java and Bali, played by a percussion orchestra of twenty to fifty players. The orchestra is made up of bronze metallophones (similar to xylophones) of different sizes, played with metal, hammer-like mallets, and metal gongs of varying sizes along with hand-held drums that register the beat. The music is based on repetition and simultaneous variations of a melodic, pulsating sound. No one instrument dominates. The orchestra performs by itself or for dancers and the Shadow Play. I found the music hypnotic.

Julie preferred the more restrained and, in her view, refined Gamelan of the Kraton (Palace) of Yogyakarta, while I was partial to the faster and more emotional Gamelan of Bali. Given that Julie is a visual person, she was particularly impressed by the simple dignity of the older Kraton players and the elegance of their dress—navy-blue shirts, blue-black caps, and red and blue sarongs.

Bali gave us the opportunity to repeatedly see a wide variety of dance forms. We enjoyed the graceful and fluid Legong performed by two female teenagers (from ages eight to fourteen) who are dressed in "gold" with a floral headdress, and we were thrilled by the energetic and mesmerizing Kecak (also known as the Ramayana Monkey Chant): one hundred bare-chested, barefoot men standing in a circle and chanting at a progressively faster beat, "chakke, chak ke chak, ke chak," while rhythmically moving from side to side. They build a circle around a fire of large embers, and near the end of the dance one man in a trance moves into the bed of coals and kicks them out toward the audience. Water is thrown on the embers as they almost reach the viewers. A hard lesson we learned was to not sit in the first two rows. This dance has its roots in the trance dance history of Indonesia. Because the dancer is in his trance state, he feels no pain from kicking the fire coals. He appeared unhurt. We would see other trance dances in small villages high in the mountains of Bali. Although Julie and I loved both of these dances, my favorite was the Kecak, and hers was the Legong.

In Yogyakarta we saw a performance of the famous Wayan Kulit (leather puppets) Shadow Play. Wooden puppets are called Wayan Golek. The Wayan Kulits are cut from large swaths of leather to represent characters from the Hindu epics of the Māhabhārata or the Ramayana (both depicting good winning out over evil) and the clown-servants of the royalty (Punakawan) that provide comic relief. The Wayan are delicately painted in many different colors but always including gold. Attached to the puppets are buffalo horn handles and control rods. The puppet master (*dalang*) sits behind a screen lit by an oil lamp (now mostly a halogen electric light) and manipulates the puppets while at times singing (gamelan music accompanies the dalang) and voicing the many characters in the play. He also manipulates a Tree of Life puppet that symbolizes good energy and is twenty-five inches high. It is used to open the play and separate the acts. I joined the local children at different times during the performance, going behind the screen and watching the puppet master do his thing. The juxtaposition of reality and magic only highlighted the talent of the man behind the screen. Traditionally the play would run from midnight to dawn. Although Julie was up for more, we were both happy it was now performed in hour-long segments. After the performance, we were invited back to the shop where the Wayan were made. Watching the talented artisans create the puppets was a treat, and of course we had to purchase a number of them for our home.

I would be remiss if I didn't note that Indonesia is famous for its fabric and weaving. Our house is filled with examples of both, and my closet holds numerous silk and cotton batik shirts that I continue to wear eleven years after leaving Indonesia. Two of these are made from batik fabric that the governor of Riau Province, Saleh Djasit, gave me as a gift.

Batik is a technique of wax-resistant dying applied to cloth either by "canting"—drawing dots and lines with a spouted tool—or by printing the wax with a designed copper stamp called a "cap." The designs and colors of the batik differ depending on where they are made. Yogyakarta and Solo still produce the best examples of traditional batik. Our conversation with a ninety-year-old artisan who handmade batik at a factory and museum in Yogyakarta indicated that handmade Batik might be a thing of the past, as the young are not interested in mastering this art form.

LANGUAGE

Learning the language of the host country you live in is always a good thing, but for me it was easier said than done. After independence in 1947, Bahasa Indonesian based on the Malaysian language was instituted as the common language of the country. The authorities thought this might help in developing a common ethos among the disparate islands and ethnic groups with their own local languages.

Julie and I went to a language school in Yogyakarta. She needed to talk with our staff in Bali, and I needed to be able to talk to senior government officials who spoke no English. The school was excellent, but when we returned to our hotel after four hours at school, Julie would go poolside with her vocabulary cards to memorize new words, and I would retire to my bed with a headache. My headache did not stem from the difficulty of the grammar of the language but from my inability to memorize words. I blamed it on my age, the fact that I worked during the day, and on and on. The reality was that I stink at languages and was too lazy to put in the extra effort. I could still do my job because most of the people I worked with spoke English. Julie became pretty good at speaking Indonesian. There is no doubt that not speaking Indonesian somewhat limited my experience in the country. It was my loss and her gain.

CORRUPTION

My friend Hattari used to joke that "Indonesians let England rule the waves, and we waive the rules." But Indonesian bureaucrats can be sticklers for rules when it suits them. The dilemma is to know which version of Indonesia applies. Both allow for corruption. There is the corruption of a civil servant adding to his meager salary, and there is a government official requesting, and a private entity adding, substantial kickbacks to the cost of a project. Although both can have a negative impact, I would argue they are not in the same category.

In 2004, when I attended the inauguration of Ismeth Abdullah as governor of Riau Island Province, I sat next to the head of the new Democratic Party, President SBY's political party. I was one of a handful of whites invited. He made the point to me that SBY (short for Susilo Bambang Yudhoyono) would be happy if he could reduce corruption from the current 30 percent of GNP to 10 percent. I thought his position was interesting from two points of view: realism and impact on economic growth. Given the entrenched forces that benefited from big-time corruption, I thought 10 percent would be difficult but perhaps still doable.

A paper comparing Indonesia with Nigeria (both had large oil reserves) found that corruption above the 10 percent level had a negative effect on economic growth.

When I arrived in Jakarta, the town was abuzz with a World Bank scandal. An audit had revealed that 30 percent of World Bank project funding had disappeared. Corrupt government officials had siphoned it off. The upshot would be new World Bank financial controls and the retirement of the country director, who was sacrificed to calm the troubled waters. World Bank Washington had equal responsibility for the fiasco, but no one at headquarters was also "retired." As the private financial sector began to play a more central role in funding development projects, it would become more difficult to hide corrupt payments to government officials. That did not mean they would not try.

SBY's anti-corruption program had some effect as a number of government officials, especially those in local government, were tried and sentenced to varying times in jail. However, many officials and private citizens with enormous wealth and the right political clout kept going unscathed. It was my impression that his administration did not reach the 10 percent goal. Although SBY should get credit for making a start within the government, he does not deserve any for reforming the courts and police.

The depth and venal nature of corruption during my time in Indonesia can be demonstrated by the following anecdotes.

Tommy Suharto had been convicted of murder and sentenced to time in prison. A close friend who had done business with the Suharto family told me this story.

Tommy was kept in the VIP section of Cipinang Penitentiary Institution in Jakarta. His carpeted cell had a twenty-one-inch TV and a private bathroom. He received a steady stream of business and political visitors. In contrast to ordinary prisoners, he also had conjugal visits. My friend held several business meetings with Tommy in the prison warden's office. He told me that Tommy would visit Jakarta several times a week and occasionally meet with him on business matters. The only thing that changed for this convicted murderer of a judge was the location where he conducted business. Corruption was alive in the prison system. When these privileges were reported in the press, they stopped. He was released after serving less than one-third of his sentence because of what was said to be normal Eid al-Fitr (the end of Ramadan) clemency together with good behavior reductions.

Another case involved Manulife, a Canadian life insurance company that had been in Indonesia for over fifteen years. Manulife was one of the country's largest life insurers and a great supporter of foreign companies doing business in Indonesia.

Manulife's local Indonesian partner, Dharmala Group, was experiencing severe financial difficulties. Manulife let Dharmala's creditors know it was prepared to buy back Dharmala's 40 percent stake in Manulife. But the prominent Chinese-Indonesian owner of Dharmala saw that offer as an act of war. Perhaps it was not only a financial issue but also one of keeping face.

What followed was a textbook example of corruption in the courts and the police, pitting the power of a financially and politically powerful Chinese-Indonesian family against the international community.

Dharmala filed a criminal complaint with the police claiming Manulife executives had forged their shares and that the real owner of the 40 percent Dharmala shares was a hitherto unknown Virgin Islands company.

Although on its face this was a flimsy claim, several of Manulife's executives were hauled into a police station and questioned. Two were held without charges: the Canadian CEO for a couple of days and the Indonesian vice chair for nearly three weeks. The CEO was released only after the Canadian prime minister intervened to warn President Abdurrahman Wahid of adverse consequences. A travel ban was placed on one of Manulife's expat managers. The police seized the $17 million that Manulife had paid into an account to acquire the 40 percent stake. In contrast to the speed with which the police acted on the Dharmala complaint, they sat on their hands for a year before acting on Manulife's complaint. By then key players had disappeared. All the Western embassies joined with the Canadian government demanding that Manulife be treated fairly by the Indonesian justice system.

Based on the flimsiest argument, a three-judge commercial court in Jakarta declared Manulife bankrupt. Under Indonesian law, this was the end of doing business in Indonesia. The ruling came down even though the company had posted a net profit of nearly $9 million the year before. It was clear to most observers that corruption was behind the decision. The outcry from the international community was deafening. It appeared that President Megawati (who had replaced President Wahid) heard the outcry, and within four months the Indonesian Supreme Court reversed the lower court decision. Yes, the court was not truly independent. The lower court judges had been investigated and had resigned, but no criminal action was taken against them or the family that owned Dharmala. Manulife survived because a concerted international effort coupled with Indonesia's need for foreign investment had for once overcome corruption.

The most horrendous example of corruption I know involved the murder of a foreigner in a botched holdup. The perpetrator was caught, but the police did not forward the case for prosecution. When the widow met with the senior police official in charge of the case, she asked why the case had not moved forward. He responded, "The suspect has offered me fifteen thousand dollars not to move forward with the case; what will you offer for us to forward the case to the prosecutors?" She was so disgusted and deflated by this encounter that she gave up trying to get action on her husband's murder and returned to Canada.

Corruption touched me personally in a number of situations, and it was one of the reasons why we eventually decided to move back to the US. I thought I could expand my business by getting contracts from other governors to provide services similar to those I had delivered for Ismeth and Saleh. Both governors had offered their assistance and support in setting up meetings with their counterparts. The problem for me was that many of my prospective governor clients were corrupt. One asked for a million-dollar kickback on a $10 million project. Another wanted me to kick back part of my fee to a local Muslim charity that the governor in turn would use for his election kitty. Another did not accept a proposed USAID project to clean up the trash in the mangroves on Bali because there was no money in it for him. My potential client base was shrinking. The brother of a governor blocked my being hired for fear I might expose his kickback arrangements. As I said, President SBY was prosecuting corruption, but not to the level of scaring off many governors from participating in it.

I myself did participate in the practice of paying an "extra fee" to civil servants to obtain a driver's license without taking a driver's test. Of course, if I had taken the test I might have been asked to pay an additional fee to pass.

We also once paid an "extra fee" to get our goods out of customs when Julie had mistakenly shipped them to herself. She had no independent legal status in Indonesia; only I had that. Thus, the customs bureaucrats would not release our belongings. An "extra fee," however, made everything "legal," and our goods were released. Customs agencies in third-world countries are notorious for corruption.

On her first trip to Indonesia Julie called from San Francisco Airport in a very upset state. She explained that her passport would expire within six months, and Singapore Airlines had informed her that this was against Indonesian entry law. They would allow her to fly to Singapore, but they could not guarantee she would able to fly on from there to Jakarta. I told her not to worry. I called Ismeth Abdullah, the chairman of the Batam Industrial Development Authority (BIDA), who later became the governor of Riau Island Province, and explained the situation. He said that she should come to Batam and he would handle the matter. BIDA Singapore staff met her plane and escorted her to the Batam ferry. Ismeth and I met her ferry in Batam, and after he talked to the immigration officials, they stamped her passport and she was welcomed into Indonesia. When she left to fly back to the SF Bay Area from Jakarta, an immigration official said with a smile, "You have friends in Batam."

Maybe wrongly, I never had any guilt in these situations of working the system. Indonesia was and, my friends tell me, still is the land of small or big dollar corruption and influence peddling.

TWO GOVERNORS: BOSSES, FRIENDS, AND FAMILY

Between 2001 and 2007 I became a senior advisor to two governors. During this period I was often the only white face among a sea of brown faces, and got a deeper insight into how Indonesia works.

During my time at Ernst & Young, I had been a panelist at a seminar on good corporate governance. My fellow panelist, Hattari (like many older Indonesians, he only used one name), was a second-tier member of what was known as the Berkeley "Mafia." He was a few years older than I and had an engaging smile and a mild demeanor. As was true of most Indonesians, he loved to laugh. The first tier of the "Mafia" were economists who had received their PhDs at the University of California, Berkeley, and had run the Indonesian government for many years. After the seminar, I invited Hattari to lunch at the Hyatt Hotel, one of a number of hotels that were meeting grounds for the Indonesian elite. We hit it off, and he made the unusual offer of inviting Julie and me to his house for dinner. I say unusual because as a rule, Indonesians did not invite foreigners to their house for a meal.

Dinner started off by our being offered sweet cakes and tea in the veranda, then we moved to the dining room where another dietary problem presented itself (especially for me as a recovered minor heart attack patient) as Indonesians eat all the organ meats of any animal and cook with a lot of palm oil. Julie and I preferred having lunches or dinners at restaurants where we could better manage our dietary concerns. An additional challenge for Julie was the Indonesian custom of separately seating men and women at table. Shopping conversations are not exactly her cup of tea.

Hattari and I became good friends, and he was my entrée to meeting Ismeth Abdullah, who several years later became the governor of Riau Islands. At that time he was the chairman of the Free Trade Zone, called the Batam Industrial Development Authority (BIDA). Ismeth was a tall man who was schooled in the ways of the West and spoke almost fluent English, having worked for the World Bank.

The upshot of the meeting that Hattari had set up was that Chairman Ismeth hired me. I would be his senior advisor for the next six-plus years. I never moved to Batam but continued to be based in Jakarta as I needed to network with the foreign ambassadors and companies as well as with senior members of the central government. The modus operandi I used was simple. After establishing an interest on the part of ambassadors and companies in Batam, the chairman would extend an invitation to visit Batam. Invariably they would be impressed by the sophistication of BIDA and the number of first-rate companies already operating out of the Free Trade Zone (especially electronics, shipbuilding, and oil and gas platform and pipe construction companies.) I would then arrange through the ambassadors to meet with interested companies in their countries to determine if it was worthwhile for Chairman Ismeth to visit and make a presentation. Ismeth and I traveled the world together looking for companies willing to physically locate all or parts of their business (factories or distribution units) within the Free Trade Zone in Batam. Later, when he was elected governor, we were looking for foreign companies to build and invest in infrastructure projects in the province of Riau Islands. I assisted in getting $11 billion in foreign investment for Batam and managed to get Rolls-Royce power plants built in Batam and the Province.

At my request, Rolls-Royce acted as a free advisor to Ismeth in developing infrastructure strategies and programs. I again experienced how the super-rich live (I remembered well the private Financial Fund dining rooms of my Bimintara time) when I worked with my friend Bernard Duc, a member of Rolls-Royce's Advisory Committee and a former senior advisor to Gulfstream and Bombardier, makers of smaller (twenty-five to forty passenger) propeller planes. We utilized his private jet to visit several airplane companies in Europe. It was a method of travel I could easily get used to. The airports for private jets were always closer to the central city, passport and customs control involved no lines, and your driver could meet you at the bottom of the stairs. Alas, this would be my only private jet experience to date. Bernard was known at the best restaurants in the world. After we jetted to Madrid on his plane we had a dinner at a five-star restaurant where I had the best foie gras I ever tasted. Not in Paris, but Madrid. The maître d' gave us special attention. The next morning, after Bernard had breakfast with King Carlos, we met with the plane manufacturer.

I was seeking aircraft that would better tie the many distant islands of the province together, as an efficient transportation system is essential for economic development. I would later seek to develop a high-speed ferry system for the same reason.

Mike Gray set up a trip to Norway for Governor Abdullah and me to visit Rolls-Royce plants that produced hydrofoils for high-speed ferries. The key Rolls-Royce executive who oversaw these operations flew in from London to meet us. As was his want, the governor changed his travel plans at the last minute. His staff called me at 4:00 a.m. to tell me to meet his flight at 6:00 a.m. Together with members of the Indonesian consulate and Rolls personnel, we raced to the airport to meet the governor, only to learn that he had gone directly to the hotel. Ismeth's last-minute improvising when he traveled caused great consternation for Rolls-Royce and myself. I learned from this and other experiences to shut off my phone at night. Ismeth never created this kind of problem for me again.

After visiting the Rolls-Royce plants and attending a brief welcoming ceremony with the mayor of Alesund (this town of 45,000 is located on the west coast of Norway and is famous for its fairy-tale architecture), we boarded a small boat that local Rolls-Royce executives had arranged to take us for a reindeer lunch at the famous Hotel Union Øye, located at the end of the small but exquisite Norangsfjord. Kaiser Wilhelm used to be a frequent visitor of the hotel. I loved the lunch and the fact that we were there in May and had twenty-three hours of light. The latter made for lively evenings for many young people in restaurants along the wharf.

The trip was a success, but Ismeth's coming legal problems prevented us from finalizing a deal.

Ismeth introduced me to the governor of Riau Province, Saleh Djasit, who hired me to be his senior advisor. Saleh was a former general with a wonderfully impish way about him. When I once pointed out how different he was from the many generals I had met, he said, "That's because they are killing-generals, and I was a lawyer-general." I worked for him for two years and also traveled abroad with him, but not as extensively as with Ismeth. During the two years I worked for Saleh I also continued working for Ismeth. Neither job required my full-time attention. Saleh was not as sophisticated as Ismeth, but he had a charm that won people over. He understood that he needed to speak English to win the confidence of foreign investors and was taking lessons when we met. He would jokingly start his speeches by saying, "Al has ordered me not to read my speech but to connect with my audience—you." He also was more straightforward and less guarded than Ismeth.

THE TOWERS GO DOWN, SEPTEMBER 11, 2001

On September 11, 2001, I entered the dining room of my hotel in San Francisco and was met by Saleh Djasit, the governor of Riau Province, and thirty other members of his Indonesian entourage. They were lined up to give me their personal condolences. I had not followed my usual on-the-road-habit of watching the news first thing in the morning. I was therefore perplexed. What was going on? We were in America as part of a promotional tour for Riau Province. They told me that two terrorist planes had hit two of the World Trade Towers in New York City.

I told the governor I would be in touch, immediately went back to my room, and turned on the TV. For the next few hours, in horror, I could not take my eyes off the screen. I would later learn that an ex-law-partner's wife died in the Pentagon crash.

I called Saleh in his room and told him our meetings for the day would not take place, but we could probably still host the vice chairman of Chevron for dinner the following night. He had run the Caltex (a subsidiary of Chevron) operation in Riau Province for years. Caltex had contributed $1 million to develop a master plan for Riau and had generously supported other community projects in the province. Chevron's corporate offices were in San Francisco. The governor said the Indonesian women wanted to know if they should remove their hijab (head scarf) when they left the hotel. I was very happy I answered yes when it was reported the next day that a Sikh somewhere in the Midwest was mistaken for a Muslim and killed. I told the governor it was best for the group to stay around the hotel until told otherwise. That night I took the governor and a small group of the delegation out for a fabulous Chinese meal at the House of Nanking (my favorite) in Chinatown. Although the US was in turmoil, San Francisco was calm, and however upset I was, it made no sense to isolate the governor and his senior group of Indonesians in their rooms. Plus, I thought they would be safe with me. I also knew that to be epicurially happy, Indonesians cannot be separated for long from their rice.

To salvage the next day, I rented a car and organized a sightseeing tour of San Francisco for the governor and the leader of the Riau legislature. The tour included a portion of Lombard Street that is often called the "crookedest street in San Francisco" with eight tight turns in six hundred feet of road. It was a relief not to be fixated on the TV in my room and the horror of what had befallen America. The rest of the delegation was free to do what they wished. The women went shopping (which is what Indonesian women like to do, especially on foreign trips.)

That night we had the dinner for the delegation and the vice chairman of Chevron at Il Fornaio, a well-known Italian restaurant on Battery Street, not far from Broadway. The fun part of having the dinner there was that my nephew, Richard, was the chef. We had planned the menu together. Given the overall circumstance, it was a lively and fun night and a small way for the governor to give thanks to the vice chairman of Caltex for his support of Riau Province and the important role Chevron continued to play in Riau and Indonesia.

The next day, after conducting a severely reduced number of business meetings, the delegation traveled to St. Helena in the Napa Valley for an already planned late lunch at Tra Vigne. Perhaps I had scheduled one too many Italian restaurants for the Indonesians. I smiled to myself when the group at one of our tables brought out the hot sauce to add to the perfectly prepared, delicate salmon sauce. In addition to rice, you also cannot separate Indonesians from their hot sauce for long. It was my fault for loving Italian food, and this restaurant in particular. Luckily the governor enjoyed it all. He bought wine and olive oil in a store in St. Helena. Yes, some Indonesian Muslims drink in the privacy of their homes.

I had stayed in daily contact with the secretary of my longtime friend Mickey Kantor (President Clinton's secretary of commerce) to see if our meeting on September 17 was still on. Even though I knew he was in Korea with Richard Blum (Senator Dianne Feinstein's husband) and foreign air travel had continued to be banned after the attacks, she kept repeating, "Don't worry, he will be here." I had not taken private jet travel into account. It had not been banned.

We were on the first United flight to Washington, DC, from San Francisco after the airport reopened on Friday, September 14. I don't mean the whole delegation, just five of us—the governor, his attaché, the leader of the Riau legislature, a *bupati* (county official) and me. Other passengers, who had arrived earlier, had taken all the seats except the five we managed to get.

I had told our group that, given the circumstances, we should arrive at the airport three hours early. I should have said five hours. When we arrived, it was utter chaos. The United line stretched for what seemed like several blocks. Everyone was trying to get rescheduled. We lucked out with our five seats. The rest of the delegation would come as soon as possible.

During this time I was also in daily contact with my friends Muchi and Fred Fisher, who owned the Westover plantation on the James River, south of Richmond, Virginia. Their house was a splendid example of early Georgian architecture in America. It was located across the river from Jamestown, the first permanent English settlement in America. They had previously agreed to host a luncheon for the governor and a reduced number of delegation members at the plantation. It would introduce them to American history and give the governor, who grew up farming, an idea how Americans did it. On Saturday the five of us drove down to Westover. The day was a success, and I have fabulous pictures of the governor "running" a tractor.

The meeting with Mickey on Monday was also a welcome success. We started the long process of attracting US finance and companies to Riau Province. To our relief, the rest of the delegation safely joined us in DC on Sunday. After our meeting with Mickey, we visited the Indonesian embassy and planted the seeds for their assistance in our strategy and programs. Economic development in the third world is a slow process.

Airplane travel was still tricky, so I rented a car and we hired a bus to get us all to New York City on September 18. The same five who went to Westover would go by car.

On our way to the Lincoln Tunnel, on the New Jersey side of the Hudson River, the car became very quiet as we stared at the smoke from the smoldering fires of the Twin Towers. The streets of New York were empty as we drove to our hotel.

The next morning we had meetings with the Indonesian consulate and with my law school classmate Michael as well as several of his partners who represented funds and other financial institutions. It was very eerie to meet with them as their offices had been obliterated and several employees killed. Our meeting took place in the offices of another law firm that had graciously taken them in. Michael had survived the destruction of the Towers because of his lawyer habit of coming to the office after 10:00 a.m. and leaving late. He was shaken but eager to get down to work. Again, we gained promising leads to follow up on. We did so with meetings the next morning.

After our business was concluded, I suggested to the governor he might enjoy a horse carriage ride in Central Park. As we walked there he commented on the good job I had done and said he wanted to "tip" me. I told him he was already paying me as his consultant. He repeated twice more, "I want to tip you!" After the third time I asked him, "What do you have in mind? " He said: "Five thousand dollars ." I said, "Thank you." He reached into his jacket pocket, retrieved an envelope, and peeled off five thousand dollars' worth of $100 bills. Welcome to the world of consulting in Indonesia.

Late that afternoon, the delegation was scheduled to fly from Kennedy Airport to Vancouver, BC. My brother, who was the head of the School of Architecture at UBC, and my law school classmate who also resided there both thought they could provide solid business and real estate construction leads for Riau Province.

I was sitting in the first-class lounge with the governor when his attaché entered and asked me to accompany him to the business class lounge where the rest of the entourage was waiting for our Air Canada flight. It turned out that six of our party, including the governor's son-in-law, had been taken into custody and were being interviewed in separate rooms by the airport and NYC police. Their luggage had been removed from our flight. I found the officer in charge and asked him in my best New York accent, "What's up?" He explained that the six who had been detained were suspicious. The only thing I could ascertain about their being suspicious was that a few of them had the name Mohammed. I told him the people he was holding were Indonesian officials and that he was creating an international incident. I also informed him that the delegation had just met with the vice chairman of Chevron and a former secretary of commerce. He asked if I had any proof of the meetings. I pulled out invitations and thank-you letters from both of them. He told me to wait a minute, dialed a number, and after a minute of talking into the phone handed it to me and said, "Talk to this guy!" I inquired, "Who is he?" He replied, "The FBI." After having the same conversation with the agent (with more emphasis on "an international incident in the brewing"), he said I should make copies of the letters and leave them with the NYC policeman in charge. We were free to board our plane. Since we were the entire business and first-class sections, Air Canada had held the flight until we boarded, thirty minutes late. The luggage of the six was returned to the luggage hold, and we were off to Vancouver. Sitting next to the governor, I asked him, "Did we make a mistake? Is he a good son-in-law, or should we have left him at Kennedy Airport?" We both started laughing.

Because I would not accompany the delegation back to Indonesia (I would spend a few days visiting my brother) and they were booked to return to Indonesia via San Francisco, they accepted my recommendation to avoid the US and return to Indonesia via Toronto.

When I returned to Indonesia, they all continually thanked me for my assistance, and we joked about the "almost international incident."

GOVERNORS AND POLITICS

Both Ismeth, as chairman of the Batam Industrial Development Authority and governor of Riau Islands, and Saleh, as governor of Riau, had to deal with the politics and consequences of hiring a white foreigner as their senior advisor. Their enemies would use my hire as a pretext to gin up nationalist opposition to attack them for diverse reasons.

After a year, each governor had to reduce my remuneration because of nationalistic politics. Saleh was not re-elected due to money politics. After two years I no longer had a consulting role in Riau Province. The new governor, whom I knew well, did not want to hire "Saleh's man." I suspected he did not want me to see how he conducted the affairs of the Province. After five years of employment, I told Ismeth that I would work for him for just expenses and the possibility of finder's fees. To avoid a conflict of interest, I made full disclosure of any finder's fees I might receive from private entities involved with Riau Islands Province. As it turned out, I never received any fees or was reimbursed for all my expenses because Ismeth lost his governor's power.

In time, the quirkiness of Indonesian law would have Ismeth and Saleh criminally convicted for causing the state to lose money. The judges in both cases ruled neither defendant had financially benefited from his governmental contract award decision. But this did not save them, as personal benefit was not required for a guilty verdict. Their convictions seemed a very strange outcome to this Western lawyer. Foreign means foreign.

I could see that the real causes of their convictions were powerful business interests. In Saleh's case it was about who would benefit from water being piped to Singapore, and in Ismeth's it was about contracts for development. Powerful businessmen could use their influence with the central government to remove any stumbling blocks to their financial gain.

Many ambassadors and the Western community in general had repeatedly maintained that Ismeth and Saleh were the best of local government. They said, "They worked to improve their citizens' situation." One ambassador told me about both governors, "Unlike many others, neither man ever asked, 'What is in it for me?'"

RUNNING A PROVINCE FROM PRISON

I left the hotel and stepped into a province car that had been sent to drive me to the prison in Jakarta where Ismeth Abdullah, the governor of Riau Islands, was imprisoned. Ismeth would run the province from prison for a month until President SBY, the only person with the power, finally formally removed him from office.

We drove alongside the very high concrete prison wall with barbed wire topping until we arrived at a huge iron door where the guards checked our papers and waved us through. In a large courtyard the driver stopped by a smaller metal door where the governor's assistant met me. The driver pointed toward his parking place at the end of the courtyard. He said, " Call me on my cell, and I will pick you up."

The governor's assistant, whom I knew well, gave me a hug. We walked one hundred feet to a guard station where I was introduced as Ismeth's senior advisor and asked for my passport. The guard and I made small talk: "How long have you been in Indonesia?" "Where in America are you from?" He then handed me a pass to hang around my neck. I would repeat this procedure on the many times I visited the governor. The conversation would become more relaxed and there would be more joking as I became a known repeat visitor.

The guard buzzed me through the metal gates, and the assistant walked me through the hallways that seemed like a labyrinth. We passed by many muscular men with head-to-foot tattoos. These men were clearly not in prison for political or corruption convictions. Finally, we entered a small room where Ismeth was seated at the head of a table and his staff was gathered around him. It was just another day at the office, except the governor wasn't going home at the end of the day. As time went by, his power was diminished. Getting the staff to follow through became more difficult, and my getting paid or reimbursed for my expenses was also a problem. In this regard, it became clear who on the staff continued to have a personal loyalty to him and who didn't.

After his removal from office but while he was still in prison, the governor, filled with emotion, told me that I was one of the few people who continued to visit him. But he never lost his ironic sense of humor. His belly would shake with laughter. I was lucky to be the exception to his habit of keeping his cards close to his chest.

By that time we now no longer met in a prison office but in an open space with two metal chairs, not far from the tattooed gentlemen I mentioned earlier. His perks were reduced. I no longer had his assistant to lead me through the labyrinth, but this was not a problem for me as I had already memorized the way. Sometimes I had to wait as long as half an hour to be buzzed through while the prisoners were either taken from the prison to court or returning therefrom. Because of the danger of physical violence, neither the authorities nor I wanted us to bump into each other.

On one occasion, I stayed for dinner which was brought by his wife and grown children. For someone who was used to the privileges of office and was widely respected (he won the highest civilian award given for service by Indonesia), he handled his situation with grace and strength. He was released from his three-year prison sentence after one-and-a-half years and started an economic development business. I saw him many times before I stopped going to Indonesia. From time to time we still exchange messages through mutual friends.

THE LARGEST GOLD MINE IN THE WORLD

I had traveled with five ambassadors from Jakarta on a six-hour trip to Timika, Papua. When we exited the Freeport-McMoRan company plane, all the cell phones of the five ambassadors began to ring in unison. Apparently, the *Jakarta Post* had reported fighting between two Papuan tribes—men who fought with bow and arrows and spears. Several people had been killed and fifteen hospitalized. We did not go as planned to the hospital but added two medical clinics to our schedule.

We had come at the invitation of the general counsel and the president of Freeport to visit the Grasberg mine and to see how Freeport was using the 1 percent of its revenues dedicated for schools, medical care (including a seventy-five-bed hospital), eradication of malaria, and other programs in support of the community. Freeport had been forced by the community to make this contribution to avoid violence. That evening and early the next morning we would get briefings from employees and consultants to Freeport on many subjects including public participation, health care, education, environment, and agriculture. I had been hired as a consultant by the general counsel to organize the trip. The ambassadors were from smaller Western countries, among them the ambassadors from Spain and Chile, who were friends of mine and had helped to get the group together. All of them had expressed interest in helping the communities surrounding the mine. The Chilean ambassador was a suave man with a great sense of humor and the reputation of being a lady's man. By contrast, the Spanish ambassador was a thoughtful and serious man. Freeport hoped to enlist support for its community efforts and to allay Western countries' environmental concerns over the extraction of gold and copper from the mine. Grasberg is an open-pit mine and the largest gold mine and second-largest copper mine in the world.

To get to it you pass through two tunnels and climb an incredibly steep road that took eight years to build and is so dangerous that drivers need a special permit to traverse it. The road partly paralleled a river where many families could be seen panning for the tailings of gold that had been dumped into the water after processing. Sadly, many of these people die each year because of flash floods, but the potential financial rewards make it worth the risk. It's impossible to keep them out of the river. Ironically, on each of my two visits to the mine I was presented with a small vile of tailings consisting of gold, copper, and silver. Unlike what could be found in the river, my tailings had almost zero worth.

The next morning we left the oasis of our four-star Sheraton hotel in Timika for the mine. I say oasis because of the stark contrast between the hotel and the town. Timika is an ugly town of mainly poor Papuans who have come from all over the province seeking work of any kind. The town is a dirty, crowded sprawl of unsightly buildings. Many of the inhabitants have the vacant eyes of those who have unsuccessfully and for too long sought work. The tension between the locals and the migrants is palpable. The police and military have a strong presence here. By stark contrast, the hotel, as is the case in many parts of Asia, is clean and luxurious with a carved wood lobby and meeting room. My room looked out on the encroaching jungle. The hotel had a golf course that a nongolfer like me used to bird-watch. The sulfur-crested cockatoos, red-cheeked parrots, and Blyth's hornbills of the course were a joy to behold.

We slowly rode to Grasberg in tank-like buses up the steep and dangerous dirt road. At the steeper points the driver stopped the bus and shifted to a very low gear before proceeding. The constant rain and heavy downpours had eroded the road in many places. At the steepest point, serrated concrete had been placed to give the bus the necessary traction to climb. I was told that it took a German engineer from Bechtel of San Francisco many years of trial and error before he was able to get the correct road angle and mix of concrete to hold. The seventy-two-mile road is indeed an astonishing engineering marvel, but constant maintenance is required; otherwise the rain and the jungle would reclaim it.

Halfway up we came to Copper Town, where most of the over 20,000 employees (60,000 including dependents) lived. It featured air-conditioned markets with a wide variety of American goods, modern apartments, and recreational facilities. Once inside one of these markets you could not be faulted for not knowing what country you were in. The road ended at the old underground mine where we caught an aerial tramway to the top (shades of a skiing resort) and the Grasberg mine at 14,000 feet. Given the quick altitude change, we had an ambulance trail our buses up the mountain. A few of the ambassadors did become unsteady but did not need oxygen. I felt very light-headed, but was not incapacitated and was able to continue the tour.

I was struck by the enormity of the operation. Grasberg operated twenty-four hours a day, seven days a week. All the heavy equipment to build the road had to be brought in by helicopter. The road, crushers, three pipelines to the seaport seventy miles away from the mine, the port, airstrip, power plant, and Copper Town construction cost were part of the $3 billion spent to develop Grasberg.

After exiting the tramway we were taken to see the crusher and grinder operation. We saw four crushers breaking the large rocks into smaller ones and a conveyer belt that brought them, in the same complex, to two semi-autogenous grinders, forty feet in diameter, that used chemical reagents to create a slurry of gold and copper that was then transported in three pipelines to the seaport. The slurry would be dried and separated and shipped to smelters worldwide. The tailings and slurry overflow would be dumped into the Aikwa River and eventually wind up in the sea.

Standing at the top of the two-mile-wide open-pit mine, I felt like a dwarf in a land of giant machines and overwhelming scenery. The ambassadors expressed similar feelings. They were very impressed by the operation. The mine was at that time 1,804 feet (a 167-story building) deep. Twenty-feet-high dump trucks (each costing $2 million) with ten-feet-high tires traversed the dirt road like a colony of ants and picked up their load at what seemed the bottom of the earth. Looking around, I could see three majestic mountain peaks, including the 16,024-foot Puncak Jaya, the highest mountain in Southeast Asia. With a touch of sadness, I realized I was standing on what was once another magnificent mountain. Nature "giveth" and man "taketh."

Grasberg produced over 1.1 billion pounds of copper and 1.2 million ounces of gold in 2013. The total deposit was worth at least $100 billion. The mine makes more than $1 million a day. Between 1992 and 1998 it provided taxes and dividend royalties to Indonesia of $1.27 billion, and between 1998 and 2002 the mine produced another $1 billion in taxes and dividends. Freeport is the largest foreign taxpayer in Indonesia. Because the Indonesian government is a stockowner of a substantial part of the company, the government receives dividends as well as taxes from the mine operation.

As is usual in third-world mining operations, Freeport has a long-term relationship with the Indonesian army and police that are hired to provide protection and keep trespassers and local people off the mine land. Some of the soldiers or police have been involved in violence against activists, but we will never know if the violence was ordered by Freeport or if the military/police were acting on their own. A complex web of political and military ties helps protect Freeport from the democratic pressures of labor unions, environmentalists, and Papuan activists. It would take a book to explain these ties based on monetary self-interest. The same applies to the mine and the environment. It is interesting to note that Freeport does not, as it did in the past, totally ignore the issue. It runs a $3.5 million environmental lab to determine if vegetables, citrus, and fruit trees can be planted on ninety square miles of wetland destroyed by waste from the mine that jumped the banks of the river and had the consistency of wet cement. The jury was still out during my visits. Freeport consultants went to great pains to defend their method of mining, including the fact that they do not use arsenic. The reality is that even in an environmentally conscious operation, mining cannot take place without environmental damage. Can the damage be mitigated to an acceptable level? Who defines acceptable? There seems to be too much money involved to find a path that all the stakeholders would agree on. Many Papuan activists feel the company has leveled a mountain sacred to the indigenous people, fouled the streams, and cut down its forests for profit while the locals remain poor.

It turned out that the ambassadors were not ready to recommend community financial assistance to their governments. They felt Freeport had the money to fund the projects itself, and that the issues of the army's role, the environment, and the independence movement were too much to take on. I agreed with their decision. My second trip to Papua and Grasberg with the British ambassador and his wife resulted in the same outcome for similar reasons. Freeport's hope for foreign government assistance was not realistic to begin with.

Three months after my last visit there was an ambush of several cars on the Grasberg road, killing three teachers, including two Americans. After a lengthy investigation by the Indonesians and the FBI, the American government concluded that the ambush was conducted by lower-level Indonesian soldiers who feared Freeport was going to cut back on their dollars and perks. The ambush was a warning to the company.

As a result of this incident, the road and mine were closed to visitors and I was not able to carry out a plan with a few of the ambassadors to go on a birding trip and a one-hour hike to the glacier above Grasberg. I never returned to the mine.

MY LUCK RUNNING OUT

After Ismeth could no longer pay me a consulting fee, I obtained a one-year contract with a law firm to be a rainmaker. Ismeth gave the law firm one Riau Island Province contract, but I could not produce more. Therefore, after a year, my role in the law firm ended, but I stayed on good personal terms with the partner who had hired me. During this time I was also hired as a consultant for several months by the general counsel of the American mining company Freeport-McMoRan, the owner of the world's largest gold mine located in Papua, Indonesia. My task was to bring in foreign ambassadors to view their operation in hopes that they would provide funding for their community programs.

There are thirty-four provinces in Indonesia, many of which are not attractive to foreign investors. They either lack raw materials (oil, gas, coal, timber, gold), or an advantageous location (for example, Riau and Riau Islands). They have insufficient government finances to partner with a foreign investor, or their population is too small.

Moreover, given the blatant corruption I experienced with some Indonesian governors, and the fact that most of them were unwilling or unable to pay for foreign consulting services or that the senior staff did not want to share their power with me, gave me pause. It became clear that over my last two years in Indonesia my consulting gigs in Riau and Riau Islands had been unique and most likely could not be replicated. My luck in generating any type of contract was running out, and I was getting tired of trying.

Julie and I decided it was time to go home, to be near family and long-term friends. Although we loved the sweetness of the people, in the end, Indonesia was not our country or culture.

PART 6: INDONESIA AND BEYOND

My work on behalf of Governors Ismeth Abdullah and Saleh Djasit of Riau and Riau Islands provinces provided me with the opportunity to travel in other countries in Southeast Asia, Australia, the Middle East, the Gulf States, and eastern and western Europe. Most unexpected to me was that my work in Indonesia opened a door to exhilarating experiences in England.

ROYAL TENNIS AT HAMPTON COURT

Rolls-Royce wanted to be part of several new power plants in Riau. Mike Gray, the CEO of Rolls-Royce Indonesia, decided it would be helpful if the senior management of Rolls-Royce in London had business meetings with Governor Saleh Djasit, and he showed Saleh the sights and wined and dined him. After the London visit, the governor, his delegation, Julie and I would go on to Paris, Berlin, and Zurich to meet with other companies. On prior trips to these cities on behalf of the governor I had set up meetings with potential sources of finance and companies who might invest in Riau Province. In Paris, Rolls-Royce gave Saleh a fabulous lunch at the La Grande Cascade, located in the Bois de Boulogne, which was arranged by their advisory board member and my friend, Bernard Duc. Rolls-Royce hoped the governor would remember their largesse in awarding them power plant contracts.

The day after our meeting with Rolls-Royce senior management, including those in charge of the power plant division, CEO Mike Gray organized a day at Hampton Court Palace. A distant member of the royal family, who was knowledgeable and had the charm and manners of the British aristocracy, would be our private guide. Her bleached blonde hair was perfectly coiffed, and her teeth were flawlessly white. The tour she gave us was as if a "family" member were describing her history. In this case the "family" history started with Henry VIII in the early sixteenth century and ended with Queen Elizabeth. The last monarch to live in the palace (a combination of Tudor and baroque architecture) was King George II. We admired the garden and got happily lost in its maze.

The highlight of our visit, however, was playing Royal Tennis in the palace, on a court first built in 1530. King Henry VIII played the game with gusto on that very court (albeit restored several times). Queen Elizabeth I was a keen spectator of the sport. In France, Francois I was an enthusiastic player and promoter of Royal Tennis. The game thrived among the seventeenth-century nobility in France, Spain, Italy, and the Netherlands. In Victorian England, Royal Tennis had a revival, but broad public interest soon shifted to the new, much less difficult outdoor game of lawn tennis. Royal Tennis continues to be played by a relatively small number of aficionados in England, France, Australia, and the US. It was featured in the films *Sherlock Holmes and Sigmund Freud* and *The French Lieutenant's Woman*.

It turned out our guide's husband had been a repeat world champion of Royal Tennis, so we found ourselves on the court playing doubles; Julie was watching from a protected gallery at floor level at one end of the service court. The court itself reminded me of a four-wall handball court with revisions. There were only three playable walls, one of which had a deep, open indentation that created many angles for the ball to slide down. The Royal Tennis ball is smaller and harder than a tennis ball and does not bounce high. The racket's head is at a thirty-degree angle to the handle and smaller than that of a tennis racket.

In a photograph of the four of us on the Court, the champion, who was six-foot-two with Hollywood good looks, is dressed all in whites, and Mike Gray, a small man with a cherubic face, wears his tie. The governor, a small, wiry man bursting with energy, and I are in our running shoes.

Although I was a decent tennis player, I failed at Royal Tennis. I couldn't acclimate to the low bounce of the ball and the angle of the face of the racket. I was so bad that I was switched from being the governor's partner to being the champion's. The governor was quite good, and Mike was okay at the game. You could see from his ease of play why the champion was a champion. We played for thirty minutes. Even with my pitiful display of no talent at the sport, it was a thrilling experience.

DINNER AT THE HOUSE OF LORDS

On the same trip, my friend the Baroness Doreen Massey of Darwen graciously hosted a dinner at the House of Lords for Governor Saleh and the delegation. The baroness was very active in the Labor party leadership in the House of Lords and was named a Labor Party Life Peer in 1999 for her work in the health field.

I met Doreen through my law school classmate Taylor McMillan, who comes from a small town in North Carolina. They met while Taylor and her husband were in graduate school at Yale. My previous trips to the Parliament for drinks and/or dinner with the baroness were always a pleasure. On one occasion, over drinks and a view of the Thames, I had an interesting conversation about British politics with the leader of Labor in the House of Lords. Doreen or her husband would meet me at the security station and walk me down the corridors of the Parliament—a walk through the history of Britain. I would pass many statues of people I knew and many I didn't. Doreen would give me a history lesson as we strolled along.

Now the Indonesian delegation walked the corridors of the Palace of Westminster and there was pointing and the low hum of hushed conversation. They were as impressed as I had been on my prior visits. Before we went to the dining room for dinner, the baroness took us to the House of Lords chamber. Since it was not in use, we were allowed to enter. Once in the chamber, conversation stopped and we all were overcome with awe.

Unlike the House of Commons that we saw through the glass in the entrance doors (a peer cannot take you inside the House of Commons), the Chamber of the House of Lords is truly elegant. At the far end we saw the impressive royal throne, the gilded wall behind it and gilded ceiling above it, the baby blue carpets, the red stuffed "couches" where the peers sit, and the beautifully carved wood panels behind them. The chamber was simply a knockout, as was the central lobby with its different-colored marble floors and paneled walls.

The dinner was lively, with the baroness and the governor asking questions about how things worked in Britain and Indonesia, and members of the delegation chiming in from time to time. The entire experience was a complete success.

Throughout the remainder of the trip it was no longer, "Good morning, Al," or "Good morning, Julie," but rather, "Good morning, my lord," "Good morning, my lady."

LECTURES AT OXFORD

My friend Leonard Van Hien, the CEO of Jardine Matheson (the multinational conglomerate that was the inspiration for James Clavell's series of novels, including *Tai-Pan*), invited me to attend a lecture on third-world development sponsored by the British Chamber of Commerce in Jakarta. The lecturer was Sir Tim Lankester, a tall, elegant man with silver-gray hair. In the Q&A I asked Sir Tim a question, and we continued the conversation after the formal program ended. We bade our farewells and went on our way.

The next morning I was at the residence of British Ambassador Sir Richard Gozny for our once-a-month breakfast when I saw Sir Tim walking toward us from a guest bedroom in the rear of the residence. We had just started our breakfast. He joined us, and after a lively conversation between the three of us, he invited me, on my next trip to London, for drinks at Corpus Christi College, Oxford (the third-oldest college). He became the president of the college after having been a private secretary to Margaret Thatcher and permanent secretary at the Department of International Development.

Two weeks later I took a train from London to Oxford to meet up with Sir Tim. I met him at the college, and we walked over to the president's house where he resided. During cocktails (mine was soda water) and dinner, we talked about American and Indonesian politics and the difficulties of working in development in a third-world country. He said he wanted me to return to Oxford to meet some of the dons and to think of different topics for a lecture I might give to the grad students at Corpus Christi. He asked me to send him a list of three topics that could be the subject matter for the lecture.

Back in Jakarta, I emailed him the list. "One American's View of War with Iraq" was the one he chose over "The Pitfalls of Third-World Development" and another topic I cannot remember.

On my next business trip to London, I again took the train to Oxford, this time to have dinner at the college with Tim and the dons he had previously mentioned. "Wow," I thought, "a first-generation American-Jewish boy from 163rd Street in the Bronx, having dinner in a sixteenth-century building with the president and dons of the third-oldest Oxford college. What a marvelous world."

I met the five dons over drinks in a room with beautifully carved wood panels adjacent to the large dining room of the college. After a stimulating conversation we moved to the head table in the dining room. A don sat on either side of me, and the conversation continued. The students sat at long tables perpendicular to the head table. Our meal was typical college cafeteria quality—nothing special, but adequate. One of the dons was a scholar of ancient Mesopotamia who expounded on his view that it would be a tragic mistake for the US to invade Iraq. Among his many reasons was that the first loyalty of the people of Iraq was not to the country but to their tribe or clan. He felt America would squander lives and treasury in such an endeavor. His analysis proved spot-on.

After dinner we adjourned up some stairs to a wood-paneled room for coffee and then, farther up the stairs, to a turret room for sherry, cognac, and cigars. The evening was a success, and as Sir Tim and I walked back to the president's house, where I spent the night, he asked me to give the president's lecture on "One American's View of War with Iraq."

Several weeks later, fifty graduate students gathered in the living room of the president's house to hear my lecture. I particularly enjoyed the Q&A after my talk. It was very stimulating and great fun, and reminded me how much I enjoyed being among students. In the seventies I had taught a seminar at the University of California Law School in Berkeley. I explained why I thought it was a mistake to go to war with Iraq, but also told the students that I thought President Bush would do just that.

It turned out the students enjoyed the time as much as I did, and Sir Tim invited me back a year later to discuss the war and American politics. On that occasion I particularly remember a female British grad student who became visibly upset and started to cry when I said that even though the war had been a mistake, President Bush would be re-elected.

Sir Tim, who had become simply Tim, and I became friends and we would get together for dinners or lunches in either Jakarta or England. Years later he arranged for Julie and me to stay in the president's room at the college and for our friends to stay in the don's room. He gave us a wonderful tour of the grounds and buildings, and I enjoyed returning to the dining room and having breakfast with the students. Tim later resigned his post as president of the college, but we are still in touch.

BIRDING ON A PAPUA ISLAND

In the fall of 2006, after nine years of living and working in Indonesia, Julie and I decided to go on a birding trip. We chose Raja Ampat Islands (Four Islands) in Papua, Indonesia, a seven-hour plane trip from our home in Bali. The islands are famous for their remoteness, their unspoiled beauty, and the Birds of Paradise. My Julie is a true birder, whereas I simply love the colors, the excitement of spotting the birds, and being in nature.

The challenge was to find a reliable local tour guide. Google led me to the Papua Bird Club. The club reported it led the world-renowned naturalist Sir David Attenborough on a trip that resulted in his book and TV program about the Birds of Paradise. Sir David had acknowledged Kris, the head of the Papua Bird Club, with special thanks. The Brits are avid bird-watchers, so I looked for another "Twitcher" who could verify the club's bona fides. After some calls I found a few people in the British embassy who sang the praises of the man-and-wife team who led the tours.

Kris was a short, muscular man with a gentle way who had moved from Sulawesi to Papua to help preserve the unique bird life there. His wife, Sita, was a beautiful, smart lawyer who had left Jakarta for the wilds of Papua to marry the man she loved. We decided to follow in the footsteps of Sir David.

Aside from the Birds of Paradise, Raja Ampat is home to one of the most spectacular reef sites in the world. The Nature Conservancy has called the reefs of Raja Ampat a natural phenomenon of enormous underwater biological diversity. Experienced divers come from all over the world to see the famous variety of seahorses and other wonders of this serene and pristine place. We planned to join them and spend a day snorkeling the teaming reefs around the island of Kri.

Raja Ampat is in the land of Wallacea, named after the naturalist Alfred Wallace (1823–1913). Wallace, who was a colleague of Darwin, discovered and supplied the specimens that substantiated Darwin's theory of evolution. Many people (not including Wallace) thought that he, not Darwin, should be credited with the theory of evolution. His nineteenth-century journals are a fascinating account of his travels in the Malay Archipelago. They are an example of one man's courage and steadfastness in the face of incredible logistic obstacles and illness. He was rewarded by discovering a treasure trove of specimens leading to evolutionary breakthroughs. The famous Wallace Line is the line that separates the Asian from the Australian tectonic plates, running north-south, just east of Bali. He proved that the separation of these tectonic plates caused one enormous land mass to divide into islands and separate land masses surrounded by water, creating changes and adaptations in once-similar and related species. Species on one side of the line do not exist on the other side (e.g. the kangaroo). Certain birds only exist on several islands in Wallacea. Birders, who are into keeping lists of "lifers" (first-time sightings of a species), will travel halfway around the world to Wallacea for a day or two, just to add the Wilson Bird of Paradise and Victoria Crowned Pigeon to their list. The 2011 movie *The Big Year* describes with humor the mania that can break out among "listers."

As Sir David did, we would follow the path Wallace took more than 125 years ago, without suffering his trials and tribulations. Timing is everything.

After flying from Bali to Sorong, Papua, we were greeted by Kris and Sita and transferred to our small, thirty-two foot boat for the three-and-a-half-hour journey to the island of Bantana. We visited three of the four Raja Ampat Islands.

Kris and Sita had built a tiny one-room house (twelve feet by twelve feet) for Sir David on the outskirts of a small village on the southern coast of Bantana. The house was made of wood from the massive virgin Ironwood trees (150-plus feet tall, 7-plus feet in diameter) that run down from the mountains to the shore. These virgin Ironwood groves are fast disappearing due to illegal logging, and Wallacea is one of the few places where you can still see them in all their grandeur (think of California Redwoods to get an idea of their majesty). We slept in sleeping bags on mats set up on two opposite porches. Sita made gourmet meals for us over a wood fire. The outhouse was a few minutes' walk on the edge of the forest/jungle, and there was no seat, only two planks of wood around a hole on which to balance. This was a challenge, and in addition, I was ever vigilant for whatever might creep, crawl, or slither out of the jungle.

We arrived during a village holiday and were paid the honor of being invited to join the festivities that included boat races and lots of food. It was strange to watch children (ages fourteen to nineteen) who already had their own children (from babies to six-year-olds) all equally enjoying the activities. The isolation of the village produced these early marriages. I was struck by the way the place where you are born determines the life you lead. It does not necessarily determine your happiness, but it can certainly determine the scope of your life.

From Bantana we took a ten-minute boat ride across a channel to the always-visible island of Salawati to go birding. Two friends of Kris and Sita greeted us with coconuts that had just been plucked from the trees and sliced in half. On Salawati we saw the rare Victoria Crowned Pigeon, a blue-gray pigeon with an elegant deep-blue and white-lipped crest, maroon breast, and red irises. It was named in commemoration of the British queen and is the largest surviving species of pigeons. It can exceed thirty-one inches and weighs over seven pounds. (An average American Pigeon is eleven to fourteen inches long and weighs between nine and thirteen ounces.) We also saw the Red Bird of Paradise on Salawati. Even though it was high in a tree, we could spot its long, glossy red tail feathers and yellow beak.

Before leaving the island of Bantana, we took a two-hour hike up the mountain where we spotted the King Bird of Paradise with its cotton ball-white abdominal feathers that offset red back feathers. We also saw the Superb Bird of Paradise with its mainly black plumage and iridescent green crown. On our way down the mountain, Sita quietly came up to me and said, "Knock that black creeper off Julie's collar." I removed my hat and immediately wacked it off. I don't remember what it was, only that it was tarantula-like, many-legged, monster-sized (as big as my fist) and apparently dangerous. A hike in Papua is not a walk in Central Park. Vigilance is key. Many things can cause you harm. The byword is to watch where you put your hands as you steady yourself against a tree on a downward slope.

The next morning we left Bantana for the two-hour boat ride to Kri Island that was halfway to the island of Waigeo. Kri housed Max Hammer's world-famous dive "hotel," which we used as a staging area before taking another two-hour boat trip to Waigeo.

The boat ride to Kri Island was thrilling, as we skipped over the exceptionally clear (ninety-foot visibility), shimmering turquoise-blue water. On the way we stopped at a small, unspoiled white-sand beach island to visit a friend of Kris's. Only his friend, wife, and children lived on the island.

Hammer's dive hotel consisted of basic huts on poles over the sea. We washed with brackish water and had our meals communal style, in a large one-room building connected to the kitchen, where we could interact with our fellow guests. Kris took a day trip to the island of Waigeo to make sure that a Wilson's bird of paradise was present and to build a blind for viewing the bird. We snorkeled the teaming reefs close to the hotel and walked around the island, spotting Buff-Breasted Paradise Kingfishers with their large red bills and dark blue or purple capes, and the olive-colored Varied Honeyeaters with darker streaks. We also saw the delightful, large-eyed cuscuses (marsupial) and monitor lizards on Kri. Kris returned that evening and said it was "a go" for the next day.

Manned with our flashlights as warning lights, we boarded our boat at 4:00 a.m. for the two-hour trip to Waigeo. We were met by our local Papuan guide in his simple, tiny (twelve feet long, three feet wide) one-person outrigger canoe, not the big varnished ones you see in Hawaii. He had just traversed the same open ocean we had in his little boat. Simply put, he was amazing. He and Kris had built the blind with wood struts, woven grass, and large leaves. He led our boat to the point where we would go ashore and begin our two-and-one-half-hour climb, straight uphill and single file through deep underbrush among the massive Ironwood trees. We had our headband lamplights on, as the sun had not yet fully risen. Without our Papuan guide we would still be lost today among the massive trees, without a clue in what direction to turn. Everything looked exactly the same to our eyes. I have a picture of Kris appearing as a dot against the giant ironwoods.

The thrill of seeing a Wilson's, this incredible multicolored bird, close up is hard to put into words. Its turquoise skin cap, red and scarlet-black body, yellow mantle, blue feet, and violet spiraling tail feathers make a feast for the eyes. Mesmerized, we watched him clean leaves and sweep twigs from his mating space to attract a female to join him. Kris played a tape recording of the voice of a female to fool the bird into thinking a real female was "speaking" to him. But as no female appeared; he performed only the cleaning part of the mating ritual and never displayed his feathers. After several hours of uncomfortable sitting and looking, we descended to our boat and said our thanks and good-bye to our guide. We motored back to Kris Island in a state of spiritual bliss. Julie and I did not speak, but later commented on the smiles on our faces.

On our last evening on Kris, we joined with a few other guests and took a wooden skiff with an outboard motor for a one-hour ride over the sea to a large rock outcropping to see hundreds of New Guinea Red-Sided Eclectus Parrots roost at sunset. The cackle of the birds was deafening as we were treated to a magnificent sunset of pinks, yellow, and reds. This sunset did the impossible—it was even more breathtaking than those of the previous nights. Spice was added on our return trip when the winds picked up and water splashed over the sides of the skiff, making our hearts beat faster.

We said good-bye to Kris and Sita with sadness in our hearts, as we had become friends. It turned out that Kris had been struggling without complaint through pain from a cancer that had returned. He would die three months later at the age of forty-two. Sita continued to run the Papua Bird Club to keep his memory alive.

CHAPTER 14

DON QUIXOTE GOES TO HOLLYWOOD: LOOKING TO REGAIN PIZZAZZ

Several years after I left the Carter Administration, I recognized that I missed the pizzazz of DC. A vacation trip with Susanne (my ex-wife) to Thailand in1984 changed that. We met an American expat who set me on a Don Quixote-like quest to produce a Hollywood movie and regain the pizzazz I missed.

PART 1—THE ADVENTURE BEGINS

Susanne and I were having a Thai-barbecue dinner on the banks of the Chao Phraya River with the brother of her friend from Vancouver, BC, and his Thai wife, when we mentioned our desire to see the hill tribes of Northern Thailand. He had lived in Thailand for many years and said he knew many people in the tour business and would inquire. One day later we had cocktails with Bill Young, our prospective guide in Chiang Mai. His melodious voice and soft manners instantly won us over. He was in his fifties, six feet two with a muscular body and a kind, handsome face. His good looks contributed to Susanne's having an instant crush on him, and she would not be the only one.

During our several-hour meeting, Bill told us that a prominent Thai general had recently cheated him out of his inheritance in a supposed real estate development, and to make a living he was setting up a tour/trekking business to the hill tribes. Unlike real estate, he would do what he knew well. We would be his first customers. Discussion focused on a four-day itinerary: we would drive to the first village in his trusty Range Rover, called "Betsy," and trek to three more villages. His hill tribe assistant would drive "Betsy" to the last one to take us all back to Chiang Mai. The villages were usually not visited by tourists. His description sounded exciting. We hired him on the spot, and the next afternoon we started on our adventure.

In our first village, Susanne and I slept on a creaking bamboo deck next to our host's hut. Bill slept inside the hut. Our beds consisted of bamboo mats with blankets over us and my jacket as a pillow. Bill had observed my unsteadiness climbing the stairs without railings to the deck. While he and Susanne danced up and down the stairs, my lack of balance and fear of heights were obvious. In a quiet tone he said to me, "These stairs are tricky." This act of kindness made me feel less incompetent and endeared him to me.

We brought enough chicken, rice, vegetables, and fruit to feed both our hosts and us. The meals (dinner and breakfast) were cooked inside the hut over an open fire and eaten inside the hut, with the dissipating smoke filling our lungs. The lack of a flue in the huts caused rampant bronchitis and lung problems, especially for the children. Susanne joined Bill in partaking of our village headman's newly distilled homemade booze. The still was in a separate hut where one could sit on chairs and drink the lovingly prepared brew. I passed because I was tired and did not want to face the stairs in the dark.

The next day we started our trek through the mountain forests. The views of the valleys and Wats (Temples) were magical. As we walked along, Bill pointed out different spots where the regrowth of the mountainous jungle had erased airstrips that the hill tribes under his command had built for the CIA. To protect his true identity, they called him Colonel Tibbets. We were not on the usual hill tribe trek, and I was fascinated.

Bill's father, Harold, had already worked for the CIA gathering intelligence in southern China in the 1950s. On his recommendation, Bill was recruited into the CIA when he was in his early twenties, but he said he had left the CIA after ten years when his boss refused to pay for expensive medical treatment in America for his Thai-American son. Along with other tales, I would learn more about his parents, wives, and children on my many return trips to meet with Bill.

At one point on our trek that day, Susanne wandered off as was her wont toward a warehouse-type building in the middle of nowhere. Bill immediately went after her and gently said, "I don't think it is wise to go in that direction." He later explained that we were in opium country and that she was headed for a heroin processing plant. She would be an unwelcome visitor. He explained that the opium fields lay across the border in the mountain valleys of Laos and Burma, and the processing plants were built in the mountains of Thailand. The US Drug Enforcement Agency (DEA) had requested that the Thai government outlaw poppy growth on its side of the border. This setup, he said, was the Thai response. I was delighted that we were able to gain insights into how the drug trade operated in this region.

I knew from the brother of our Vancouver connection (who had arranged the meeting with Bill) that he was part of a famous Methodist missionary family. And as we walked in the rugged terrain, Bill filled in the blanks.

His grandfather came to Burma in the 1880s as a Methodist missionary. His father, Harold, although an American, became a major in the British Army during World War II. He arranged for his family to leave Burma for the relative safety of India. After the war, Harold became a high-level administrator in Burma, first for the Brits and then for the Burmese. A deal for power sharing between the hill tribes and the lowlanders fell apart with the assassination of Nobel Peace Prize winner Aung San Suu Kyi's father, who was scheduled to be prime minister, and war broke out between the lowlanders and the hill tribes in 1947.

Harold was ordered to arrest a number of his hill tribe friends but refused. He knew his refusal would cause his arrest, so he immediately moved his family and their possessions out of the country to Thailand. Bill's life would mirror the divided loyalties of his father. When Bill told me the story of his exodus, I saw it all in visual terms like the opening scene in a movie. A wide pan of elephants and donkeys packed with all their earthly goods trekking over the mountains from Burma to Chiang Mai. Loyal household staff and animal handlers can be spotted. Then a cut to closeups of thirteen-year-old Bill, his seventeen-year-old brother, and Harold showing the stress and fatigue of the five-day journey. Even as a youngster, Bill proves his grit when he refuses to ride an elephant, as do his sister and mother. He insists on walking with his father and brother and facing the dangers of the forest jungle. An overlaid flashback conversation between his father and mother explains the reason for the exodus. What a fabulous, auspicious beginning to a movie this scene would make. It made me curious to know more, and over time the "layers of the onion" of Bill's life would be peeled away.

I learned about the schools and infirmaries Bill's missionary grandfather and father had set up for the hill tribes. A substantial part of Bill's time was devoted to keeping them running, especially after his father's death. On future trips I would see his family's "good works" firsthand and understand why they were held in high regard. Several of the tribes viewed Bill's dad as a god, and the revered king of Thailand had honored Harold by inviting him to many state dinners in Chiang Mai and Bangkok. I glimpsed the extent of the exalted position the family held when I accompanied Bill to a village where he was checking on a school they had sponsored. When we were served tea, the woman server, as an act of respect, never let her body rise to the level of Bill's belt buckle. The people of this Lahu village had transferred the god-like status of his grandfather to his father and then to Bill. I thought this scene had to be captured in the script. Later, Bill told me he had a fantasy of retiring, moving to the US, and pushing a lawn mower across his front lawn while dressed in Bermuda shorts and flip-flops. The pressure of his god-like status imposed a burden of never being able to fully relax.

Harold, who was an influential part of the life of Chiang Mai, donated a zoo to the people of the town. I imagined a flashback scene showing Bill alongside his brother in the wilderness of Burma and in the Northern Thailand rain forests, hunting and capturing the big cats: black panthers, South-China leopards and tigers for the zoo. Bill told me, "I felt that I was born to be in the wilderness."

On the plane ride home, an outline of the movie fell into place. I saw Bill as a larger-than-life Southeast Asian hero version of Lawrence of Arabia without the mania. Similar to Lawrence, who had the split personality of a mild-mannered bureaucrat turned warrior, Bill had the split personality of a missionary and warrior. He found himself conflicted in doing God's work while working for the CIA and DEA. He was providing health clinics and schools for the hill tribes and at the same time he was "Colonel Tibbets" leading them in battle against the Communist Pathet Lao in Laos. As was the case with Lawrence, he had a similar naïveté that got him into avoidable trouble, as I would later learn.

There would remain gaps in my knowledge of his life story, but several things stayed constant: his missionary work with the hill tribes, his close hill tribe relationships, his ability to speak a number of their languages in addition to Thai, his comfort in a jungle setting, and his ability with weapons and hand-to-hand combat. He utilized all these skills in dangerous assignments over many years both for the CIA and the DEA.

The movie had to evoke his Asian manner and the mode and texture of the dangerous intrigues he was involved in for the CIA and DEA (think *A Year of Living Dangerously*). Someone had to make a movie of Bill's incredible life with the exotic Northern Thailand as a costar.

I imagined the dense rain forests, with killer snakes hanging from trees, the colorful hill tribes, and the many Wats of Chiang Mai. A decaying hardwood framed Wat on the edge of the Mekong River could be shown with yellow and saffron robes drying on the balconies, while monks of all ages would be deep in conversation or chanting prayers. All this would be essential for the flavor of the movie.

A major theme, however, would capture the juxtaposition of the Asian polite, calm, kind, and gentle part of Bill's personality with his sharp nose for lurking danger and his unflappable courage.

Once when we (my present wife Julie was with us) attended a major village ceremony, a drunken man started to act erratically and hostilely toward several village men. With great patience, over what seemed like an interminable period of time, and without ever raising his voice, Bill kept gently talking in his hill tribe language to the man until he left the ceremony peacefully with several of his friends.

At this same party, two drunken, out-of-uniform Thai soldiers were behaving badly. Bill did not let on that he spoke fluent Thai in order to overhear any plans they might be concocting to harm us. He was afraid they would think we would report their behavior to the authorities. Years earlier, at another village ceremony, he had overheard Thai soldiers plotting to rob and kill him and his companion, an American woman. His language skills and cunning allowed him to take a different road out of the village and avoid disaster. This time, too, he led us on a different route to safety.

PART II—LET'S MAKE A MOVIE

I didn't think I could weave these themes together myself and write a gripping script. But there was one thing I could do: produce the movie and find a good scriptwriter for the story. The tempting thought kept playing through my mind.

I had long been fascinated by moviemaking. Indeed, when I graduated from law school a fellow classmate and I discussed at length our going to Hollywood and using our degrees as a way to get a job in the business as a lawyer or …? Receiving a federal clerkship offer from a judge in the Southern District of New York had ended this line of thinking for me.

Throughout my career I had excelled at networking, building relationships, and putting together the pieces and people (especially those with expertise in the field) necessary to move a project forward. As an anti-poverty lawyer I organized coalitions to bring about new regulations, legislations, and programs. In the Carter administration I had guided savings & loans into funding real estate projects in the inner city. After I left the administration, I was appointed by Federal Savings and Loan Insurance Corporation (FSLIC) to the boards of two bankrupt institutions where we did $4 billion of loan restructuring "workouts."

Why not use these same skills to produce a movie? In my mind, the role of a producer was similar. I had learned the buzzword language of government, international development, finance, and real estate and now would use the same for moviemaking. In all these ventures, I'd had expert friends showing me the way—step by step.

Four months after our Thailand vacation, I returned to Chiang Mai to discuss with Bill the idea of making a movie based on his life. He was excited by the prospect and agreed to sell me the exclusive rights for a percentage of the net profit and also be paid a fee for his role as a location and hill tribe consultant. The percentage and his consultant fee would be determined once we knew the budget for the movie. At that point in time Bill had no permanent job. He had left the CIA long ago and was freelancing for the DEA on specific assignments. As I noted earlier, a lot of his time was spent on the family's missionary work—raising money, buying medicine and books, and finding teachers, nurses, and doctors. Whenever there was a hitch, Bill would help fix it.

Four years later, Bill was actively involved with a Kachin hill tribe princess supplying medicines to Burmese students who had escaped from Rangoon after the collapse of the August 8, 1988, "student-monk-housewives" uprising. The students who led the uprising were city folks and had a difficult time living for a long periods in the jungles. After spending time with the princess and seeing her assistance-operation, I understood why Bill was supporting her. Over time, I raised a few thousand dollars from friends for her. I also helped, from time to time, loading medicines and mosquito nettings into four-wheel-drive SUVs for delivery to the students.

Bill related a story about his CIA role with Air America in Laos. Air America was a covert CIA airline that started in 1950 to carry equipment and personnel into places like Laos and Cambodia where the US military could not go because of treaties or politics. He was called upon to rescue three Air America operatives from a downed helicopter in Laos. The helicopter had crashed between two densely forested hills, one of which was commanded by the Communist Pathet Lao "bad guys." After a two-and-a-half-hour trek from his base village camp through jungle forest, he and his team reached the helicopter, which was under heavy fire. Bill and his troops had to leave the tree cover of their hill and descend into the open crash site below. They discovered that only one of the operatives was alive, although badly wounded; another was dead, and the third was in pieces. "We put the pieces in a body bag, along with the dead man, and carried it together with the wounded man to safety." Neither he nor anyone on his team was hurt in the operation. However, he confided to me, "Fifteen years later, I still wake up in a cold sweat from nightmares about the operation." "Wow," I thought, "a scene about awaking in a state of cold sweats, with a flashback to the rescue operation, would be a great moment, equal to or surpassing any adventure movie scene I could remember." This story reinforced my desire to make a movie about this man who would without hesitation follow the call to duty and risk his life to save others.

I was not the only one who took notice of Bill's role in answering the call to duty with the CIA and the DEA. In the seventies and eighties, his exploits were mentioned in three books that also showed the different faces of Bill.

The first, *The Politics of Heroin in Southeast Asia*, by Alfred W. McCoy (1972), describes Bill Young's activities as a CIA agent in Laos and Thailand, where he oversaw the building of numerous airstrips to facilitate CIA activities in these countries. It has been widely reported over the years that the CIA supported the growing of poppies, although no "courtroom" facts have been shown to prove this claim. McCoy makes a case for this and describes how the drug trade affected the US and the countries in the region politically. Did Bill's role in the Air America operation make him a knowing participant in the CIA drug trade, or was he a simple soldier in the anti-Communist efforts of the US government? I could believe either story.

Bill had a great deal of knowledge about the drug trade in Southeast Asia, but I do not think he personally profited from the trade. The book also details Bill's work for the CIA as the leader of the Yah and Lahu tribes in battles against the Communist Pathet Lao guerrillas. The fact that he agreed to be interviewed by McCoy demonstrates the Inspector Clouseau-part of Bill's personality.

The publication of McCoy's book put Bill in mortal danger. It revealed operations and local players connected to the heroin trade and to CIA operations in Southeast Asia, including names of top-level Thai and Burmese military operatives. When the book came out, Bill went into hiding. Months later, after tempers had cooled, his father was able to use his influence and esteem to get the sanctioned "hit" by certain Thai generals on Bill lifted. Not a simple undertaking. Bill told me he thought McCoy was in fact from the CIA. Given the obviously sensitive nature of Bill's information, why didn't he check him out with his CIA superiors? Out of politeness, I never asked him this question because I didn't want to give the impression that I thought he had been stupid.

The second book, *Air America* by Christopher Robbins (1979), confirms the Lawrence of Arabia part of Bill's personality described in McCoy's book. He sets forth his exploits with admiration. And the third book, Frances Belenger's *Drugs, the US, and Khun Sa* (1989), describes Bill as "perhaps one of the most effective American agents ever" because of his knowledge of the hill tribes, his ability to speak many of their languages, and his facility for spending long months of solitude in the jungles.

At some point, Bill told me the US government was thinking of having talks with the Laotian government over the prevention of drug traffic into the US. They wanted Bill and his loyal hill tribe members to enter Lao and find out if any of the senior government officials were involved in the drug trade. Through his connections among the hill tribes of Laos, Bill confirmed that the vice president of Laos was indeed involved. This mission was risky at many levels, especially if the Lao government had got wind of it. Weeks after Bill related this story, I was home in California, picked up the *NY Times,* and read that our government was opening normalization talks with the Laotian government. This was realpolitik in action, and risks to life and limb in fact-gathering be damned.

On another occasion, I was sitting in Bill's house in Chiang Mai when one of his hill tribe lieutenants rushed in and excitedly told Bill that they had found the largest refined heroin cache ever. The cache was located deep in the jungle near the Thai border. If this cache could be seized, the DEA folks and Bill would receive a promotion and a large bonus. Excitement was in the air, but Bill was skeptical. He explained that members of the Burmese Wa tribe, who were famous for their ferocity in fighting, were guarding the heroin. To go after the heroin, the DEA needed the cooperation and approval of the Thai Border Patrol. Given their known fear of the Wa, Bill thought they would delay or not give permission for the operation. When I next met Bill he told me the DEA conducted a flyover of the site and confirmed the cache of heroin. Nonetheless, the Tai Border Patrol refused permission. No bonus for Bill, no promotions at the DEA! The largest cache of heroin ever located would find its way onto the streets of NYC, Chicago, and other American cities.

The night before I left Thailand, I discussed with my friend, the general manager of the world-famous Oriental Hotel, my idea to shoot a scene on the terrace of the hotel, where months earlier this exhilarating adventure had begun. He was excited about my request and agreed to it.

PART III—DON QUIXOTE BEGINS NETWORKING

Upon returning home, I started networking. I was aware that I was Don Quixote, the outsider without wealth or position, entering the Hollywood labyrinth that one has to maneuver to get a movie made. It was worth the effort to tell Bill's astonishing story of being both a missionary and a warrior.

In my previous enterprises, I usually had an expert to guide me when I entered uncharted waters. I needed a Hollywood insider, a Sancho Panza, to guide me through the process and past the roadblocks.

I would quickly learn from several people I knew in the business (including lawyers and my actor brother-in-law) that the best way to get a movie made would be to get an A-list actor and/or director attached to the project. (See, I learned the lingo.) The problem was, if you did not know any of these folks personally (neither I or my friends did), you had to access them through their agent. The agent would ask, "Is the project funded?" When I said no, that was the end of it. You might ask, why didn't I fib? First, this would have been a lie and not a fib. Second, the agent would have wanted to see the funding documents, and my word has always been my bond. My reputation is my most valuable commodity.

I did get past this problem with William Hurt's agent, who loved the concept and thought Hurt would make a great Bill. But Hurt did not follow his agent's suggestion. In any event, at that time he was no longer an A-list actor, and his drinking had made obtaining production insurance iffy.

The "is it funded" question was understandable, given that these folks are flooded with scripts and it makes no sense to commit to a project that might never get made. A real, full-blown project opportunity would be missed because of a commitment to me. Had I been a rich man or had access to big development funds I could have guaranteed a sum of money to the A-list actor or director. But I was not and did not have such access. I was faced with a catch-22 dilemma. I needed a funded project to get an A-list player to sign up, and I needed an A-list player to get the movie funded. But I knew from my contacts that it was possible to cobble together the pieces even without big development funds. It had been done before, successfully, especially with the $14 million to $20 million it would cost to make and advertise my movie. Even back then, this was not a big sum in the business.

It reminded me of my time in the Civil Rights Division of the Justice Department where I found myself in a similar merry-go-round situation with the Sailors Union of the Pacific that discriminated against blacks. It was a time of well-paying jobs on ships sending goods to Vietnam. Blacks were kept from getting these jobs by the following scheme: To get a union card, you needed a job on a ship. To get the job on a ship you needed a union card. Only whites were given both a job and a union card. Back then I was able to stop the scheme by having the FBI photograph the union records that demonstrated the racial discrimination of the scheme.

I thought by networking I could find "a player" who loved my movie concept as much as I did and who would help me find either a source of development funds or an A-list actor or director to move the project forward. It became clear that I could not move it forward based on only a concept. I would need a script. Since I faced a similar "is it funded" dilemma in enlisting an A-list writer, I would have to find the needle in the haystack: a gem of an unknown writer who would work for a small fee and a percentage of the profits. A very good script was a key component (not a guarantee) to opening the gate to everything: talented actors, directors, funded production companies, and studios. *Good Will Hunting*, which jump-started the careers of Matt Damon and Ben Affleck, is a great example of this fact. They would not sell their script unless they could also act in it. The power of the script convinced Robin Williams to take the risk and attach himself to the project, and a studio picked it up.

PART IV—MOVING TOO FAST

It is probably a repressed memory category of Freudian-Jungian psychology that I cannot remember exactly how long it took (but it was long time), or how I connected to my first writer. I was in and out of Los Angeles a lot during this period, and in all probability a friend introduced us. I liked him personally, and I thought I had lucked out. The writer gave me a full script of his to read that had been made into a movie, shot in Southeast Asia. I loved the writer's descriptive powers of the settings in Thailand, but I did not pay enough attention to his dialog or structure—after all, as I said, the script he gave me to read had been made into a movie. The irony in hiring this writer was that he turned out to be a member of the Writers Guild and could not work for less than union scale—$25,000. I didn't have the confidence that I would ever find another writer if I rejected this one.

Over time I would contribute $25,000 to the project and raise another $25,000 for my development fund from personal friends and law school classmates who were eager to participate in a Hollywood adventure. I did not want to mix funding for a movie with my potential needs for financing on business projects, and I did not want to involve my political connections from whom I might need a political favor. Without my asking, a friend and law school classmate contributed the last $5,000 tranche (he was aware of my efforts to raise money) that allowed me to move forward. He said, "Everyone should have a chance to follow their dream." At the time I thought, "Why didn't Susanne get this?" She thought I knew nothing about the movie business, and we could ill afford to lose our investment. She feared the embarrassment of losing friends' money. To her the whole endeavor was irresponsible.

Another factor in my mind behind hiring the first writer was my hope that he might be of assistance in raising funds, or at least connect me to "players" who could help get the movie made. I even paid for a trip for us to go from Bangkok to Tokyo where his purported "funders" resided, to renew contact and present his full fledge "Bill Young" script to them when he finished it. We stayed in an expensive hotel to impress them when they came for drinks, but we never let on that we shared a room or avoided the expensive breakfast and eight-dollar coffee at the hotel. Appearances are everything in the moviemaking world. I was still drinking at that time, and maybe my thinking was simply typical Alcoholic grandiosity, not rationale thinking.

It turned out his contacts were iffy even before presenting his "Bill Young" script, and they disappeared altogether after reading it. "Oh well," I told myself; it was just an expensive way to be a tourist in Tokyo. Given our economic status at the time (I was consulting, and although my fees were not paid every month, at year's end I made a good income) Susanne's misgivings made sense. A part of me thinks I should have paid more attention to her financial fears, but I didn't know how to do that without giving up my dream.

My eagerness and enthusiasm did not allow me to slow down and seek other points of view about the full script the writer gave me to decide if I would hire him. I didn't even seek input from my actor brother-in-law. Looking back, I was in fear; I was not willing to hear any criticism of his writing. It takes a special talent to judge a script and translate it in your mind to the big screen. I met an industry lawyer who told me he had read the original script of *Lawrence of Arabia* and advised his client not to make it. When I read the scripts of both *Lawrence* and *The Year of Living Dangerously*, I had a better understanding of the complexities. The *Year* script did not exactly overwhelm me, whereas *Lawrence* pulsated off the page. The lesson I learned from *Year* was that a great director and talented actors could turn an okay script into a first-rate movie. I didn't know the fatal difference between an okay script and a bad one. I was convinced my idea was powerful enough to come through any script.

The writer and I traveled together to Thailand to have him meet Bill and soak up his stories and aura. I was pleased to see that he was as impressed with Bill as I was. He was thrilled by the project and shared my excitement. A clue I missed was that he did not bring a laptop with him. He could not quickly edit what he wrote, and it slowed down the whole process. I had to wait for a long period before I received a full *Bill Young* script.

PART V—NETWORKING WORKS, AND HOPE SPRINGS ETERNAL

After returning from my trip to Thailand and Tokyo with my enthusiastic and smitten writer, I called my friend Marilyn Melkonian, the lawyer who set up Lucas Ltd. She had worked with and was close friends with two men at Lucas Ltd. One was at that time a vice president at Paramount Pictures and the other, Sid Ganis, was a vice chairman of Columbia Pictures. They both adored Marilyn. (More about Sid later.) She liked the concept I had outlined on the phone (there was no script yet) and said she would set me up with both of them. I told her, "Let's try the guy at Paramount first." My networking skills seemed to be working. I met the Paramount vice president in the Studio Cafeteria. It was filled with actors in costume, members of the crew gangs working on the lot, and studio executives. I loved the pulse of the place. Pizzazz was growing. We first talked about Marilyn and what she was up to. Then we discussed, in depth, my concept about a movie based on Bill's life to be filmed on location in Thailand. He was a soft-spoken and kind man without the outsized ego of many in Hollywood. We met for over an hour and a half. He said I should get him the script when it was finished. He invited me to join him again for lunch when I was back in town. Contrary to what I had heard, all the executives I met in Hollywood were generous with their time and eager to help if they could.

Two weeks later, I was going to be in Los Angeles again on business and called him to set up a second luncheon. I liked him, and the pulse of being with him was fun. Even though the script was not yet done, it couldn't hurt to get to know each other better. Apparently, he enjoyed me too as he took time from his very busy schedule to set up a no-agenda lunch at a chichi Rodeo Drive restaurant in Beverly Hills. The second thing I noticed, after the richly appointed décor (Louis XIV), were the expensive watches on the men in suits, and similarly expensive watches worn by the men in designer jogging outfits. Taken together, the value of the watches could have funded development of my movie. Unlike my lunch partner and myself, most of them had deep tans. Most of the women looked as if they had just stepped out of a beauty parlor. When we arrived there were no vacant tables. Within a flash the maître d' had the staff bring out a deuce table, moved aside tables of several seated patrons, and squeezed us into the middle of the restaurant. All the other lunch guests were from the movie world. Many of them stopped by our table to say hello and "kiss the ring." He could make or break the careers of these folks. I experienced a touch of the thrill I wanted back in my life.

During this time, whenever I was in LA, I visited the Polo Lounge of the Beverly Hills Hotel. This is where Hollywood came to see and be seen. The wannabes and the famous all frequented the Polo Lounge for a drink or dinner. It had already been a drinking hole for Spencer Tracy and Douglas Fairbanks. On my visits I spotted Sharon Stone, James Caan, Tom Cruise, and Steve Martin. The maître d' ushered you to a table in the rear if you were not an A-list person and in the front if you were. Most of the time I would sit at the bar and take in the scene. The first time I noticed a very tan, short, bald Jewish man in his eighties sitting with a twenty-something statuesque blond. He was smoking the requisite monster cigar. I chuckled to myself and thought, "He must be a producer, too."

As you walked into the lounge there were three booths facing the entrance. These were the top status locations. A producer dictating something urgently to a secretary always occupied these booths. People would stop by to say hello. This man had an office somewhere, but the deal was "to see and be seen." Another status symbol was to receive a phone call at the lounge and have the maître plug in the phone at your table. You must be someone important! Of course I had a friend call me at the lounge to demonstrate my importance. I had tipped the maître d' and informed him that I was expecting a call. My visits to the Polo Lounge were great sociological fun, provided some laughs and a bit more of the excitement I was seeking. But it did not move me any closer to having my movie made.

After a parent's meeting at my son's boarding school at which Julie Andrews and her husband Blake Edwards (of *Pink Panther* fame) were in attendance, Susanne and I went off to dinner with the father of one of Noel's friends. He was the highly respected and very tough head of production at Paramount Studios. I steered the conversation toward the movie I wanted to make. Susanne commented how foolish it was for a novice to try to produce a movie, pointing out all the pitfalls in the process and my lack of knowledge about how the industry works. He responded by saying, "Every man should follow his dream." In response to his kind offer, I sent him the finally finished *Bill Young* script. In retrospect, his reaction was predictable, but he was very kind in his turndown. The problem is that Hollywood executives don't say, "You have the kernel of a great story here, let me put my writers on it and we can move forward together." There is no reason they should, except in my Don Quixote fantasy world.

Another networking connection I wasted was an entertainment lawyer/agent couple I had met in Acapulco, to whom I had given the script. They were escorts to events for many female stars and were well known in the industry. They gently suggested it needed more work before they could present it to their contacts. The same reaction came from the vice president of Paramount Studios a month after I gave him the *Bill Young* script. He said that although he still liked the concept, it was so far off the "marketable" charts that it was impossible for him to be of assistance. I had made a horrible mistake in submitting the script and wasting a very promising contact.

Instead of the golden egg I hoped for, the first writer's script was beyond my wildest nightmares. He'd fallen in love with Bill and forgotten the basics of screen writing. Although his scene setting was great, his script was without an arc and was filled with terrible dialog. It was written in the following manner (I am exaggerating, but only a little): "Bill awoke, brushed his teeth, and got dressed, he visited the DEA and went out and killed people."

But I was unwilling to see the flaws. I was convinced that the spectacular settings and Bill's fascinating personality would shine through and carry the day. This was the case even after my actor brother-in-law and his actor wife, who between them had fifty years of experience in the industry, read the script, hinted at its failings, and offered to write a new one. I was not open to the possibility that they could write a great script; in my mind they were actors, not screenwriters. I was in fear and denial. I said to myself, "Okay, the script is not great but, as the Indonesians say, it is good enough." I was on the D express train and could not get myself to pull the emergency cord. Given Susanne's strong opposition and other doubters of the whole project, I could not bring myself to admit that the script was unusable and regroup. I wasn't sure how to do that. Again, I did not have a trusted and knowledgeable Sancho

Panza to advise me that the wisest course was not to go forward with what I came to understand was not even an okay script but a disastrous one.

You might ask, "How could I be so unaware?" To this day I don't have a fully satisfying answer. I know that normally I would never use my entire "seed" fund to hire a writer, but I did! Maybe it was rebellion against Susanne's opposition to my quest? She had read the script, but not until much later in the process did she let me know how terrible she thought it was. To be fair, I don't know if I would have listened to her anyway. My determination to make the movie became the catalyst for our ending the marriage. I was definitely in the mode of "I will show you and other doubters." A psychologist friend aptly put it this way: "If the movie gets made, you will be a genius. If it doesn't, you will be a schmuck."

I had exhausted my development fund and had spent a bunch of money of our own that only added to the tension between Susanne and me. I could not spend more of our money or raise more from friends, and I had no clue how to find a better writer who would move ahead solely on spec. I felt I was dead in the water and had no choice but to continue networking, using the *Bill Young* script in the process. This was a major and irreparable mistake on my part because my networking efforts worked, but I did not have a saleable product. No lance I carried could punch through the barriers I faced because of the dreadful script I was pushing. Too late, I finally understood my basic error: my impatience in hiring a scriptwriter and my unwillingness to admit to myself that my blindness about his talent doomed my quest from the beginning.

I finally fired him. He could not accept that his script was "not up to snuff." It was a difficult meeting for me. I had liked him. He was a sensitive guy who shared my love of Bill and the magic of Thailand.

PART VI—DEATH AND RESURRECTION

Seven years after I first met Bill in 1984, the project was dead in the water. But two years later, in 1993, I connected with Michael Vickerman, a young writer from Sylvester Stallone's production company, and as with Lazarus, the project was restored to life. Given how long it had been dead, I thought of it as a miracle. The truth was, I had never completely given up on my dream. And from time to time I would mention it to people who might help. After Susanne and I had separated I met and moved in with Nancy. In time, I told her about my Hollywood experience and my dream of moviemaking. She mentioned a girlfriend who was married to Stallone's main bodyguard, and after a phone conversation I flew to LA to meet with him. He was six feet, two inches tall, muscular, very handsome, of Hawaiian-Irish descent and proficient in a number of martial arts. He was also a likable, gentle man. He wanted to become a producer and quit the bodyguard business, so I agreed to his having a producer role in the movie. He suggested I meet with Vickerman the next day. Vickerman would be the writer who could save the day.

Vickerman was in his late twenties and had the polite and "nice" personality of a mid-westerner. We talked for hours about his movie business background and the movie I wanted to make. He said he would work for a percentage of the profits, but wanted producer credit as well. He sent me a sample script he had written on spec with well-written dialogue and a good storyline. Soon after I hired him, we had a first draft. Thereafter, we continuously collaborated until we had a script that we were ready to show to others for comment. I found the process fun and exhilarating. Pizzazz!

My actor brother-in-law and others in the business agreed: I finally had a professionally written movie script, and the project could move forward again. But I was still without a connected and knowledgeable Sancho Panza.

PART VII: WANTED: THE ONE PERSON IN THE ROOM

I gave Vickerman's script for comment to Ted Post, the father of my friend Bob Post who would become the dean of Yale Law School. Ted was the director of the anti-Vietnam War cult movie *Go Tell the Spartans* starring Burt Lancaster, and the hugely successful *Magnum Force*. He graciously gave me his time and expertise in the business. To get the movie made, he thought the script needed one more thing: a unique dimension, "something that has never been done before." But after many rewrites with Ted's active input, we could not come up with a unique and viable approach. To write a totally new movie, with a new approach, was out of the question as that would have required raising additional substantial funds to pay Vickerman, or someone new, for another script. For me, Ted's advice fell into the same category of others who suggested I first write a book about Bill, get it published, and then sell it to a producer in Hollywood. Both were "a bridge too far." I did raise another $5,000 (from a Hollywood-enamored couple from my law school) to pay Vickerman for a rewrite of a scene or two. Maybe twenty years earlier, Ted Post could have been my Sancho Panza, but he no longer had the clout or connections to get a movie made. Maybe his suggestion was just wrong.

I continued to network. Through a lawyer friend's secretary I was able to have famed director and producer Sidney Pollack read Vickerman's script. He turned the opportunity down to direct my project, which was now titled *Divided Loyalties*. In a kind rejection letter he praised the professional writing (later confirmed by my friend's secretary), but stated that before giving up two years of his life to making a movie, he had to be enthralled by the story (e.g. *Out of Africa*). He said it was a well written and interesting story but he was finished with this genre.

Through my brother-in-law we had the *Divided Loyalties* script passed on to Mark Harmon of *NCIS* fame. Networking! But it turned out he wanted a break from TV and moviemaking. In addition to a good script, you need the heavens to align to get a movie made.

My friend David Rosenthal grew up in Detroit with Bob Shaye, the founder and CEO of New Line Cinema. He arranged for us to meet at Shaye's house in Beverly Hills.

We stopped in the Valley at Art's Jewish deli to purchase lox, cream cheese, bagels, and white fish as an offering to the studio head who could green-light my movie. I suppose our offering was the modern version of the magi bringing presents to the baby Jesus. In Hollywood fashion, we would gather at the pool to make the pitch, submit the script, and gather advice. Shaye had the air of a very successful man.

Although I had gained a lot of knowledge in the last ten years about how to operate in Hollywood, I still had gaps in how to play the game. I made another fatal error in not asking Shaye to read *Divided Loyalties* himself.

He gave it to one of the young readers on his staff. Later, I happened to be in an office of one of those readers and understood why he recommended to Shaye not to do another "Vietnam War action movie." The reader's office was decorated with wall-to-wall scripts, and the floor was carpeted with more. There was no way he could read so many scripts. At best, he could just quickly glance through the pages. Asian setting, violence, and CIA equaled "Vietnam War action movie" rather than an adventure movie about an American expat, the grandson of a famous missionary family, who found himself in a conflict over doing "God's work " while at the same time working for the CIA or the DEA. His categorizing *Divided Loyalties* as a Vietnam War action movie stretched credulity. But you only get one shot. Another lost opportunity because of my lack of savvy.

David Rosenthal wanted to meet Bill and get a feel for the hill tribes and locales for the movie. We would first meet Bill in Bangkok, then travel on to Chiang Mai and from there into the hills.

In our phone conversations, before we left California, Bill said that the vice chairman of the "freedom fighting" hill tribes, who were still fighting the Burmese central government, wanted to meet us and get our assistance. Hollywood meets world politics. Although Bill and his father had long lived in Thailand, they had continued to nurture their relationships in Burma and provide financial assistance to the rebels in their fight against the central government. David and I agreed, and we met in my room at the Oriental Hotel in Bangkok. The vice chairman was an articulate and proud man. He wanted our help in building international support and in convincing the Reagan administration to assist the tribes in their cause of gaining a role in the central government of Burma.. He also said he wanted our help in raising funds for his group. They would clandestinely reopen a sapphire mine, have us sell the stones in America, and use the majority of the profits to buy weapons. We would keep a minority of the funds for our efforts. Bill, David, and I discussed producing a documentary for the cause, and before the meeting ended the vice chairman invited us to meet a week later with him and the chairman in their jungle hideout in Burma. This would entail leaving Thailand and entering Burma on boats along the Mekong River with heavily armed rebel "soldiers" to protect us. Caught up in the romance of the moment, David and I foolishly agreed. Bill's feeling that it was not a problem to visit the jungle headquarters figured greatly in our decision.

That night we flew to Chiang Mai, and the next day Bill provided David with a "tourist day," visiting several hill tribes. When we returned to Chiang Mai that evening we were excited about going "up river" to meet with the chairman in his jungle hideout. Bill said he would check with the wife of one of the leaders about the status of our trip. He returned with big news. The enclave had been attacked the day before by the Burmese army, and our trip was off. We were saved by one day. That night I kept having images of our dead bodies face down in the Mekong River. David and I agreed we had been saved from our own stupidity.

I used my contacts to get a call through to the lead producer of Tom Brokow's *NBC Nightly News*. I wanted NBC to fund a documentary about the ill treatment of the hill tribes by the Burmese government, or at least do a segment on the *Nightly News*. He told me Americans had no interest in Burma; Burma was the Asian Albania. He would "take a pass" on both requests. In time, he would be proved wrong about both countries. So ended my efforts to publicize the plight of the Burmese hill tribes. I felt I could not attempt to produce the movie and a documentary at the same time.

Now that I was fired up by my last adventure with Bill and David, and since I had a good, professionally written script in hand, I contacted the second of the two leads my friend Marilyn Melkonian had given me. The first, you may recall, was the vice president of Paramount Studios.

Sid Ganis was then a vice chairman of Columbia Pictures. He would go on to be chairman as well as chairman of the board of the Academy of Motion Pictures Arts and Sciences. When I was ushered into his office by his secretary, Sid introduced me to Danny DeVito, who was just leaving. It gave me a chance to say how much I enjoyed his work and to have a brief conversation with him about nothing. I liked him. I said to myself, "Not a bad beginning to make small talk with an A-list star, what a great Hollywood hit!" The office walls were lined with pictures of Sid and many stars. I was indeed in Hollywood.

Sid was a torrent of energy. There was no seat at his desk. The desk reminded me of an architect's drawing table, but in beautiful polished wood. While I sat on a couch, he burst around the room in continual movement. He could not stay still, barking orders to his secretary just outside his door. After small talk about how Marylyn was doing, I handed him the script and asked that he personally read it (I had learned my Shaye lesson). He said he would. We shook, and I left his office on a high. I thought if he liked the script, my movie would finally get made.

A month later, when I picked up the phone, it was "Vice chairman Ganis calling." His secretary, who had initiated the call, said he would have to call me right back. Busy men juggle several calls at the same time. My present wife (Julie) was with me in my apartment at the time. We knelt down together alongside my bed and I said a prayer to the effect of "your will, not mine." I was turning the outcome over to the universe. When Ganis got on the phone, he said, "I loved the script, but my therapist says I cannot do everything I love." He went on to say that he had given the script to others to read who had said it wasn't "commercial." I hung up, and after a few moments my first reaction was, "That's Hollywood—no one says it straight." Hollywood folks might work together on another project, and therefore it is best be vague, indirect, or even lie. Soon thereafter, upon reflection, I thought even if he was less than honest, I probably would not like to be told directly and bluntly that the script was not good enough. I knew this time it was.

Divided Loyalties was definitely commercial. Maybe the problem was a 1995 film about the Burmese uprisings, *Beyond Rangoon*, that starred Patricia Arquette and had been a failure at the box office. Columbia Pictures had distributed it. In typical Hollywood fashion, they probably blamed the locale rather than the movie itself. Although I usually loved Arquette's acting, when I saw the movie it felt flat and boring. Maybe she was miscast, or it was the direction and/or the script, I do not know. I just knew my film was better. If only I'd had the Vickerman script years earlier, before the failure of *Beyond Rangoon*. Alas, I don't control the universe, to whom I had left the outcome. I do have gratitude to Ganis for the time he spent with me. As I said earlier, the leaders of Hollywood I met were kind to me.

An outsider trying to get a movie made could be the basis of a funny, annoying, and poignant movie itself. For me the poignant parts were: 1) I lost $30,000 of friends' money, 2) becoming a "producer" was a catalyst to ending my marriage, and 3) Bill Young died without the world getting to know about this exceptional man.

Looking back, I am struck by how my personality affected the outcome. My impatience led to a fatal error of judgment in hiring the first writer and using his incompetent script. You only get one chance at the gold ring. There were other things that should have warned me off or stopped me in my tracks. Why didn't I walk away from trying to make a movie about Bill when he said he had found full-time work with the DEA and didn't want to repeat the McCoy book mistake? He was okay with a fictionalized flick that used a number of his stories, but not with one that was directly about him. He felt it might cost him his job and maybe his life. I certainly did not want either outcome for him. But I simply could not walk away from the project.

I had already spent most of the money I had raised and did not want the result of all my efforts to be a big fat zero. I also was smitten with the glamour of being a Hollywood producer, even if it would be only of a good, but not outstanding, flick. As time went by I understood that from a moviemaking point of view, fictionalizing Bill's story was probably a good idea. It would make no sense to produce a documentary-like movie. Maybe that was the problem with *Beyond Rangoon*. *Lawrence of Arabia* and *Out of Africa* demonstrate that you need a compellingly dramatic script to hang an extraordinary life story onto. My sojourn into La-La Land was over for good this time. No money, no leads, no hope, and no energy left.

Years later (2011), I was very saddened to learn that Bill had committed suicide at the age of seventy-six (he was four years older than I). The press gave many unflattering reasons for his suicide, including owing money to powerful drug lords he worked in concert with. But I believe that his ill health was the true reason. Bill's high blood pressure and other maladies made me feel he was a mere shell of his former self, and he found his reality deeply depressing.

My life has been enriched by my time with Bill and the experience of Hollywood. As a friend said, "You lived a movie trying to make a movie." Even though my movie was never made, I do not feel like a schmuck. Today, I appreciate walking in nature in Petaluma and abroad with my wife Julie, writing this memoir, and enjoying friends and family. I no longer need the drug of pizzazz.

CHAPTER 15

RECOVERY

As I write this chapter I am eighty years old and have been clean and sober for thirty-three years—twenty-eight of which have been in a 12-Step Program.

In my first five years of sobriety I learned that I could operate without booze and did not yearn for it, but the first six months of not drinking or using marijuana were not a walk in the park. I found not drinking especially difficult on my work trips between San Francisco and Washington, D.C. I missed the camaraderie on the 747 United Airline flights with a group of guys from Lockheed who were regulars on this flight. They would bring their own small, hotel bottle-sized booze on the flight. This was the time when the top of the 747 was a bar-lounge. We started drinking when we left Dulles airport and continued until we landed in San Francisco, all the while standing at the bar-lounge. It was great fun. "Alas," I thought, "no more." Other times in early sobriety that proved difficult were celebrations when the Champagne flowed.

My first 12-Step Program meeting, called "Rap-at-Noon," took place in the old YWCA building in downtown Oakland, California. We met in a large room laid out with folding chairs. In the rear, big pots of coffee and hot water for tea stood next to platters with doughnuts and other treats. Ashtrays stood ready around the room (people still smoked in those days). The fifty to seventy attendees were a racially, educationally, and economically diverse group. Men and women, young and old, doctors and lawyers mixed with people just out of prison. (More young people have joined over the years as my 12-Step Program opened its doors to the dual-addicted who were using both booze and drugs.) There were low bottom alcoholics (living on the streets or who had been found guilty of vehicular homicide) and high bottom drunks (who had not yet suffered big-time negative consequences), maintenance (all day and every day) drinkers who did not get sloppy drunk but who needed a certain glow to survive, and periodic drinkers who did get sloppy drunk. The attendees verified the fact that alcoholics are made up of different types, from the Bowery to Park Avenue, from the Tenderloin to Pacific Heights. It was a "speaker meeting" where one person told their story to the group in fifteen to twenty minutes—what caused them to seek help and what program suggestions worked for them to stay sober. Then other members of the group who wished to spoke about themselves for three to five minutes. One suggestion (there were no rules) of the group was that there be no cross talk. People should not comment positively or negatively on an attendee's talk. Your focus should be on just talking about yourself. This helped foster a safe place to be. It took me many meetings to recognize the similarities between us instead of the differences. I had been on a path of becoming terminally unique. In time, however, I came to realize that although our stories were different, our struggle was the same.

It struck me, from the first meeting on, how welcoming the group was. This was also true in meetings I attended in London, Paris, Moscow, and other cities in the US. The other wonder of the meetings was laughter. Although dealing with alcoholism is a serious matter, the commonality of our outrageous behavior and the excuses we used elicited knowing laughter. Meetings were upbeat because we had found a way to have gratitude for what we did have and not focus on what we did not. We could also laugh at ourselves for our continuing denial that we had a problem with booze and/or drugs. We began to understand the difference between needs and wants. We may want a fancy house but all we need is a roof over our heads.

I stayed in the Program because it gave me a positive way to deal with life, not because I was afraid I would drink or use again. In the first years I attended meetings three to six times a week. In Oakland it was easy to find many meetings I liked. These days I continue to go every Sunday to a meeting in Pt. Reyes, California. I drive forty minutes from my house in Petaluma because of the wisdom I gain from the long-term sobriety members, the honesty of all the attendees, and the reminder from the newcomers how grateful I am that I no longer drink or use. For a long time now I no longer need to look over my shoulder while driving to check if cops are behind me, or make a problem worse because of my drinking and resultant personality change. Even all these years later, it is still a delight to awaken without a hangover or having to repair a negative situation I caused.

I had to unlearn being the fastest mouth and put-down artist in town. I saw that these survival tactics learned on the streets of the Bronx and from becoming a lawyer no longer served me well. Always being right and winning every argument may have served my clients, but it made me edgy and argumentative outside of my professional role. Not a winning formula in any personal relationship! Adopting the Program's saying, "Being open to change, willing to heed sound advice, and honest about my character traits that no longer serve me well" allowed me to open new doors and ways of seeing things differently.

Stephen Levine's meditation on wishing for others what I wanted for myself allowed my resentments toward my ex-wife Susanne to slowly dissipate. (Stephen Levine was a teacher of guided meditations and healing techniques. His workshops and books focus on conscious living and conscious dying). Our working on "our side of the street"(changing ourselves not others), has allowed Susanne and me (and her husband) to spend holiday dinners, our big birthdays (e.g. his and my eightieth) and our grandchildren's birthdays together. Thich Nhat Hanh's mindfulness meditations and poems were very helpful in bringing me degrees of calm and relaxation. Lao Tsu's *Tao Te Ching* parables also opened my eyes to a spiritual path of living my life. He was a sixth-century BC Chinese writer and philosopher who created Taoism. Meditation and doing my eighth and ninth steps allowed me to begin the process of self-forgiveness and letting go of shame and guilt for the consequences of my heavy bouts of drinking. Slowly, around the edges, I softened.

Let me be clear, as the Program would say, I have been involved in a process of "progress and not perfection" in changing what I consider negative traits. The Bronx is still a part of who I am, but I am not as aggressive. I don't need to win every argument and can most of the time "promptly admit" when I am wrong. Sometimes my admission is not prompt but it does occur, even if it takes days. (Sometimes I still forget apologies entirely.) I am less judgmental and more accepting of all our flaws. I love the observation that alcoholics look down on others from the gutter.

None of the changes in me came quickly. They came, then they disappeared, and then reappeared and took hold. The changes were not without a struggle.

Due to my 12-Step Program I became a better listener, kinder, more empathetic, and better able to focus on things that I have gratitude for instead of the negatives in my life. It took two years after I joined the Program to finally admit that the first step applied to me. I was "powerless over alcohol" and [my] "life had become unmanageable." I could see it was the first drink, not the last, that got me drunk. After taking the first, I never knew how many thereafter I would have. The fact that I had to regularly apologize to Susanne for my behavior after too many drinks showed the unmanageability of my life. It took a full year of doing Stephen Levine's meditation before my heart would begin to open to her. It is said that relationships with family members, especially exes, are the most difficult. I had to accept that Susanne was not ready to read my fourth-step amends letter for many months, much less accept it. As the Program says, this step is for you to get rid of walking around with guilt, but the subject of the amends does not have to accept it. It requires diligence not to allow a nonacceptance to create resentment.

As I followed the steps and went to meetings, over time I softened and became less self-absorbed. It was not a linear forced change, but rather as if by magic the work I was doing in the Program to live a useful and positive life altered my personality. Remember it is about progress, not perfection. I still can be triggered to return to the old Al of judgments and putdowns. My changing is not simply my opinion but is confirmed by my adult children, my wife, and old friends. I am especially grateful that the Program gave me a way to talk to my children that they find helpful: without judgment, waiting to be asked for my opinion, and sharing how others in the Program dealt with similar issues. They both cite my entering the Program as producing a different dad. For the prior five years I had been a "dry drunk"—not drinking or using, but still in my "alcoholic thinking" of me, me, me and behaving as if I was always right and special.

It is a wonderful feeling to now have a great relationship with them both. I was very touched that my daughter and her husband generously contributed the lion's share to the cost of my eightieth birthday party and that my son and his wife made it possible on their very tight budget to fly in from Taipei. It was a great day filled with love and fun. A fabulous Zydeco band contributed to the upbeat spirit in the room. I relished the fact that forty friends from the Program mixed easily with ninety of my drinking friends and family who enjoyed the wine and beer we provided. It was a catered affair, and my brother-in-law brought pounds of pastrami with him from a great Los Angeles Jewish deli. It was a hit with everyone.

In the beginning, many of the 12-Step Program sayings that were taped to the wall at the "Rap-at-Noon" and other meeting places made me want to vomit. The one that repelled me the most was "Let go and let God." Another troublesome one was "One day at a time." Today I see the wisdom behind both. I substitute the word *universe* for God and don't "future trip" too much. Over time I noticed that most of us have anxiety about the future. Many times our fears are not realized. We waste a lot of energy on things that do not happen. I slowly saw the wisdom of these sayings and freely use them in conversation. Sadly, I no longer meditate regularly; I find it interesting how we don't always do what we know is good for us. I can use the excuse of too many things to do in a day, but I am fully aware that I could make it a priority if I chose to. I do go back to it from time to time when I am in pain. The Program teaches that pain is a part of life but that suffering is optional. It also teaches that neither the bad nor the good lasts forever. Your attitude toward either is crucial. I drank to keep the fun going, I drank to avoid pain, and in the end I drank to excess because I am an alcoholic.

Over the years, sitting in my chair at meetings, I witnessed how members dealt with clinical depression, childhood abuse, losing a job and a house, children going to prison for being drunk behind the wheel, dealing drugs, or killing someone in a bar fight. I saw a number of them face the death of loved ones and their own mortality with dignity and strength.

During my beginning meetings, people pointed out that I did not need not to be a believer in God to move forward. My "higher power" did not have to be in the Judaic-Christian mode but could be defined in any way I wanted. In the end what worked for me was to understand I was not God. I was not in control of outcomes.

The first two steps are about reflection, but the next ten are about taking action. The twelve steps gave me a program and tools to deal with life in a positive way and to help others. It also allowed me to be at ease with my past. In the language of the program, I have to take care of "my side of the street," have the right thoughts, and take thoughtful action; do whatever I can to produce a good result. The hard lesson to learn is that even with taking good action, I might not get the result I want. I can try to produce a movie or write a memoir, but I am not in control over the movie being made or the memoir being picked up by a publisher. The secret is to be okay with this. I learned there are many excuses to go out and drink again, but only one to stay in the program: I am an alcoholic, with all the attendant negative consequences; if I resume drinking, my life will get steadily worse. Alcoholics who "go out," drink, and never come into the Program continue on a downslide that many times results in jail or death. The kindness I witnessed toward people who went out and returned to the Program was uplifting and instructive. No judgment, just support. People would say the person just needed "more research." Luckily, I haven't needed "more research."

The lesson I learned early on was that I alone am responsible for my sobriety. What others do (from aggressive behavior to suicide) should not be used as an excuse to drink again. It is suggested that as a newcomer you find a sponsor to help you through the steps (including facing many things you are ashamed of), hear your ongoing resentments, and act as a sounding board for your proposed actions. It is said, "Be sure to call your sponsor before you take a drink as a solution to any problem." It turned out that my sponsor, who had five years of sobriety and who took me through the steps, had continued to use cocaine on a regular basis. I am not sure why I intuitively saw this as his problem and not as a betrayal of me, but I did. I severed our relationship but did not have any resentment over it. Over the years I have used close friends in the program as my sponsors.

Two weeks after my first sponsee approached me after a meeting and asked me to be his sponsor (this is the usual way of finding a sponsor), he put a gun to his head and killed himself. It turned out that he could no longer deal with the fact that his mother had repeatedly tried to kill him when he was young. Because of the very short time I knew him, I was aware that his act had nothing do with my sponsorship. The Program has written many useful suggestions on the sponsor-sponsee relationship. Many of my sponsees had spent more time in the Program than I, but liked what I said in meetings and wanted me to be a sounding board for their proposed actions. Some wanted to do the steps again.

Although I feel a great responsibility to be there for my sponsees and was saddened by the desperate act of my first sponsee, it did not put me in a tizzy. By contrast, the suicide of a friend in the program sent me back to meditation and leaning on the folks in the Program to talk about my feelings to ease my pain. He had a five-month-old baby, but still stuck his head in the oven. He had resumed drinking the day he committed suicide. Although he had successfully opened and run a winery that he then sold for big bucks, he could not get his father's negative voice out of his head. Alcoholism is a dangerous disease that can be fatal.

In the language of the Program, alcoholism is "cunning, baffling, and powerful." I had one sponsee who "went out" after twenty years of being clean and sober even though he had experienced all the benefits of not drinking. He was lucky, however, and returned to the Program. I became his sponsor, and he is still in the Program twenty-some years later. Others I have known who did not return wound up homeless, estranged from family and friends, and usually dying alone from this disease. Others report after "going out" that the Program had ruined their drinking and using and made them return to the Program after all. Why do some people continue to drink after two DUIs, fully aware that a third will put them in jail for a year or more? Yes, it is true: alcoholism is "cunning, baffling and powerful." One friend's story perfectly illustrates this truth. He was in the hospital awaiting a liver transplant when he began fantasizing that his IV was filled with whiskey.

Today I have two sponsees; One just turned seventy and has been clean and sober longer than I. The other, after sixteen years in the Program, went out for three before returning. He is in his sixties. Both are professionals who operate at a high level. I gain much wisdom directly and indirectly from them. Being a sponsor is always a two-way street. Sometimes I only learn from their experiences about how not to deal with a problem.

I have watched over the years as people in the Program worked on this important lesson, especially when it comes to family relationships. The recognition that the only person you can change is yourself produces incredible results. This is an extension of knowing "you are powerless over alcohol" and recognizing you are powerless over others. This extension of the first step was and is the hardest for me. The other hard ones are steps eight and nine. "Making a list of persons we have harmed" and then making amends to such people isn't easy. Not regretting your past but owning it is a very difficult task for many. It is important to accept your past because it got you to the present that you are now experiencing.

Over and over again I watched relationships repaired after having been breached for years. Once a member acknowledged that they could not change a parent's, sibling's, child's, or friend's behavior, accepted all of who they were (the good and the bad), and began the process of letting go of their resentments, the relationship dramatically changed for the better or, at the very least, the anguish lessened.

The toughest period in my sobriety has been dealing with my brother Sandy's decline and death. It will be six years this October (2019), and I am stilled touched with sadness when I think of him. But I do not think of drinking to erase the sadness. That was my modus operandi before the Program. For about a year after his death, seeing a picture of him would greatly upset me. As I write these paragraphs, I am filled with emotion. We were very close. He told me after he started to decline that he had always viewed us as united together against the world. We covered each other's back. We were each other's protector even as our relationship changed from older-younger brother to brothers who were friends and equals. At the same time he would always be the brother who carried me down the movie theater stairs when my legs locked from rheumatic fever, and who drove me around Miami Beach on the back of his Schwinn bike. He bought me an exact replica of his Columbia University jacket so I could pretend to be older than I was. He was also the one who taught me how to carry three cups and saucers or three or four plates at a time before I went to work as a waiter in the Catskills. I was the one who took on my father when he treated Sandy badly. We both thought the reason was that he visually reminded Dad of Mom. At Sandy's request, I took on the responsibility of making sure there was no flare-up between Mom and Dad at my nephew's bar mitzvah. I convinced Sandy that he would regret not coming to our father's funeral in Miami. Although I could cite many more examples, I think, dear reader, you get the picture.

In the last year and a half of his life our relationship grew even closer, fueled with love and laughter. I would drive the two-and-a-half-hour round trip from Petaluma to Oakland once a week to be alone with him and discuss everything, including personal life issues. After he survived a bout of sepsis, he had to undergo an operation on his knee to remove the knee replacement hardware placed there years ago. Given his condition of chronic heart failure and diabetes, it was fifty-fifty whether he would survive the operation. The infection that brought on sepsis had settled in his knee.

The doctors told him they could not guarantee that the infection would not return and suggested amputation. Sandy had told me many months before he wanted my presence at doctor meetings and input on the path forward. He knew he could rely on my honesty, analysis, and opinion regarding a situation.

Luckily, no amputation was necessary. He spent weeks in a rehab center in Berkeley where I visited him almost every day, with a few breaks to recuperate from the toll of driving. Until he died months later (he had returned to his home) we continued to laugh together, discussing our youth and life in general. When I shared at my Sunday meeting about Sandy, people in the meeting would come up afterward, give me a hug, and tell me they could literally feel the love between us. I was a very lucky man.

Months later, at the request of his wife, Vivian, I presided over the Celebration of Life ceremony, which took place in a large gathering room in one of the senior citizen projects he had designed. Over a hundred people attended. I continuously feel gratitude to the Program for giving me the tools to be present for my brother, his wife, and his kids. Without it I would have focused on my own pain and drunk Scotch or whatever to avoid facing the reality. My drinking had always made me the problem rather than simply being a man who had a problem.

The Program has also allowed my relationship with my wife, Julie, to deepen. I don't always need to be right! And most importantly, I have learned that even when I feel I am right, loving-kindness is more important. We try not to allow resentments over small or big issues to fester. Talk about it and try to let it go. I try to remember that expectations can be a resentment waiting to happen. The Serenity Prayer (I use it as a meditation) proves very useful in my dealing with my spousal relationship and many other things. Acceptance is the key.

The Serenity Prayer

God [Universe], grant me the serenity to accept

> *the things I cannot change,*

Courage to change the things I can [usually me],

> *And wisdom to know the difference.*

It is okay that Julie and I are different, and I can learn from her way of seeing the world.

I would be remiss if I did not mention a very useful bit of advice I received from our one-time couples therapist: "Think of doing housework as foreplay."

Looking back over my life with its ups and downs, I feel lucky for being able to help others and grateful for the beauty, fun, and love I have experienced. I believe this ordinary man has had an extraordinary life. Maybe I will write a supplement to this memoir when I turn ninety.

Printed in Great
Britain
by Amazon